branded

branded

adolescents converting from consumer faith

katherine turpin

THE
PILGRIM
PRESS
Cleveland

To my parents,
David and Linda Turpin,
co-creators of my first circle of grace

The Pilgrim Press
700 Prospect Avenue
Cleveland, Ohio 44115-1100
thepilgrimpress.com

Printed in the United States of America on acid-free paper

11 10 09 08 07 06   5 4 3 2 1

Library of Congress Cataloging-in-Publication Data
Turpin, Katherine, 1971-
    Branded : adolescents converting from consumer faith / Katherine
Turpin.
        p.   cm. – (Youth ministry alternatives)
    Includes bibliographical references and index.
    Includes bibliographical references (p. [205]-223).
    ISBN-13: 978-0-8298-1738-6 (alk. paper)
        1. Consumption (Economics) – Religious aspects – Christianity.
2. Christianity and culture. 3. Christian life. 4. Youth – Religious life.
5. Church work with youth. I. Title. II. Series.
BR115.C67T87 2006
241′.68 – dc22
                                                        2006008910

Contents

Part three
Nurturing contexts for
adolescent ongoing conversion

Foreword

For three decades the task of conceptualizing youth ministry has largely been left to independent commercial enterprises that have failed to recognize the importance of denomination, theology, ethnicity, class, and other cultural particularities for shaping Christian discipleship. In addition, youth ministry as it has evolved over these decades lacks significant critique of the shift in the social roles of young people in the second half of the twentieth century and into the twenty-first century, in which youth are increasingly ghettoized as passive consumers rather than treated as agents of faith influencing the common good.

Decades of domestication, marginalization, and trivialization of youth ministry by theology schools, denominations, and publishing houses has distorted our imagination of what counts as youth ministry. The image of youth ministry as trivial or pragmatic has left many hungry for youth ministry approaches that include social critique and engagement, theological sophistication, faith formation, and a genuine knowledge of and respect for the unique youth of today. The Youth Ministry ALTERNATIVES series has been jointly conceived by The Pilgrim Press and David F. White and Faith Kirkham Hawkins to address that hunger.

The Youth Ministry ALTERNATIVES series aims to clearly articulate approaches to youth ministry that embody social awareness and theological reflection and foster the distinctive gifts of youth for the church and the world. The series will highlight approaches to youth ministry that embody the following commitments:

1. **Dialogue with Living Communities.** This series will highlight approaches for fostering dynamic dialogue between the Christian traditions and youth and adults in living communities of faith.

2. **Deeper Understanding.** This series will engage this dialogue to deepen understanding of youth, theology, and youth ministry. Of particular interest is the wisdom emerging from a variety of underexplored sources that will be identified and interpreted, including the following:

   • the wisdom of youth

   • the wisdom of communities engaged in youth ministry

   • the contexts of youth, including their inner landscapes, communities, cultures, and physical environments

   • the resources of Christian tradition

3. **Transformative Practices.** From these conversations and the wisdom gleaned from youth, communities, and their contexts, this series will especially highlight a range of practices for engaging youth in ministry, such as:

   • doing theology and ministry with youth

   • taking youth seriously — their wounds, blessings, and gifts

   • mobilizing and enhancing youth agency and vocation

   • enhancing formation and transformation of youth as they journey in faith

   • articulating clear approaches to youth ministry

   • discerning a congregation's unique youth ministry

In *Branded: Adolescents Converting from Consumer Faith*, Katherine Turpin explores the impact of consumer culture on young people, particularly upon their vocational imaginations. Her book not only describes these significant inhibitions to the Christian vocation of young people, but, by drawing upon John Wesley's theology of ongoing conversion together with the educative and supportive function of small communities to support countercultural transformation, she persuasively and practically shows us how we can help enliven the imaginations and agency and faith of young people, and how many young people already model such a conversion from faith in consumerism.

DAVID F. WHITE AND FAITH KIRKHAM HAWKINS
Series editors, Youth Ministry Alternatives

Series editors Faith Kirkham Hawkins and David F. White are respectively Director of the Youth Theological Initiative and Assistant Professor of Youth and Education at Candler School of Theology at Emory University in Atlanta, and C. Ellis and Nancy Gribble Nelson Associate Professor of Christian Education at Austin Presbyterian Theological Seminary in Austin, Texas.

Acknowledgments

This book has been at least six years in the writing, and during this time I have been graced with my own circle of saints who have played important roles in the various stages of its creation. I am keenly aware of the gifts they have offered through their sojourning in the process, and I offer sincere thanks for their generosity of spirit. While I will take responsibility for the mistakes and limitations of this book, whatever useful knowledge it offers owes much to their insight and companionship.

To those who know my mentors, their influence will be evident all over these pages. I owe an enormous debt to Chuck Foster, Mary Elizabeth Moore, Brian Mahan, Jim Fowler, Rod Hunter, Ted Brelsford, and Elizabeth Bounds for the ways in which they have shaped my thinking and writing about these issues. I can only hope that my teaching of graduate students approaches the ways in which they gifted me during my time at Emory. Michael Warren of St. John's University took me seriously way before I did on this topic, and graciously offered support and inspiration during its early stages.

My faculty colleagues at the Iliff School of Theology granted me the research leave to finish this book both the first and second times. Their convivial companionship and collegial challenge make me a better scholar and teacher. Leslie Greer, Carla Engbretson, Vanessa Owen, Anna Mendelstamm, and Sara Rosenau read early versions of this material and offered helpful suggestions to make it both more reader-friendly and grammatically recognizable.

My years of working with the Youth Theological Initiative at Emory University and FaithTrek at the Iliff School of Theology endlessly enlivened my imagination about the possibilities of youth ministry. Both programs were funded by the Lilly Endowment, Inc., whose commitment to adolescent theological reflection under the leadership of Craig Dykstra has generated an entire scholarly conversation about youth ministry that was not present ten years ago. The many YTI and FaithTrek participants who graciously let me interview them inspired me with their faithful imaginations and alternate vocational paths. What for you was an hour of time taken away from an exciting program became months and years of pondering and writing for me. Your gifts of candor and beautiful living have inspired me no end. My colleagues on the staff of these two projects have been central to my development as a teacher of both youth and adults. At FaithTrek, Anne Carter Walker and Allyson Sawtell have been constant conversation partners these past three years. The communion of saints of YTI is too numerous to name adequately, but I owe particular thanks to Tim Van Meter, who initially got me involved in the project; to Mark Monk-Winstanley, who hired me as the research coordinator and encouraged me in the interviews that so enlivened this book; and to David White and Faith Hawkins for introducing me to Ulrike Guthrie, who has been the most compassionate and encouraging editor I could ever have wanted throughout the process of readying this book for publication.

All of my colleagues in ministry at Trinity UMC in Atlanta: Rex Kaney, Ron Anderson, Janna Wofford, Mary Jane Kettler, Mark Schmidt, Tim Porter, Gretchen Kaney, Ellen Maynard, Will Studstill, Chris Gibson, Lillian Bolster, Hannah Logan, Josh Rasor, Laura Gibson, Martin Frederick, Rachel Kaney, Geno Stroupe, David Harbin, Patrick Kaney, Frank Stroupe, Anna Alexander, Rachel Scott, and all of their parents taught me most of what I know and reminded me of what I didn't know about youth ministry. The members of that congregation continue to be a true mentoring community to my family and a gathering of the saints like no other. The good folks of Mountain T.O.P. (Tennessee Outreach Project), especially Judy Rogan, hired me at seventeen for my first job in youth ministry and shaped many of my gut instincts about the importance of inviting young people into serious work in the world through solidarity with the poor.

My fine colleagues in PCRP at Emory: Leah Horton, Kristin Hanson, Kimberly Buchanan, Helen Blier, Robin Ficklin-Alred, Barbara McClure, Gordon Mikoski, Tim Van Meter, HeeJung Kwon, Veronice Miles, Lynn Bridgers, and so many others taught me that the search for truth should always occur in community. They both sharpened my questions and fed my postpartum family; I could ask for no better companions in the academic venture. Amy Cottrill and Ken Wheeler were soulful friends during those Atlanta days and continue to be an integral part of our extended godfamily. Three dissertations and four children later, may the rest of our friendship be as fruitful!

My sister, Krista Turpin; my in-laws, Bob and Janet Blackmun; and our local godparents Jeffrey and Louise Mahan provide much-needed familial support and fellowship and serve as key players of my children's "underground" formation. The phenomenal teachers at the Fisher Early Learning Center of the University of Denver love and nurture my children during the hours while I sit at the computer. I am ever aware that my freedom to work is directly proportional to my confidence in their skill and dedication, and they come through with flying colors every day.

I owe special thanks to my husband, Andy Blackmun, my partner in all things. You have loved me and lived with me through graduate school, the transition to full-time academic life, parenting, and so many other moments of joy and struggle, bringing whole new levels of meaning to "I couldn't have done it without you." My delightful and determined children, Elizabeth and Christian, were birthed alongside this project. In addition to helping me keep it real, they remind me every day that I need to practice what I preach on this whole consumer thing.

Introduction

All cultures, of course, have socialized their members to think and act in ways that support the social, economic, and political arrangements, but until recently none has possessed the technology necessary to inform, entertain, and condition massive populations continuously and cumulatively.

— Margaret Miles[1]

One day last spring, I went to pick up my daughter Elizabeth from daycare. After we had exchanged greetings, I turned to chat with her teacher about her time at school. The teacher prompted my daughter to share with me that she had been violent all day on the playground. After a hurried conversation in which I was relieved to discover that she had actually been "Violet" all day on the playground, my next question was to find out what that meant. It turns out that Violet is a character from the Disney/Pixar film *The Incredibles*. She is an adolescent superhero who can turn invisible and generate force fields on command. My three-year-old daughter had been acting out scenes from this movie with her preschool playmates in their free play time at school.

Despite the fact that I had deemed this film inappropriately violent for my young daughter, I soon discovered that she knew all of the character names, their superhero powers, and the basic outlines of the plot. She learned all of this from her classmates, many of whom had received copies of the DVD as Easter gifts. Over the course of the spring, she attended birthday parties with Incredibles cakes and favors, she pointed out the characters on T-shirts and toys in discount

1. Margaret Miles, *Practicing Christianity: Critical Perspectives for an Embodied Spirituality* (New York: Crossroad, 1988), 2.

1

stores, she noticed posters advertising toy giveaways as we drove past fast-food restaurants, and she saw candies in the grocery store branded with characters from the movie. Despite the fact that we had intentionally chosen to avoid exposing our daughter to this film, her peers educated her to be completely familiar with the characters used to generate children's interest in buying all manner of items, from bedsheets to clothing. And so it begins.

I recently heard a statistic on a radio program that the average American child recognizes over five hundred brand names before they reach the age of five. Because I heard the statistic on the radio, I can't tell you how the researchers came up with that number. After I heard the statistic, I began listening carefully to my now four-year-old daughter to see how many brands she recognizes and uses in her daily description of the world. After just a few days, I realized that she is well past the five hundred mark already. She knows names of restaurants, department, and grocery stores and recognizes their signs even though she does not yet read. She knows characters from Disney and Nickelodeon and the Sesame Street Workshop, and recognizes them when they show up on products in the grocery store, even when she has not seen the movies or television shows from which they come. She knows a few brand names of food items, particularly breakfast cereals. All of this is particularly remarkable because she has never watched "commercial" television.

Branding is just one aspect of the continuous and cumulative conditioning that consumer culture offers to its participants of all ages. Our desires, our self-image, our taste, our leisure activities, our surroundings, our values, our sense of efficacy, and so much more are fundamentally formed by our participation in the system of acquiring and consuming goods. Despite my parenting efforts to decrease the impact of this system on my young daughter, there is no way to live in the United States and avoid the powerful and relentless formation that the system offers. We can't even conceive of a world without brand names, malls, corporate sponsors, or mutual funds. Consumption is at the heart of the way that we shape our lives, ever present and ever powerful in both our conceptualization of the world and the institutions we navigate on a daily basis.

Although I start this book with a story about my own parenting struggles with consumer culture, I actually began to reflect on the relentless formation into the role of consumer twelve years ago when I began work as a youth minister in a local church. I had chosen the church that employed me because the community of believers gathered there held significant commitments to urban ministry. Many of the members were involved in nonprofit work, education, or other vocational paths involving service to people on the underside of the economy. I was inspired by the countercultural ways in which they structured their lives and modeled an integrity of faithfulness to some of the more radical economic demands of the gospel. These were not people who worried about keeping up with the Joneses.

However, when I began working closely with the adolescent children of these adults in the church, I was surprised to find some of them to be quite committed to the pursuit of wealth and the acquisition of status-granting goods. I had already come to recognize the strength of consumer formation in my own life, but I had been raised in suburban contexts without the influence of parents or church with strong counter-consumptive commitments. If these young people who did have strong models of counter-consumer commitment all around them still fell under the sway of consumer formation, I wondered if any young people could resist the strong formation of consumer culture. Short of moving onto a subsistence-farming commune, avoidance of consumption is nearly impossible in our culture. The question quickly becomes how we help young people negotiate within consumer culture in such a way that it does not dominate their formation.

Despite the fact that I think everyone from infants to elders in our society is strongly influenced by the formation of consumer culture, I continue to be interested in its particular impact on adolescents. Adolescents are at a critical moment in the formation of their vocational sensibilities, they represent a hugely targeted market, and they are on the cusp of entering the economic world under their own auspices. All of these reasons make addressing consumer formation in adolescents important in any setting, secular or religious. However, this book addresses primarily the religious formation of adolescents, and in particular the impact of consumer culture on their vocational understanding in a religious sense.

The relentless formation of consumer culture has a powerful impact on young people's sense of what is important to pursue in the world. More than a system of economic engagement in the world, consumer culture offers a story of meaning and purpose to define human existence. Specifically, consumer culture offers the story that the key to a good life lies in acquiring enough money to obtain the goods that offer happiness, status, protection, and comfort. The right car or clothing may attract the interest of other persons and lead to companionable relationships. The right money management firm will lead to security in old age. The right choice in restaurants or amusement parks will lead to a good time regardless of who your companions are or why you find yourself in need of distraction.

Every aspect of this story is challenged by any major religious tradition and even by common wisdom about the meaning of life. However, our collective fascination with acquiring and consuming goods indicates that these counternarratives perhaps chasten, but do not eradicate our faith in the consumer story. And no wonder. We are inundated by the gospel of consumption through every means imaginable, from SkyMall catalogs in airplane seat pockets to corporate names on public school signs. We work long hours so that we can have money to pay mortgages, to feed and clothe our families, and to indulge in the occasional whim purchases. Consumption is at the heart of our corporate life together; it binds us together as a nation and, increasingly, as a globe.

As adolescents imagine their adult selves and begin to make life decisions to move toward those adult imaginings, this consumer formation defines their sensibilities about lifestyle, status, and self-worth in ways both conscious and unconscious. In order to offer young people the freedom to listen fully for an authentic calling not completely defined by what will make them the most money given the skills they have, an educational process reducing the impact of this formation is critical.

As I have sought to address the issue of adolescent vocation and consumer culture in my own religious educational practice, I first approached it as an educational problem that required increased critical awareness in adolescents about the consumer context in which they are living. I came to realize that the problem ran much deeper than cognitive awareness: at stake was the shaping of imagination, agency, and the most basic structures of meaning making. Simply being aware of the ways in which consumer culture worked in the United States and its ecological and economic impact on the rest of the world is not enough to transform the power it has to define our sense of the world and how it works. What has to be transformed is not our understanding of consumer culture, but our faith in it. In short, adolescents require educational structures to support an ongoing conversion of faith.

My own thinking about these issues has involved keeping three elements in conversation: the problem of consumer culture and its distortion of adolescent vocation, the dream that adolescents would discover the freedom to live into a vocational path not dominated by consumer culture, and the search for a process of enlivening agency and imagination that would allow for such freedom of vocational development. I have found "ongoing conversion" to be a helpful category to gather up my thinking about these three elements and to provide clues to appropriate pedagogical approaches given the context in which American adolescents live. In addition to these three elements, another emergent concern is the relationship of individual processes of conversion to broader social transformation around the issue of consumer culture.[2]

---

2. Karl Barth understood conversion itself to be a social rather than an individual matter. He notes that conversion is not an end unto itself, but rather an entry into the service of God to the whole of creation. He notes: "When we convert and are renewed in the totality of our being, we cross the threshold of our private existence and move out into the open. The inner problems may be most urgent and burning and exciting, but we are not engaged in conversion if we confine ourselves to them.... When we convert and are renewed in the totality of our being, in and with our private

I write as a practical theologian who stands in the discipline of religious education, which shapes both my concerns and my methods for addressing them. I first recognized the generating problem in my practice as a religious educator in a local congregation in which I had primary responsibility for the youth group. Thus, part 1 of this book describes the problem of the religious formation generated by consumer culture among adolescents beginning in that context and moving to situate it more broadly in an American context. Part 2 of the book explores ongoing conversion as a framing metaphor to explore religious educational practices that support adolescents as they seek to shift from faithful participation in consumer culture to faith in alternative meaning systems. Part 3 of the book focuses on nurturing small pedagogical communities that support ongoing conversion in adolescents.

In order to explore this issue, I have chosen conversation partners who are not only involved in a theoretical discourse about personal and social transformation, increasing agency for resistance, and imagining alternatives to a dominant culture, but who are also thinking pedagogically and politically about how transformation occurs, often having worked with communities and persons who are attempting to embody an alternative discourse. In other words, I have chosen practical theologians as conversation partners, persons whose theological and theoretical work is prompted by specific situations and contexts and is designed to speak back to those contexts.

As a starting point for my exploration of ongoing conversion, I have chosen the work of John Wesley. As a lifelong United Methodist, my understanding of conversion as a process has been both tacitly and explicitly informed by Wesley's theology. The more I worked with his sermons and teaching strategies, the more I appreciated his strange relevance to the issues with which I wrestle. Wesley's proximity to the start of the Industrial Revolution, his close attention to

---

responsibility we also accept a public responsibility. For it is the great God of heaven and earth who is for us, and we are for this God." Karl Barth, *Church Dogmatics* IV:2, trans. G. W. Bromiley, ed. G. W. Bromiley and T. F. Torrance (Edinburgh: T & T Clark, 1958), 565.

the issue of money and its effects on the souls of believers, his interest in the entire moral psychology of the person in the process of
transformation, and his lifelong practical theological concern as an
educator of persons involved in the Methodist movement make him a
particularly appropriate conversation partner for this project.[3] Wesley's reflections on the *via salutis* (way of salvation) paint a picture
of the ongoing character of the struggle to resist sin and to embrace
a life of love in the image of Christ. Here, I am using the broad concept of ongoing conversion to capture the process to which he refers
in various places as regeneration (restoration of the image of God),

---

3. Wesley's sermon on the uses of money points rather presciently to his concern
about the direction of consumption and its function in the religious life of believers. He notes: "Do not waste any part of so precious a talent merely in gratifying
the desire of the eye by superfluous or expensive apparel, or by needless ornaments.
Waste no part of it in curiously adorning your houses in superfluous or expensive
furniture; in costly pictures, painting, gilding, books; in elegant rather than useful gardens" (John Wesley, "The Use of Money," in *John Wesley's Sermons: An Anthology,*
ed. Albert C. Outler and Richard P. Heitzenrater [Nashville: Abingdon Press, 1991],
353 [hereafter cited as *Sermons*]. He also recognizes the way in which consumption
is a demanding master of desires: "Who would expend anything in gratifying these
desires if he considered that to gratify them is to increase them? Nothing can be more
certain than this: daily experience shows, the more they are indulged, they increase
the more.... When you lay out money to please your eye, you give so much for an
increase of curiosity, for a stronger attachment to these pleasures, which perish in the
using" (354). Although Wesley was deeply concerned about the plight of the poor
and the impact of poverty on believers, his social location in history made him seek
individual rather than social reform of these issues. At the same time, he emphasized
the need for works of mercy to both spirit and body, and refused to separate issues
of economics and faith. His cautionary words in his sermon on the uses of money
seem relevant even today, particularly the famous trifold instructions: gain all you
can, save all you can, and give all you can: "But this it is certain we ought not to do:
we ought not to gain money at the expense of life; nor (which is in effect the same
thing) at the expense of our health. Therefore no gain whatsoever should induce us
to enter into, or to continue in, any employ which is of such a kind, or is attended
with so hard or so long labour, as to impair our constitution. Neither should we
begin or continue in any business which necessarily deprives us of proper seasons
for food and sleep in such a proportion as our nature requires" (350). Wesley goes on
to denounce working environments that involve exposure to toxic chemicals. Finally
he denounces any gain that hurts our neighbors, whether in substance, in body, or
in soul. Wesley's association with those who were workers in the early Industrial
Revolution led him to see the great harm that exploitative working conditions could
cause to body, mind, and soul.

sanctification (increase in holiness of heart and life), and Christian perfection (perfection in love of God and neighbor).

As a religious educator, whose primary contexts are the seminary classroom and local congregations, I am also interested in the function of small communities that educate. Thus, another set of authors that I am in conversation with are a blend of theologians, ethicists, and educators who are all interested in the formation of political agents for the transformation of basic faith or ethical understandings in individuals and broader social groups. These persons, such as Sharon Welch, Paulo Freire, and Rosemary Radford Ruether, are concerned primarily about social transformation but are looking at small communities as the pedagogical base to create it. These more contemporary authors are informed by political dynamics in a different way than Wesley, and they pay attention to generating resistance to dominant culture and formation in alternative cultures.

By putting a theologian of ongoing conversion with pedagogical insights into sustaining changes in faith commitments in conversation with theorists interested in resistance to and transformation of dominant modes of making meaning, I hope to illuminate some key aspects of educational efforts to assist adolescent conversion from faith in consumer culture. Using the resources explored, I begin to describe the shape of a pedagogy of ongoing conversion that can address the particular challenges of this age group in a variety of contexts.

Throughout the book I keep my examples and imagination focused on adolescents and the practice of religious education with young people. Many of the stories come from my own practice of youth ministry in local churches and residential theological academies for youth. I also draw on a series of interviews conducted over the years with participants in these settings. I hope you recognize the young people in your life in their stories and find in these pages resources to support your own ministry of creating circles of grace where young people can be free to respond fully to God's call in their life in the midst of consumer culture.

Part one

Adolescents and consumer culture

One

Must they go sadly away?

Adolescence, vocational imagination, and consumer culture

As [Jesus] was setting out on a journey, a man ran up and knelt before him, and asked him, "Good Teacher, what must I do to inherit eternal life?" Jesus said to him, "Why do you call me good? No one is good but God alone. You know the commandments: 'You shall not murder; You shall not commit adultery; You shall not steal; You shall not bear false witness; You shall not defraud; Honor your father and mother.' " He said to him, "Teacher, I have kept all these since my youth." Jesus, looking at him, loved him and said, "You lack one thing; go, sell what you own, and give the money to the poor, and you will have treasure in heaven; then come, follow me." When he heard this, he was shocked and went away grieving, for he had many possessions.

— Mark 10:17–22[1]

The rich young ruler, Michael, and me

The young man in this story experiences a moment of vocational crisis. Raised as a faithful member of his religious tradition, he is well-versed in its commandments. He even claims to have kept the commandments of this tradition since his youth. Upon meeting a powerful teacher within his tradition, he questions what he is called

---

1. New Revised Standard Version, copyright 1989, Division of Christian Education of the National Council of the Churches of Christ in the United States of America.

11

to do to please God and be named among God's heirs. He wants to follow a vocational path that will be acceptable to God, marked in the symbol system of the story as the gift of eternal life. The answer he receives from Jesus is not what he is expecting. By inviting the young man to sell what he owns and to give the money to the poor, Jesus demonstrates to him that there is still something in his life that is more important than responding to God's calling. The story ends somewhat tragically: unable to release himself from his possessions, the young man turns sadly away from following Jesus in a God-centered life, at least within the confines of the narrative.

I wrestled with the implications of this story while growing up in upper-middle-class Protestant congregations. The text came up often in our educational programming, perhaps because the issue it addressed aligned closely with the spiritual struggles of fairly well-off American United Methodists. The story served as a proof text for the problem of materialism, a sort of warning about the perils of loving things too much. More radical interpreters among our Sunday school teachers and youth group sponsors understood it as a condemnation of the rich. It was a frightening text that called into question the easy marriage of Christian discipleship and our economic lifestyle.

As I have continued to listen to this text, I am less convinced that it is a text of condemnation. It is true that immediately following this encounter in the text, Jesus turns to his disciples and begins to teach them how difficult it is for the wealthy to enter the kingdom of God. For both the disciples and the young man, the idea that owning many possessions could inhibit entrance into the kingdom of God is a surprising notion. The young man is "shocked" by this information; the disciples are "perplexed." Apparently, people in ancient times assumed the salvific nature of possessions much as we do in contemporary times. In Mark's narrative, Jesus uses this encounter to disabuse the disciples and the young man of the notion that owning many possessions would lead to salvation. Instead, wealth makes the ability to enter the kingdom of God more rather than less difficult. However, Jesus carefully points out that it is not impossible. One of the important elements of the story in Mark's version is the lack of condemnation from Jesus for the young man. In the moment where Jesus calls the man into a life following him without the burden of his possessions, he looks at the seeker and "loves" him. Rather than a story of denunciation of the wealthy, this is a story in which Jesus demonstrates compassion for and insight into the complexity of a young man's relationship to his possessions, even as he graciously calls him into a different life.

It's a story that has become rather emblematic of many young people I have encountered in my work as a Christian religious educator. Often adolescents formed in the Christian tradition truly desire to live out a vocation that expresses their love for God and neighbor. Yet they find themselves coopted by social scripts that emphasize their own potential for success as indicated by the accumulation of wealth, status, and possessions. Often, their nascent dreams of living out a God-centered vocation are pushed to the side by the concerns of an alternative definition of success embodied by two of the primary institutions of adolescence: schools and mass media.[2] Alternatively, they may continue to articulate vocational statements that are couched in the language of Christianity, yet their behavior and living situations express a different set of values.[3]

As a religious educator in a local church, I began to wonder what sort of educational efforts could counter young people's formation into consumer roles promulgated by a broader U.S. culture. One incident stands out in my mind as an example of how this formation is expressed. I gave "Michael" a ride to the Sunday night youth group meeting every week. Normally, my conversation with Michael on the

---

2. I name school and mass media as primary institutions for adolescence because they are the institutions outside of the family within which most American adolescents spend the majority of their time: approximately thirty-five hours at school and on average forty hours a week using mass media. For a comprehensive study of the use of the media by children and adolescents, see Donald F. Roberts and Ulla G. Foehr, *Kids & Media in America* (Cambridge: Cambridge University Press, 2004), 139.

3. For an insightful and deeply nuanced discussion of this phenomenon, see Brian J. Mahan, *Forgetting Ourselves on Purpose: Vocation and the Ethics of Ambition* (San Francisco: Jossey Bass, 2002). My own thinking on this topic has been deeply influenced by Mahan's work.

road consisted almost entirely of my asking questions about things of interest to him. Michael generally was polite enough to answer, but he rarely got passionate or particularly involved in what he was saying, unless it involved a trick bike move he had been practicing. One week, however, Michael offered out of the blue: "Do you know what *really* bugs me?" I was surprised by the energy behind the statement, and so I responded with interest to hear something of what made Michael tick: "When people are really cheap," he said in a tone of utter disgust. I asked him why this issue was particularly on his mind that day. It turned out that he and his mother had been shopping for new shoes and clothes that afternoon, and his mother had wanted to buy off-brand alternatives to the clothing and shoe items that Michael had selected. He went off on a small rant about how people should be willing to spend the money for quality items and how important it was to have the right kinds of shoes and clothes. He even used the words "project the right image" in this sermonette about the virtues of being a good consumer. All of this was delivered uncritically and without a sense of irony: it was a kind of gospel truth for Michael. The right brands — at least for the moment — equaled salvation from the derision of peers.

Because as an adolescent I had once had the same fight with my mother over a pair of outrageously expensive designer jeans, one would think that this conversation might not have come as such a surprise to me. I was surprised, however, because I thought that Michael's parents and the community in which he was reared had sufficiently and intentionally educated him out of this commitment to being a good consumer. Michael's parents had chosen an alternative lifestyle. His mother and father are both social workers with significant commitments to impoverished and underserved populations. His commercial television viewing had been carefully monitored and limited. Michael attended public schools with students of diverse ethnic and economic backgrounds. His church home was a congregation with a deep theological commitment to social justice, and Michael had been taught in theory, narrative, and daily life practice about issues of economic justice. Yet, despite this immersion in an alternative community with clearly articulated values, Michael was reading to me a social script about consumption straight out of mainstream U.S. culture.

As I reflected upon this conversation with Michael over the next weeks and months, I became acutely aware of the ways in which I also was deeply formed by my participation in American consumer culture. As an educator, I began to be concerned that nothing short of complete social isolation could allow room for resistance to the relentless education into the role of consumer present in our culture. This concern about Michael's and my own formation into the role of consumer has prompted my interest in adolescent vocational formation within the context of consumer culture.

I often wonder how the encounter between Jesus and the young man with many possessions might turn out differently in a modern context. How might someone be transformed so that she is not imprisoned in the grasp of her possessions, but rather is free to respond to the call of God and move into a life that more fully embodies the love of God and neighbor? More specifically, how might North American adolescents who are deeply shaped by the context of aggressively targeted marketing and recruitment into the role of consumer be given the space to make vocational choices that do not merely replicate the social scripts of success through wealth accumulation, but rather open up the possibility of a variety of ways of defining and living into a meaningful life path for themselves?

Generating problem

The generating problem of this book is a theological problem with strong ethical components posed by the context of the United States: how can Christian vocation develop in adolescents in the midst of a strong alternative formation of vocation offered by the cultural-economic system of consumer capitalism? Participation in the cultural context of the United States provides powerful vocational social scripts in which working to make enough money to buy many things becomes a vocational end in itself. While the Christian tradition challenges this abbreviated understanding of human vocation, even fairly well-traditioned Christian adolescents often demonstrate little integration of Christian understandings of human vocation.

The formation of Christian vocational identity in a contemporary U.S. context is a form of countercultural activity. This claim highlights some assumptions, both sociological and theological, that I should clarify before continuing. First, there are many who would state for varying ideological purposes that the United States is a Christian society; therefore, engendering Christian vocation is not a countercultural activity. In some connotations of the term "Christian society," this is true. For example, Christians still have statistical dominance when it comes to the actual numbers of U.S. citizens who claim a religious affiliation. Historically and culturally, Christians have been the predominant religious voice in this country for the last four hundred years. Members of other religious groups have experienced the ways in which the rhythms of this society are deeply influenced by Christian religious texts, commitments, and the Christian calendar. However, to state that this religious voice has been the primary discourse for meaning making among the American citizenry ignores the impact of other deeply rooted forms of discourse that both shape and arise from the lived experience of Americans, whether the discourses are philosophical, political, psychological, or economic. In fact, there are many multilayered cultures going on simultaneously within "American" culture, with various levels of cachet in influencing human behavior. However, I risk gross oversimplification to state that, particularly in the lives of adolescents, the culture of consumption has risen to nearly hegemonic status in informing the imaginations of young people. I say more to support this claim in the pages to follow, but for now I leave the challenge that the Christian tradition (a multilayered discourse of its own) is a countercultural discourse in most adolescents' lives.

Second, despite claims that Christian identity is deeply intertwined with capitalism, famously Max Weber's work on the relationship between the Protestant work ethic and the development of capitalism,[4] Christian theological claims do not partner easily with the meanings and values of consumer capitalism. This is a theological assertion rather than a social-scientific or historical one. Basic Christian theological claims such as the love of God and neighbor, care for the alien and the orphan, reverence and stewardship of creation, and justice for the poor and oppressed fundamentally come into conflict with the basic meaning claims of consumer capitalism: more is better; beautiful, famous, and powerful people are the most valuable; and the ultimate ethical value in decision-making has to do with the bottom line and the increase of capital. In a broader context, the culture of consumption practiced in the United States has serious ramifications both nationally and globally in terms of ecological sustainability, global economic justice, ongoing colonialism, and fair labor practices. This cultural system has important material consequences. While I am unable to deal with these issues more than obliquely within the scope of this book, they are ever present in my consciousness and inform my religious commitment to engender resistance to the hegemonic values and practices of consumer capitalism in my own context.

Adolescents, identity, and culture

Since the generating problem deals particularly with the development of vocational identity in adolescence, an exploration of the particular relationship of identity, culture, and adolescence may be helpful. My understanding of adolescence draws heavily on the work of developmental psychologist Erik Erikson. He understood adolescence as the period of normal human development in which there is an increasingly consolidated and emergent sense of ego identity.

---

4. Max Weber, *The Protestant Ethic and the Spirit of Capitalism*, trans. Talcott Parsons (New York: Scribner, 1930).

There is a growing conviction "that one is developing a defined personality within a social reality which one understands."[5] For Erikson, the identity development that consolidates in adolescence is related to the social institution of ideology, by which Erikson means "some inspiring unification of tradition or anticipated techniques, ideas, and ideals"[6] that are offered to youth for their development and integration by older generations. As they venture further from home, adolescents begin to become aware of the broader themes of their social context, and they must navigate who they will be and how they will relate in the midst of these broader themes.

In Erikson's cyclical understanding of the relationships between generations, this necessary integration of ideology into ego identity allows social systems to enter into the fiber of the next generation even as the next generation serves to reject or rejuvenate them. Erikson notes: "Adolescence is thus a vital regenerator in the process of social evolution, for youth can offer its loyalties and energies both to the conservation of that which continues to feel true and to the revolutionary correction of that which has lost its regenerative significance."[7] As such, adolescence can be understood theologically as a period of life whose members serve a prophetic function for the whole of humanity. The understandings of the meaning and value of life, of human vocation, and of relational structures that adolescents confirm or deny will be those that are offered to future generations. People know this intuitively; it informs the concern that churches have when they realize that their young people are not vitally connected to the beliefs and practices that older generations hold dear.

Because of the close relationship of cultural ideology and identity in adolescents, persons in this developmental stage are particularly vulnerable to participation and furtherance of sinful structures that are proposed to them by their elders. Adolescents are thus poised

---

5. Erik Erikson, *Identity and the Life Cycle* (New York: Norton & Company, 1980; reissued 1994), 95.

6. Erik Erikson, *Identity: Youth and Crisis* (New York: Norton & Company, 1968; reissued 1994), 130.

7. Ibid., 134.

to provide prophetic voices for the renewal of understanding of human vocation and at the same time are subject to the deep influence of sinful structures lived out by their forebears. This offers a unique moment of educational intervention around issues of vocation in adolescence, particularly in the cultural context of consumer capitalism.

Many parents struggle with their adolescent children over commitments to consumer capitalism because the wrestling with consumer systems of meaning surfaces so visibly at this age. Adolescents are forced to figure out how they relate to the ideologies of wealth and acquisition as they begin to navigate their enlarging social world. Save a few adults who adopt the ideology wholeheartedly (and might own the bumper sticker proclaiming that "The one who dies with the most toys wins!"), this struggle with consumer ideology often goes underground rather than disappears as we get older. We may become more skillful in our navigation of the ideology of consumer capitalism and more refined in our self-deception about its importance to us rather than less dependent upon it as a meaning system that makes sense of our world. We may find ourselves worrying more about retirement savings and the value of stock portfolios rather than name-brand shoes, but both worries seek salvation in having the money to acquire possessions.

The particular expression of our loyalty to consumer culture also shifts as we mature. For example, in workshops where I have presented on the religious dimensions of consumer culture, I have invited participants to rewrite a familiar sacred text such as Psalm 23 to reflect a consumer rather than a Christian/Jewish religious ideology. I find the exercise helpful because groups enjoy collaborating to create relevant parallels to the phrases in "consumer speak," such as "My MasterCard is my shepherd, I shall not want." At the same time, when we read multiple versions created by different groups, we can begin to see the specific ways in which the religious faith in consumer systems takes form. I have done this exercise with both youth and adults. The differences in the ways they name the ideology are quite interesting. Youth tend to focus on the lookism, branding (especially with cars and clothes), and celebrity aspects of consumer culture. Adults tend to focus on the credit-card debt, overwork, retirement income, and entertainment aspects. The particular ways in which the groups are caught up in the culture are different, but both are deeply involved.

While vocational development begins in late adolescence, it continues to be reshaped and transformed over the entire life span. In addition to reconsidering or actually changing our professions or life priorities at different points in our lifetimes through necessity or desire, even if we stay on the same vocational path our way of following it may change. For example, we may make a move that accepts less income for the benefit of more time with family, or we may shift our focus to caring for clients personally rather than caring about what they can bring us (money, acclaim, status, power, connections). We may choose to retire or take a break in work in order to care for young or elderly family members, or we may find that our lifestyle is more than we can support economically and emotionally and decide to simplify. Negotiating our vocational commitments within consumer culture is a lifetime process. Therefore, the generating problem I am addressing affects not only adolescents but also adults across the life span in the U.S. context. While this issue should be addressed within adulthood as well, late adolescence is a time of intense vocational preparation around economic life in terms of occupational discernment, high school education, and preparation to attend college or enter the workforce. According to Erikson, it is also a time in which identity is being consolidated through the appropriation of cultural social scripts, of what "is expected."

Precisely because adolescence is a period of such intensive involvement in preparation for economic life, it is a particularly apt time for religious educational programs to begin to address issues of vocational discernment. Teens often haven't made lifestyle and relational commitments that are difficult to reverse, such as having children or taking on huge consumer debt, and thus have a bit more freedom to engage in reflection on these choices without the constraints of these

responsibilities. Also, adolescents are an increasingly aggressively targeted market, and in many cases they are already expressing concern
about their own participation in this system.[8]

Targeting adolescents

Adolescents have a unique relationship to economic life in the United
States. In the modern American context, the period of preparation
and education necessary to participate in the economy has delayed
adulthood more than a decade by comparison with earlier societies.[9]
This shift added an entire period of the "teenage" or "adolescent"
years to the course of human development (which now often seems
to extend into the mid-twenties, with the exception of those who
commit violent crimes or give birth to children during this period).
Adolescents are not only a product of changing economic situations;
they are particularly targeted within the realm of consumption as a
lucrative market. Teens are the fastest-growing population group in
U.S. society, and as such they spend enormous amounts of money.
For instance:

> Last year, Americans ages 12–19 spent $170 billion on every-
> thing from jeans to lipsticks, according to Teenage Research
> Unlimited, a Chicago market research firm that works with such
> companies as Nike, MTV and Coca-Cola.... With the current
> teen population at 32 million, the research firm expects 3 percent
> growth for 2002 based on an increase in population.[10]

The very existence of Teenage Research Unlimited, founded in 1982
as the first marketing research firm focusing solely on the teenage

---

8. See, for instance, the documentation of the resistance movement of young
people against corporate takeover of public space provided by Naomi Klein in *No
Logo* (New York: Picador, 1999).

9. For a history of the relationship between economic developments and the
institution of the "teenager," see Thomas Hine, *The Rise and Fall of the American
Teenager* (New York: Avon Books, 1999).

10. "Teen Sheens: Cosmetics Firms Targeting Girls, Their Wallets," *Atlanta
Journal-Constitution,* April 24, 2002.

market, indicates the importance of this market. For a substantial fee, some 150 brand marketers, advertising agencies, and media companies subscribe to TRU in order to receive biennial reports which include a thousand pages of analysis such as "Coolest Brand Meter," "TRUScore celebrity ratings," and other indicators of what teens will buy and why.[11]

Advertisers are also particularly keen to target adolescents because of the belief that adolescents develop brand loyalty that will keep them using a product for life. This is a somewhat twisted form of Proverbs 22:6: "Train children in the right way, and when old, they will not stray."[12] An example of this marketing to the young for lifelong branding can be seen in the efforts of sports marketers to reach the children's market, who have realized "that children will become fans and the season ticket holders of the future."[13] Marketing efforts such as creating children's areas in professional stadiums, allowing children to run the bases after games, and providing promotional giveaways for children all intend to attract children and thus to cultivate a lifelong customer. This wisdom informs the desire of television advertisers that primarily target younger viewers, and it explains why television programming is regularly skewed toward the tastes of younger audience members.

Across the retail spectrum, children and teenagers have become increasingly singled out as profitable markets over the last twenty years. This shift has occurred as advertisers, often with the assistance of child psychology professionals, have realized that children can and do strongly influence the buying choices made by their parents. New child-oriented commodities such as school supplies, clothing, toiletries, foods, and toys connected to popular brands such as Barbie or media events such as the Star Wars movies create an endless presence of commodities in children's lives. A recent *PBS Frontline* special

---

11. For more information, visit the TRU Web site at *www.teenresearch.com*.
12. New Revised Standard Version.
13. Matthew D. Shank, *Sports Marketing: A Strategic Perspective* (Upper Saddle River, NJ: Prentice Hall, 1999), 200.

about marketing to adolescents indicated that the average American adolescent encounters approximately three thousand discrete commercial messages every day.[14] Given that the average American between the ages of eleven and thirteen consumes over eight hours of media a day, and between the ages of fourteen and eighteen about seven and a half hours per day, one can understand how this immersion in commercial media with its attending advertising has a profound influence on the worldview of adolescents.[15]

Offering imaginations of selfhood

In this context of the aggressive targeting of adolescents as a present and future market, consumer culture has a powerful impact on the formation of their desires, values, and tastes. This formation directly impacts their vocational imagination, or their latent understandings of who they are called to be and what they are called to do in the world. Within a Christian theological framework, *vocation* expresses the partnering relationship between humans and God that serves as the primary source of direction for constructing a life path or journey. The word "vocation" is derived from the Latin verb *vocare,* which means "to call." One's calling in a Christian worldview comes from God. This relationship provides an ordering of the daily decisions and life path upon which a person embarks. Theologian James Fowler defines "vocation" as follows:

> *Vocation is the response a person makes with his or her total self to the address of God and to the calling to partnership.* The shaping of vocation as a total response of the self to the address of God involves the orchestration of our leisure, our

---

14. *PBS Frontline: The Merchants of Cool.* Originally aired February 27, 2001.

15. Media included in the Kaiser Family Foundation comprehensive study on children and media use included magazines, newspapers, books, television, video and audio recordings, video and computer games, movies, radio, and computers (including surfing the Web, e-mail, and chat rooms). Computers and books used for school work were not included in the study. Roberts and Foehr, *Kids & Media in America,* 13.

relationships, our work, our private life, our public life, and the resources we steward, so as to put it all at the disposal of God's purposes in the services of God and the neighbor.[16]

Fowler's definition expresses a broad meaning of vocation, something that impacts all areas of the self.

The emphasis on vocation as a total response of the self through ordering of our lives in light of larger meaning is quite similar to what psychologists Mihaly Csikszentmihalyi and Reed Larson in their research with adolescents have called a "life theme." A life theme is a meaningful interpretation of experience that helps teenagers by giving "order to the events that normally produce boredom, rage, or despair."[17] The theme transforms what often presents itself as individual or social misfortune into a goal that gives direction and meaning to the life of the adolescent. Csikszentmihalyi and Larson note that not many adolescents actually form "fully authentic life goals — most are satisfied to pursue the goals society prescribes: a college education, a job, marriage, children, and life within conventional standards of morality."[18] However, Csikszentmihalyi and Larson warn that when entropy or stressful events enter the lives of persons, they are often at a loss to make meaning out of these disordered experiences if they have not moved beyond accepting standard cultural goals to direct their lives. Therefore, for Csikszentmihalyi and Larson, a life theme or vocational understanding is cast as a positive psychological coping mechanism that allows for human flourishing in the midst of difficult times.

Another way of documenting the relationship between adolescence and the importance of vocation is noting the predominance of myths and stories about vocation targeted to young people in mainstream media. This is found particularly in the fantasy genre, with a strong

---

16. James Fowler, *Becoming Adult, Becoming Christian* (San Francisco: Jossey-Bass, 2000), 77, emphasis in original.

17. Mihaly Csikszentmihalyi and Reed Larson, *Being Adolescent* (New York: Basic Books, 1984), 262.

18. Ibid., 278.

representative sample evident in the superhero stories that are enjoying a comeback in visual and electronic media. (They have retained popularity in print media for generations.) Superheroes often discover in adolescence a dramatic calling that they must fulfill. A good example of this in recent popular culture is the television show *Buffy the Vampire Slayer*. In this series, the heroine Buffy finds out as a sophomore in high school that her destiny is to kill vampires and other forms of supernatural evil in order to save the world time and again. Only her closest confidants know of this secret vocation. Buffy struggles with this calling as she tries to balance it with the "normal" concerns of adolescence and young adulthood: grades, friends, extracurricular activities, romantic involvements. Other recent popular television shows such as *Smallville* and *Roswell* and films such as the Star Wars and Harry Potter series also highlight older adolescents struggling to live into their often supernatural vocations to fight evil and injustice in the world. These shows not only represent a fantastic sense of human achievement and fulfill a need for distraction and entertainment, they also appeal to a deep adolescent longing to know that their lives count in the big picture. The stories reflect a desire for a vocation worthy of one's commitment.

Sharon Parks explores the vocational tasks of young adulthood in her book *Big Questions, Worthy Dreams*. Parks has defined young adulthood as approximately the period between ages seventeen and thirty. Therefore, my story about Michael would represent the relationship to consumer capitalism in the younger stages of adolescence, while the period Parks describes overlaps with the movement through older adolescence into young adulthood. She notes the desire for persons in this stage of life to work out a meaningful vocation for themselves:

> Now, at the dawning of the twenty-first century, I continue to watch young adults reach for a place of belonging, integrity, and contribution that can anchor meaningful hope in themselves and our shared future — while the tides of cynicism and the prevailing currents of consumerism play big roles in charting their

course. I have observed, among some of the most talented, many who simply have been lured into elite careers before anyone has invited them to consider the deeper questions of purpose and vocation.[19]

Parks notes that, during young adulthood, a distinctive mode of meaning making can emerge around vocational concerns. Ideally, this mode includes awareness that one composes reality in particular ways, a self-conscious participation in a dialogical search for truth, and cultivation of the agency to respond in just and meaningful ways.[20] She also shares the concern that many young people move into consumer-oriented vocational paths prior to engaging in a meaningful vocational search. In my work with older adolescents at theological summer programs, I have often been troubled to hear young people who otherwise expressed theologically complex understandings of God, the world, and themselves indicate that they would be following one of a few standard career paths associated with the professional middle class: lawyer, doctor, and so on. While some named a sense of calling to caring for the sick or to defending the poor, often the reasons given for these career decisions had more to do with the income level and respect garnered from those positions than their relationship to the young person's faith life. Few recognized that the debt taken on to complete law or medical school and the implicit formation of class values that occurs would shape their commitments and the form of their practice when they emerged.

Many critical theorists and educators have explored the pervasive pedagogy of consumer capitalism and its impact on adolescent vocational imagination. A key figure in this conversation is Henry Giroux, particularly his recent work on youth, corporate power, and the politics of culture entitled *Stealing Innocence*. In this work, Giroux describes how youth are shaped within a social order that is increasingly "a culture of violence that cares more about profits than human

---

19. Sharon Daloz Parks, *Big Questions, Worthy Dreams* (San Francisco: Jossey-Bass, 2000), 3.
20. Ibid., 6.

needs and the public good."[21] Giroux wonders where children find spaces to name hopes, discuss meaningful differences, and form "non-market-based democratic identities."[22] He is particularly concerned with the increasing influence of corporate power in commercializing youth, in elimination of noncommercial public space, and the driving of institutions of education by imperatives of the market.[23] Giroux is but one example of many educators, both religious and secular, who are concerned about the relentless pedagogy of consumer capitalism and its effect on the young.

The connection of vocation and imagination is a particularly significant one in the period of adolescence as young people are beginning to envision possible vocations, that is, patterns of living and ways of being in response to the larger realities in which they find themselves. In *Seeing through the Media*, Michael Warren explores the relationship between media advertising, imagination, and vocation during the adolescent years. He notes:

> During the teen years, young people try on various "imaginations" of themselves in an effort to find one that fits. These imaginations are part of a broader project in young people's lives: they are trying to imagine the kind of person they wish to be, what their future life will be like, and the kind of person they wish to share it with. If the process of establishing an identity is, in part, a process of imagining for oneself possible forms of behavior, possible attitudes and values, possible goals, and ultimately, a possible future, then those who propose those imagined possibilities wield special influence.[24]

The media-saturated realms of consumer capitalism provide a constant stream of images and imaginations to adolescents of what it

---

21. Henry A. Giroux, *Stealing Innocence* (New York: St. Martin's Press, 2000), 23.

22. Ibid., 11.

23. Ibid., 26.

24. Michael Warren, *Seeing through the Media* (Harrisburg, PA: Trinity Press International, 1997), 9.

means to be human in contemporary society. Without intervention, this barrage of images can dominate and distort the vocational imagination of adolescents, leaving them with the guiding vocational image of themselves as consumer above all else. Like the rich young ruler, they may find that this formation in relation to their possessions makes living out a God-centered vocation difficult, if not impossible.

Two

A golden calf?

*Consumer culture as an inadequate object
of adolescent devotion*

Perhaps "idolatry" seems a rather radical way to describe the struggles that young people are dealing with today. Idolatry evokes the seminal story from the book of Exodus in which Aaron calls the people together in the wilderness to fork over their earrings so he can make a golden calf for them to worship. Worshiping a golden calf just because Moses hung out with God on the mountain a trifle long has always seemed a little ludicrous to me. What kind of people would have confidence in a statue of a cow for which they had just given the gold? Surely this kind of idolatry, casting a graven image of an alternative God and then worshiping it, would not be something contemporary persons are tempted to do.

What I didn't know as a child when I learned that story is that the image of a calf was not a random choice for Aaron. The bull was a common religious symbol of Canaanite fertility cults of which the people of Yahweh would have some deep-level awareness. In a moment of serious concern with the power of this God who had brought them out of Egypt, Aaron throws the people a bone. He offers a symbol that, in the broader shared culture of many inhabiting that region of the world, was culturally believed to have great power and meaning. He defaulted to the familiar religious language and symbol that the people would have recognized.

For us, probably the closest contemporary parallel to the fertility religions of the ancient Near East would be consumer culture and the stories it so avidly proposes as a meaning-making system in our culture. If Aaron had been leading the people of the United States in the early twenty-first century, he would not have reverted to casting a golden calf for their trust in a moment of deep uncertainty. Rather, he would likely say, "So, Moses has been detained with the Lord for a while. Don't worry! Let's take your mind off this turn of events. Let's go buy everyone a new pair of hiking boots so we'll be ready to roll when he returns! Or perhaps everybody could turn on their televisions to *Entertainment Tonight* to see how Tom and Katie are getting along this week." (You can add your own comments here about President George W. Bush exhorting the nation to go shopping as an effective response to the terrorist attacks of September 11, 2001.) Consumer culture serves as our default meaning-making system, our golden calf for our new age.

Consumer culture and meaning making

In using consumer capitalism as a category I do not intend to evoke a strictly economic analysis of structures of exchange. Rather, I am talking about consumer capitalism as a cultural system that wields powerful influence on human valuing, relationship, meaning making, and institutional structures in a U.S. context. Beyond their service as the way in which we generate and acquire the necessary goods for living, categories of consumption become a powerful and central contributor to the ways in which Americans make sense of their lives and decide what is important to them. It informs the vocational imagination of our collective identity. We live to shop. Currently, the culture of consumption in the United States seems to have reached unprecedented heights, spawning various grassroots resistance efforts such as the simplicity movement and Adbusters.

How did consumption assume this role in our contemporary setting? Economist Juliet Schor has analyzed some of the reasons that consumption has moved to become such a central piece of culture. She notes that as birth, history, and caste become less important in determining status in Western industrialized nations, ownership of goods becomes more important as a marker of status. Historically, as the middle class increased in number, access to the goods that were once only available to the economic elite became more widely available to whoever could find the income. Schor notes:

> Urbanization, formal education, and the disappearance of traditional social relationships render spending more salient in establishing social position and personal identity. Thus, in the modern consumer society, commodities take on a new kind of symbolic importance. (Consumption has symbolic importance in all societies, but in consumer society its role in establishing personal identity and social position to some extent eclipse its symbolic role in ritual, religion, and so on.) More and more, what you wear and what you don't wear define who you are and where you are located on the social map.[1]

Anyone who has walked alongside a young person through the experience of middle school recognizes the pathos of Schor's last sentence. In addition to urbanization, for adolescents the consolidation of local schools into regional high schools means that even rural, small-town teenagers tend to be in school largely with persons with whom they are not familiar. With no other readily available social information to determine status, the pressure on adolescents to wear clothing and have other personal accouterments that bear markers of status can be intense.

Schor also notes that this pressure to consume grows as the reference groups with whom persons compare themselves has shifted from the Joneses up the street (who often shared their basic economic station in life) to an understanding informed by mass media of what are "normal" kinds of goods to own. Television and movies almost exclusively portray the lifestyles of the upper social classes.[2] The proliferation of television shows that explore the daily lives of celebrities and their stuff (homes, vacations, wilderness treks) demonstrate the

---

1. Juliet Schor, "What's Wrong with Consumer Society? Competitive Spending and the 'New Consumerism,'" in *Consuming Desires*, ed. Roger Rosenblatt (Washington, DC: Island Press, 1999), 41.
2. Ibid., 44.

hunger of regular people to view the lives of the economic elite. The MTV show *Cribs* exemplifies this approach, with young sports professionals, musicians, and actors giving tours of their homes in which they gleefully point out their favorite stuff: luxury vehicles, projection televisions, Jacuzzis, and customized gourmet kitchens filled with takeout boxes from trendy eating places. Yesterday's luxury items quickly become today's middle-class necessities. For Schor, one of the outcomes of this situation is the rise of the "aspirational gap," that is, the difference between what people aspire to and the income they have available to spend.[3] This increasing gap means that at almost any level of income consumers are dissatisfied because they do not believe that they have enough.

In addition, people are more likely now than in previous generations to equate the good life with owning the right goods: "Growing numbers of people believe that vacation homes, swimming pools, travel abroad, really nice clothes, a lot of money, and second cars are symbolic of a good life."[4] This equation of ownership with virtue, the continual dissatisfaction cultured in the consumer, and the shaping of desire and sense of beauty moves the issue of consumption squarely into the realm of religious belief. Consumption becomes more than acquiring what one needs for material survival; it moves into the realm of meaning making and valuing in a structured system well beyond the individual taste of the purchaser.

This cultural system of consumption is not only supported by and embodied in institutions such as the mass media and its advertising corporations, but also has a significant toe-hold in sectors such as public schools, higher education, and even churches. The cultural system becomes invested in the corporate lives of people through something similar to Raymond Williams's understanding of "structure of feeling," which I first encountered through the work of Michael Warren. Warren notes, "Structure of feeling refers to characteristic ways of seeing and judging that emerge from the social and

---

3. Ibid., 46.
4. Ibid., 45.

cultural patterns experienced by particular generations."[5] Another term used for this phenomenon is "taste." Similarly, I am using consumer capitalism to refer to an entire cluster of cultural meanings around owning goods and their value for human life that has become embodied in human patterns of meaning making in the contemporary U.S. context. It informs the tacit understandings or worldviews of persons who live within it.

Of course, I am not the first person to notice the relationship between American forms of consumer capitalism and religious meaning making. Anxiety about the relationships among spiritual health, consumerism, materialism, and individualism seems to be growing, particularly in terms of its impact on the development of children and adolescents. An entire body of popular literature has emerged about the relationships between faith and consumption.[6] Many theologians have dealt with the relationship between religious and economic thought, and the connections are numerous and complex.[7] In this book, I am relating consumer capitalism to religious belief by describing the ways that consumer capitalism serves as a cultural system of meaning making.

---

5. Warren, *Seeing through the Media*, 70.

6. Here are a few examples from the body of literature engaging the religious and spiritual aspects of participation in consumer culture: Tom Beaudoin, *Consuming Faith: Integrating Who We Are with What We Buy* (Lanham, MD: Sheed & Ward, 2003); Marva J. Dawn, *Unfettered Hope: A Call to Faithful Living in an Affluent Society* (Louisville: Westminster/John Knox, 2003); Dell deChant, *The Sacred Santa: Religious Dimensions of Consumer Culture* (Cleveland: Pilgrim Press, 2002); Vincent J. Miller, *Consuming Religion: Christian Faith and Practice in a Consumer Culture* (New York: Continuum, 2003); and Arthur Simon, *How Much Is Enough? Hungering for God in an Affluent Culture* (Grand Rapids: Baker Books, 2003).

7. One connection between the two would be economics as a form of theology. Harvey Cox convincingly argued in "The Market as God" (*Atlantic Monthly*, March 1999) that economists writing for the *Wall Street Journal* were actually writing a form of process theology with "The Market" serving as a god with the corresponding characteristics of being omnipotent, omniscient, and omnipresent. Another way of connecting the two is through shared metaphors. For example, M. Douglas Meeks struggles to recover the metaphor of economist for God at least partly to undo the separation of politics and economy (M. Douglas Meeks, *God the Economist: The Doctrine of God and Political Economy* [Minneapolis: Fortress Press, 1989], 6–7).

Consumer culture = American culture?

Some authors have proposed that the consumption of commodities serves fundamentally as the basis for American society and culture.[8] While prominent theorists such as Baudrillard, Adorno, and Marcuse have argued that the culture of consumption is a whirlwind of deception and falsity that keeps persons from paying attention to their true needs, the depth to which it has become centralized in American culture makes it difficult to argue that it could be stripped away entirely. In this line of thinking, consumer culture represents more than the outward distractions that keep us from attending to our deepest concerns: consumer culture serves as the core unifying element of American culture which we export globally through multinational corporations. Rodney Clapp reports an incident that exemplifies the depth to which American culture is defined by consumption:

> I asked Lendol Calder, a historian in New Hampshire who devoted his doctoral book to consumerism, "When did you first begin to notice the depth and breadth of consumerism in our culture?" He recalled a Christian camp for college students of several nationalities. A get-acquainted exercise divided campers by nationality, charging them to choose a song representing their culture, one that all could approve and sing to the rest of the assembly. Most nationalities reached consensus, practiced, and were ready in 10 to 20 minutes; nearly all the groups chose folk songs from their native lands. Not the Americans. They debated over 20 minutes, then an hour.... At last they settled on the Coca-Cola jingle "I'd Like to Teach the World to Sing." The tune ringing in his ears, Lendol realized that commercial culture was what really bound these Americans — these American Christians — together.[9]

---

8. Grant McCracken, *Culture and Consumption* (Bloomington: Indiana University Press, 1988).

9. Rodney Clapp, "Why the Devil Takes Visa," *Christianity Today* (October 7, 1996): 20.

The equation of consumer culture with the heart of contemporary American culture is not uncommon. Alex Kotlowitz studied young residents of Henry Horner Homes. Kotlowitz notes that although these children are socially isolated from the cultural centers and resources of mainstream Chicago, they are still connected to people outside of their economic class. He writes: "[I]t is as consumers that inner-city children, otherwise so disconnected from the world around them, identify themselves not as ghetto kids or project kids but as Americans or just plain kids."[10] By borrowing the fashions of bourgeois Americans, they become connected to a more prosperous and secure world. The only way in which they have access to participate in this world is as a consumer: "It is as consumers that they claim citizenship."[11]

Kotlowitz explores the meaning of the sharing of fashions between poor urban and wealthy suburban teens, noting that the connections created by consuming the same fashions are not true connections. In reality, poor children do not have access to the institutional resources of their suburban peers, and suburban young people know nothing about the difficult day-to-day reality of their neighbors. He notes, "And so, in lieu of building real connections — by providing opportunities or rebuilding communities — we have found some common ground as purchasers of each other's trademarks. At best, that link is tenuous; at worst, it's false."[12] Kotlowitz strongly argues that the culture of consumption has become the defining marker of American culture.

Lest we equate "U.S. culture" with "consumer culture" in too monolithic a fashion, it is important to consider how consumer culture manifests itself in various contexts and subcultures of U.S. society in different ways. In Clapp's vignette about the group of college-age Christians attempting to find a common cultural ground, he does

---

10. Alex Kotlowitz, "False Connections," in Rosenblatt, ed., *Consuming Desires*, 67.
11. Ibid., 69.
12. Ibid., 72.

not address the reality that the difficulty in defining a single cultural song arises at least partially from the remarkable ethnic and
racial diversity of the United States. Anthropologist Elizabeth Chin
recently tackled the project of describing how consumer capitalism
manifests itself in a particular subcontext as she wrote an ethnographic study of the impact of American consumer culture on poor
and working-class racial-minority children living in the Newhallville neighborhood of New Haven, Connecticut. She notes that the
easy equation of American culture with consumer culture in analyses
such as Kotlowitz's fails to recognize the diversity embedded in consumers' lives across boundaries of ethnicity, gender, race, and class.[13]
Chin notes that contemporary commodity consumption impacts the
Newhallville children as strongly or even more strongly than their
middle-class, majority-culture peers, but that their participation in
this culture is quite different from these more privileged peers. In
her analysis, she proposes that contemporary consumption serves
as a "medium through which social inequalities — most notably of
race, class, and gender — are formed, experienced, imposed, and
resisted."[14]

Despite her claims that the economically disadvantaged young persons she interviewed were deeply impacted by consumer culture, Chin
asserts that to assume that consumers are passive recipients swayed
by the products and services offered by self-interested corporations
is to underestimate their agency and creativity in interacting with
the process of consumption. Chin argues that her young informants
confront the culture of market and critique it from their own social
location. The limited economic resources of the Newhallville children
that she interviewed mean that they recognize from an early age the
scarcity of goods to which they have access and the limits that this
places on their desires. For Chin, the consumption process includes
not only the acquisition of goods, but also the encounter with a wide
spectrum of images and ideas. Chin relates the story of two young

---

13. Elizabeth Chin, *Purchasing Power: Black Kids and American Consumer
Culture* (Minneapolis: University of Minnesota Press, 2001), 7.
14. Ibid., 3.

girls and their playful response to the Barbie doll they own. One of the youngsters, ten year-old Asia, notes:

> Okay. What I was saying that Barbie...how can I say this? They make her like a stereotype. Barbie is a stereotype. When you think of Barbie you don't think of fat Barbie.... You don't think of pregnant Barbie. You never, ever...think of an abused Barbie.[15]

The girls are testing within the realm of their own experience the stories that are being sold to them through the commodity Barbie. Through this encounter, Chin pushes her reader to broaden the understanding of the agency of consumers. She notes, "[I]t has become increasingly evident that consumption is at once a hegemonic force deserving of condemnation and a realm in which people exercise considerable power and creativity."[16]

Such careful analysis of the negotiations made by the children reminds us not to reduce consumer culture to an evil Pied Piper who seduces all persons to uncritical participation in the dance. At the same time, Chin shows us that the desires cultivated by consumer culture are not limited to those who have the economic resources to act on them. Her point is one that we are invited to consider carefully: how can consumer culture simultaneously be a hegemonic force that deserves condemnation and the locus of creative and playful expression of individual agency? The complexity of this relationship between culture and individual construction of vocational expressions warrants further investigation, which I do by considering participation in consumer culture as a form of religious faith.

Consumer culture as a faith system

To identify consumer culture as a form of a faith system requires that I explain how I am using the term "faith." Everyone has faith in

---

15. Ibid., 1.
16. Ibid., 10.

something. The idea that a person cannot survive and construct a life in any meaningful way without faith has been memorably asserted in religious educational literature by James Fowler in his work on faith development.[17] He defines faith as follows: "It is our way of finding coherence in and giving meaning to the multiple forces and relations that make up our lives. Faith is a person's way of seeing him- or herself in relation to others against a background of shared meaning and purpose."[18] Faith, for Fowler, is a universal human phenomenon that serves to help people forge purpose and meaning in relationship to the larger entities with whom they are in relationship.

Fowler draws on the work of previous Christian theologians in his analysis, most notably that of H. Richard Niebuhr, for whom the understanding of the self as a fiduciary being is a unique and persistent theme. For Niebuhr, humans can perhaps have an existence, but they cannot be *selves* without loyalty, without fidelity to a center of value that bestows worth on their existence.[19] In Niebuhr's anthropology, "to be a self is to have a god," a center of value and power that connects the narrative of one's life into a meaningful, unified history.[20] For Niebuhr, even persons who would consider themselves atheists are not faithless. To deny the existence of a supernatural being is quite different from living without trust in a center of value or without loyalty to any cause.[21] Faith can have a range of objects of loyalty or centers of value, and its relational character arises among those who share the same faith objects.

Some contemporary young persons may appear to put this idea of universal faith to the test, living a life defined by cynicism, or more drastically nihilism. While it may seem paradoxical to put nihilism

---

17. Fowler develops this understanding particularly in part 1 of James W. Fowler, *Stages of Faith: The Psychology of Human Development and the Quest for Meaning* (San Francisco: HarperSanFrancisco, 1981).

18. Ibid., 4.

19. H. Richard Niebuhr, *Radical Monotheism and Western Culture*, Library of Theological Ethics Edition (Louisville: Westminster/John Knox Press, 1993), 22.

20. H. Richard Niebuhr, *The Meaning of Revelation* (New York: Macmillan, 1941), 59.

21. Niebuhr, *Radical Monotheism and Western Culture*, 25.

and faith in the same sentence, even a belief that nothing is worth trusting can provide the organizing center of value and power for the self. The embracing larger metaphor that provides the categories by which some persons narrate their lives is something like avoidance of being made a fool by refusing to trust in anything outside of oneself. By not committing to anything larger than ourselves, be it institutions, religious traditions, political structures, or value systems, we won't be used by something bigger than us for purposes that are not our own. This can be seen in the influence of the philosophy of anarchy among the young, even young people who are protesting for social change. This ideology may be at least partially an inheritance of the distrust exhibited by their parents' generation, many of whom were part of questioning the racism, sexism, and militarism of institutions in the 1960s and 1970s. However, a life lived solely in negative reaction and/or ironic playfulness ultimately lacks hope and the ability to forge new institutions that sustain human community and life.[22] Defining our selves solely in resistance to something is perhaps enough to survive, but not enough for our lives to flourish and constructively add to the common good.[23]

In claiming that humans are only selves if they have faith, Niebuhr means something much richer than cognitive consent to a set of doctrines or to the existence of certain realities. Rather, faith refers to the experience of reliance, trust, and relational dependence on those

22. Sharon Welch similarly explores the limitations of a politics of critique in her chapter "Frustration and Righteous Anger Do Not a Politics Make": "Once we have power, and we should have it, what are we to do with it? How do we move from the politics of protest to the very different challenges of building institutions?" Sharon Welch, *Sweet Dreams in America* (New York: Routledge, 1999), xxi.

23. This claim reflects a normative judgment that will have to be tested by further observation and reflection, but it is an insight that is often embedded in educational theory and practice. An education only in critique ultimately fails to encourage the development necessary for full and vibrant participation in the world. Thomas Aquinas provided a metaphor for this insight when he warned teachers "never to dig a ditch that you fail to fill up." French educator Jacques Maritain notes about Aquinas's warning: "He knew that to raise clever doubts, to prefer searching to finding, and perpetually to pose problems without ever solving them are the great enemies of education" (Jacques Maritain, *Education at the Crossroads* [New Haven, CT, and London: Yale University Press, 1941], 50).

realities.[24] Faith is the ordering of one's life based on loyalty to a cause or a value center.[25] For example, during the devastating days after Hurricane Katrina, many people who would not profess a belief in "big government" were shocked and horrified when governmental agencies were unable to alleviate the suffering of thousands of New Orleans residents marooned downtown after the storm. Although their expressed beliefs about government may have been "the less of it, the better," they actually relied on government to intervene and save people in moments of deep crisis. In other words, they had faith in the government that was sorely tested in this incident.

While existence of those things in which we place our trust is implied, faith moves beyond intellectual assent to a relationship of reliance upon it: "Faith represents a knowing that involves personal commitment, confidence, and trust rather than a detached understanding of the nature of things."[26] The objects of faith are those persons or realities in which we place our ultimate security and reliance. They are the things we value absolutely, a "being infinitely attractive, which by its very nature calls forth devotion, joy and trust."[27] The "infinite attractiveness" of the objects of faith indicates that an aesthetic sensibility is involved in the experience of faith. Our objects of faith are not only trustworthy, they are beautiful to us. They evoke a positive response to their rightness, their fittingness.

Thus, if the human relationship to consumer culture is understood as a kind of faith, it runs much deeper than intellectual assent to an economic system or even the mindless mimetic behavior of consumption. It implies a faithful dependency that orders the self at a primary level. Humans trust in and count upon the meaning system of consumer capitalism to make sense of reality and themselves, even if they would not use this language to describe their own faith. Metaphors from this meaning system such as "bottom-line thinking" and "capital" begin to have "cash value" or "purchase" to frame and make

---

24. Niebuhr, *Radical Monotheism and Western Culture*, 116.
25. Ibid., 24.
26. Ibid., 112.
27. Ibid., 25.

sense of realities far from the original contexts of their use. Educators, for example, may talk about the "social capital" of communities when discussing the contexts of origin of their students. The language of this meaning system becomes the metaphoric base by which other situations are made sense of and explained.

In my college days, my friends and I would engage in a ritual we jokingly called "consumer therapy." When we were feeling down or bored, we would embark upon shopping trips, often for items we didn't particularly need. Thinking about consumerism as a kind of faithful participation in a religious system indicates that there was perhaps more truth to the therapeutic aspects of this behavior than we realized. The belief was that engaging in the ritual of purchasing something would lift one's spirits and reinstall a sense of meaning and purpose into life. It did — at least for a while. Some deep sense of self was invested in the ritual of acquisition and consumption of goods. Participation in consumer activities takes on the character of faith when it provides an ordering purpose to one's life based on loyalty to a center of value shared with others.

Consumer culture as religious system

This equation of consumer culture to religious faith is explored further by Dell deChant in *The Sacred Santa*. Looking through the prism of the Christmas holiday in the United States, deChant argues that the commercialization of this holiday does not exemplify the secularization of society as is commonly assumed. Rather than a secular corruption of a Christian feast, the consumer activity around Christmas functions as the high holy day of a completely different religion, one centered on consumer culture. DeChant compares the normative ritual practices and legitimating mythic narratives of consumer culture to those of cosmological religions of antiquity. Whereas ancient religious persons once worshiped the natural world as the locus of sacred power, consumer culture is a religion that reveres the economy as the divine power. A religion such as Christianity reveres a personal, transcendental god, and the locus of human meaning and value rests in the individual believer. A cosmological religion such as consumer culture has a world utterly permeated by the divine, and the locus of human meaning and value is in the social collective rather than in the individual.[28]

Consumer culture, like other religions, is at its strongest when it is practiced by an entire culture. It has its own ritual calendar (the Friday after Thanksgiving is considered "Pilgrimage Day" in deChant's schema) and normative practices. This religious system is complete with shared myths and rituals. He names the great meta-myth as "the myth of success and affluence, gained through a proper relationship with the economy, and revealed in the ever-expanding material prosperity of society and through the ever-increasing acqui-sition and consumption of products by individuals."[29] This myth is the story we know the best, the one that we tell each other and that we never tire of hearing. Our mythic heroes — celebrities and others who have mastered the process of acquisition and consumption — invite us to be like them, "to be close to the sacred world they have mastered," preferably by consuming the products they consume.[30] Through mimicry of the actions of mythic heroes we improve our participation in the religious activities of consumer culture and draw close to the sacred world that they have mastered.

Unlike my example of consumer therapy, which indicated some level of ironic self-reflection, deChant asserts that the whole point of this ritual system is that we don't think about it much: "It is just the way things are. What *is* is what *ought* to be. To say otherwise, or to think too hard about it, is not appropriate, not normal, not in harmony with the sacred order and process of the economy."[31] In this, religion is not a distinct collection of beliefs and practices but

---

28. Dell deChant, *The Sacred Santa: Religious Dimensions of Consumer Culture* (Cleveland: Pilgrim Press, 2002), 30.

29. Ibid., 37.

30. Ibid., 38. For an example of this kind of media, see the E! channel's show *It's Great to Be*. In each episode, a different celebrity is profiled solely in terms of the amount of money they make and how and where they spend it. In religious terms, it is a hagiography of consumption.

31. deChant, *The Sacred Santa*, 40.

rather a comprehensive way of being and living that connects a people together. We do not have to give conscious attention to the meaning narratives that guide this behavior. The most important thing is the ritual acquisition of products themselves.

No one has to be initiated or confirmed into consumer religion. The religious narratives are all around us and within us. One of the most ubiquitous forms of the mythic narrative is found in advertising. DeChant notes, "In these myths the most sacred entities of all insert themselves into our world. These are the commodities of consumer culture, goods and products, the sacred objects and images of ritual consumption; and their stories are of supreme importance to us all."[32] Through the immediate access of billboards, mail-order catalogs, commercials, and brand logos, the beliefs of consumer culture are disseminated and new believers are evangelized minute by minute.

In line with Fowler's analysis of the universality of the human phenomenon of faith, deChant names the religiosity of even the most seemingly secular of behaviors, such as watching advertisements and going to the mall. DeChant muses that by recognizing the religious nature of consumer culture, we may "discover just how religious we may really be and how hard it may be to be different than we are."[33] What is a side comment for deChant in his text rests at the center of this book: we cannot easily shift the objects of our true dependence and shared religiosity. The process of change involves heart and mind, desires and loves that are so thoroughly shaped within this religious milieu that they seem natural, even "God-given." The nearness of this faith to the core of individual selfhood and shared religious identity makes it difficult to transform.

The equation of capitalism with religious belief is not a recent phenomenon. H. Richard Niebuhr expressed concerns about the church and its relationship to capitalism well over a half century ago in his work *The Church against the World*. He noted:

---

32. Ibid., 62.
33. Ibid., 40.

The church is in bondage to capitalism. Capitalism in its contemporary form is more than a system of ownership and distribution of economic good. It is a faith and a way of life. It is faith in wealth as the source of all life's blessings and as the savior of man from his deepest misery. It is the doctrine that man's most important activity is the production of economic goods and that all other things are dependent upon this.[34]

Niebuhr noted that this faith is embodied in laws and social habits, transforming civilization into an economically centered enterprise. Other institutions such as education, government, family, and the city begin to be structured and dominated by the interests of the religion of capitalism. Niebuhr noted, "So intimate is the relation between the civilization and the faith, that it is difficult to participate in the former without consenting to the latter and becoming entangled in its destructive morality."[35] Success, cost-effectiveness, and efficiency infiltrate and replace faithfulness to God and love of neighbor as the cultivated virtues of discipleship for both churches and individuals.[36] In the twenty-first century, we need to shift Niebuhr's analysis a bit to emphasize the consumption rather than the production of goods, but his description of the faithlike reliance on capitalism remains convincing.

Niebuhr's labeling of this predominance of reliance on capitalism as an issue of faith has caused me to reconsider elements of my own long-term project of religious education that might generate resistance to societal and cultural norms of consumption in the United

---

34. H. Richard Niebuhr, *The Church against the World* (Chicago and New York: Willett, Clark & Co., 1935), 128.

35. Ibid., 129.

36. Michael Warren has also worked fruitfully with the idea of consumer culture as a faithful enterprise: "Consumerism is a religion promising salvation through the wisdom of the right purchase and with goods as its sacramental sins.... When worshipers who have ingested the religion of consumerism bring it unnamed and unrecognized into the place of worship, we have a radical conflict between two claims of ultimacy, the overt one of a formal religion and the covert one of the consumerist faith" (Michael Warren, *At This Time, in This Place: The Spirit Embodied in the Local Assembly* [Harrisburg, PA: Trinity Press International, 1999], 18).

States. This shift to understanding resistance to consumer capitalism as an issue of misdirected faith rather than one of inadequate knowledge opens up for me a new set of categories in religious education. In addition to something like critical consciousness according to the model of Paulo Freire, what might be needed to transform the vocational imaginations informed by consumer capitalism is something like the dynamics of ongoing conversion.

What's so bad about shopping?

So, you may be asking, what do I have against shopping? I have already confessed my ritual practice of consumer therapy. If it works, even for a bit, what's the big deal? Dell deChant, in his analysis of the cosmological religion of consumption, expresses very little concern about this development in the history of religious belief. For deChant, the economy functions well as the locus of sacred power that constructs community around itself. Unlike deChant, I am deeply concerned about several aspects of this system of religious belief, both because of its material consequences and the inadequacies of its capacity to organize meaning and enliven spiritual functioning for its adherents.

One part of my concern about the religious aspects of consumer culture centers around justice issues. First, fully engaged participation in the ritual of acquisition and consumption on the part of some persons comes at the cost of underpaid labor, uneven distribution of the earth's resources, and suffering on the part of many others. Second, the earth's ecosystems are strained unsustainably by our rigorous faithfulness to consumer culture. Third, the system creates insider and outsider status on the basis of access to the centers of consumption, something often determined by the chance circumstances of one's birth. All of these issues raise red flags about the adequacy of consumer culture as an ethical system of organizing human behavior and belief.

In addition to the systemic injustices perpetuated by consumer culture, I have concerns about the adequacy of its ability to provide spiritual grounding for its believers. The desires that are created by consumerism are ultimately artificial desires. Their fulfillment does not bring true human joy and flourishing, and they require endless repetition and escalation to sustain their religious power. The word of grace found in the invitation to conversion recognizes that consumer culture is not a gracious god to serve; its cultivated desires are not easy to fulfill. Consumer capitalism demands from even its most successful adherents regular sacrifices of relationship, rest, and community. The word of grace indicates that there are more life-giving ways to make sense of the world and one's role in it.

Consumer capitalism provides significant structuring of meaning for participants in American culture. Adolescents are particularly vulnerable to the influence of consumer culture in making sense of their lives because of their media consumption habits, their status as a targeted market, and their careful (and at times uncritical) attunement to cultural ideology. The impact of consumer culture on adolescent vocational understanding requires intervention in order to overcome its nearly hegemonic status in informing the imagination and agency of its participants.

Both Christian and consumer: On being multifaithful

Often religious persons value a completely integrated belief system in ways that do not take into account the often conflicting and multiple faith systems coexisting within most persons. For example, when my college buddies and I were engaging in consumer therapy, we would never have named that activity as religious in nature. We considered ourselves committed Christians who would not engage in idolatrous activity. Yet deChant's analysis points to the ritual nature of those shopping trips and their religious significance to our understanding of self: acquiring goods restored a sense of balance and rightness to who we were. They served as markers of our consumer religious identity. The reality of these two belief systems coexisting in us without informing one another points to a distinctive kind of faithfulness, perhaps multifaithfulness, that is not commonly acknowledged among adherents of a faith tradition.

Turning back to H. Richard Niebuhr and his normative definition of faithfulness, he claimed that the only satisfactory and rightful object of human loyalty is the transcendent source of all being, God, the One. Participating in consumer religious activity for Niebuhr would be considered misplaced fidelity, or, more strongly and religiously coded, idolatry. In Niebuhr's schema sin is defined as disloyalty to the true God expressed through loyalty to other less trustworthy and enduring realities. To organize one's life around loyalty to class, self, nation, humanity, or, in this case, shopping is to draw away life from its true center, literally to rebel against God.[37] As he notes, "It is not possible for men to be simply disloyal; they are always loyal to something."[38]

Niebuhr's normative emphasis on monotheistic faith and corresponding coherent selfhood reflects modern sensibilities in its presupposition of a unified, coherent self rather than a fluid, multi-centered one. Such a monolithic understanding of the self has been deeply critiqued by postmodern theorists of the self, who emphasize the multiple contexts and roles required of the self. For example, Kenneth Gergen notes that we now become selves in a context of social saturation, where we are bombarded by the images and interactions of persons with differing views, values, and visions from our own.[39] Each different context in which we work and socialize demands a different self from us in a way that was quite different even just one hundred years ago, when it was much more common for people to live entire lives and die just a few miles from their place of birth. Regular patterns of relocation, global migration, and even

37. Niebuhr, *Radical Monotheism and Western Culture*, 27.

38. H. Richard Niebuhr, *Theology, History, and Culture*, ed. William Stacy Johnson (New Haven, CT: Yale University Press, 1996), 276–77.

39. Kenneth Gergen, *The Saturated Self: Dilemmas of Identity in Contemporary Life* (New York: Basic Books, 1991), 15.

virtual identities demand a fluidity and multiplicity of identities for contemporary persons that is rather unique in human history.

Even as Gergen celebrates the possibilities for increased ethical living associated with allowing the perspectives of others to become part of our selves, he also expresses a sense of unease with the situation. He notes, "There is a *populating of the self*, reflecting the infusion of partial identities through social saturation. And there is the onset of a *multiphrenic* condition, in which one begins to experience the vertigo of unlimited multiplicity."[40] Gergen's language of "multiphrenic" belies a sense that perhaps this condition is unhealthy for human flourishing. Certainly, this populated self is a departure from earlier, more stable understandings of the self such as were proposed by Niebuhr. Gergen doubts the existence of a coherent self with identifiable attributes such as the one generated by monotheistic faith in Niebuhr's schema.[41]

In addition to postmodern objections about a unified self arising from recognition of the multiple roles the self must play, ethicists such as Iris Marion Young take this critique further in noting that the consolidation of a unified self can be linked to social problems such as racism and homophobia.[42] For Young, the need to suppress heterogeneous aspects of ourselves to achieve a consistency and coherence of the self can lead to the rejection of other persons who exhibit those rejected aspects of the self as their primary ways of being. As an alternative, a notion of the self as fluid and multiple might lead to increased capacity for compassion for those who represent the "other" to us. She notes, "Rather than seeking a wholeness of the self, we who are the subjects of this plural and complex society should affirm the otherness in ourselves, acknowledging that as subjects we are heterogeneous and multiple in our affiliations and

---

40. Ibid., 49.

41. Ibid., 16.

42. Niebuhr shared the concern about racism and xenophobia, although remarkably he assigned the exact opposite rationale for its genesis. Niebuhr asserted that belief in any object of faith other than God would eventually lead to worship of the tribal group the less than adequate god represented.

desires."[43] Rather than understanding the multiple self as a liability, Young notes the gains in ethical capacity offered by such a self. This raises an important question: How can such a "healthy" multiplicity of the self be understood without moving into the multiphrenic state of competing partial identities described by Gergen?

A healthy multiplicity of the self allows for flexibility in complex environments and recognition of otherness while still maintaining the coherence necessary for psychological health and functioning. Moving beyond the fully unified self advocated by H. Richard Niebuhr, we begin to see the possibility of multiple selfhood advocated by contemporary ethicists who understand its value in increased empathy and compassion for those who are "other" to us. At the same time, multiplicity has its limits. The healthy functioning of the self requires some boundaries, a level of coherence and emerging integrity in commitments and loyalties. In the next section, we turn to conversion as a way to conceive of healthy multiplicity.

Reconceiving multifaithfulness (being both is not so bad)

The complexity of identity common in contemporary contexts may mean that being a self who faiths[44] may not be as tidy as we imagine. Even those of us who claim fidelity to a particular historic religious

---

43. Iris Marion Young, *Justice and the Politics of Difference* (Princeton, NJ: Princeton University Press, 1990), 124.

44. I use "faith" as a verb occasionally because the traditional verbal form of the English word for faith, "believe," often connotes something more like cognitive assent than the dependence of the full self. James W. Fowler addresses the limitations of the English language when it comes to faith: "The English language handicaps us when we try to speak of faith. It gives us no verb form of the word. As we have seen, the Greek verb *pistuo* and the Latin verb *credo* permitted writers and speakers to say, 'I trust, I commit myself, I rest my heart upon, I pledge allegiance.' All of these paraphrases show us that faith is a verb; it is an active mode of being and committing, a way of moving into and giving shape to our experiences of life. They also show us that faith is always relational; there is always another in faith." In Fowler, *Stages of Faith*, 16.

tradition may in reality use multiple belief systems to make sense of our lives. We may trust that God will provide in our times of need, but we also believe that a good credit score can be a lifesaver. Faith is often conflicted and paradoxical. While we may want to proclaim theologically the steadiness of God's faithfulness to all of creation, human faith has a much more dynamic and fluid quality in its loyalties and relationships. Selves tend to be somewhat conflicted and divided in their loyalties. In fact, this theme has resounded in the writings of Christian theologians from the very beginning. Paul and St. Augustine, to name two rather prominent examples, both vividly expressed a phenomenological sense of themselves as divided in loyalties.[45]

The desire for the faithful self to be consistent and unified in its commitments is rooted deeply in those of us steeped in a Western form of Christianity. While Paul and Augustine described their own sense of division of loyalties, it was with anguish and desire to elim-inate it: "For I do not do what I want, but I do the very thing I hate. ... Wretched man that I am! Who will rescue me from this body of death?" (Romans 7:15, 24). Certainly my friends and I, when shopping for consumer therapy, would have been deeply troubled if someone had pointed out to us the ways in which this was reli-gious behavior with a different object of religious devotion than the Christian God.

However, this judgment of the conflicted self as inadequate often leads us to want to repress or deny these paradoxical elements of the faithful self from ourselves and others rather than to come to a deeper understanding of them and work for their transformation. Brian Mahan has written that this move toward condemnation of the self in paradox is often the very thing that keeps us from being transformed. He notes:

---

45. For a description of Paul's sense of division, see Romans 7:14–25. St. Augus-tine noted: "How can one soul contain within itself feelings so much at variance, in such conflict with each other? How does it balance them in the scale?" Augustine, *Confessions* (New York: Penguin Books, 1961), 84.

In fact, it is Percy's special genius to recognize and to point out gently that attachment to scripted images of the self as already moral — that is to say, as already beyond such petty jealousy and attachment — is more likely to inhibit practices of self-discovery than to encourage them. Paradoxically, it is the simultaneous confession and careful study of our sometimes conflicting attachments to material, social, and moral scripts that hints at the possibility of joyful detachment and of a life given over more fully to vocation.[46]

This practice of recognizing the paradoxical nature of the human embodies a certain attitude of grace toward a conflicted self that is crucial to provide the space for transformation to occur. This attitude of graciousness is embedded in ancient spiritual practices of confession and repentance within the Christian faith tradition, but it is an element that is often lacking in most communities practicing Christianity. While there is often a cultural assumption that church is the place where the people who are already good can be found, at the heart of the Christian tradition is the idea that the church is the place where sinners gather to seek healing.

Rather than assuming that the presence of multiple belief systems indicates hypocrisy and potential idolatry, we could assume that the believer is merely in the process of converting from one set of beliefs to another. The self in conversion is a self in paradox: old and new, sinner and redeemed at once. Karl Barth described this self in conversion as man "totally fallen out with himself."[47] In addition to this more conflicted understanding of selves who faith, the self in the process of ongoing conversion houses both the contradictions and the increasing integrity of various loyalties simultaneously.

For Barth, conversion extends over the whole of life. While there may be certain moments that capture and illuminate the total content of the process, sanctification through ongoing conversion involves the total life movement of persons. He notes that there is an increasing

---

46. Mahan, *Forgetting Ourselves on Purpose*, 113.
47. Barth, *Church Dogmatics*, IV:2, 574.

"sincerity, depth and precision" over time in conversion,[48] but there is a sense in Barth that even at the heart of the change one is never without one's past. While there is a qualitatively new person, the old person is still there. There is a both/and quality to the existence that cannot be written off simply as lack of coherence or integrity. Rather, it captures the complexity of the movement toward increasing holiness:

> The *vita christiana* in conversion is the event, the act, the history, in which at one and the same time man is still wholly the old man and already wholly the new — so powerful is the sin by which he is determined from behind, and so powerful the grace by which he is determined from before. It is in this way that man knows himself when he is really engaged in conversion.[49]

For Barth, it is the very multiplicity of the experience of oneself that indicates that the movement toward increasing faith is completely engaged.

Many of us judge negatively the conflicted parts of our self as incomplete rather than joining Barth in recognizing our conflict as an indication of the fullness of our engagement in transformation. Understanding the self-in-conversion as multifaithful and moving toward greater integrity, rather than as inconsistent and hypocritical, allows us to address the complexity of multiple loyalties more adequately. In the next chapter we further explore ongoing conversion as a dynamic resource for addressing adolescent faith in consumer culture.

---

48. Barth, *Church Dogmatics* IV:2, 566.
49. Karl Barth, in *Conversion: Perspectives on Personal and Social Transformation*, ed. Walter Conn (New York: Alba House, 1978), 43.

Three

Consumerism is wrong. Wanna go shopping?

From critical awareness to conversion

Hayley, sixteen, likes to wear a shirt with four images on it: an animal claw, a bare foot, the footprint of a man's shoe, and the footprint of a woman's heeled dress shoe. The caption underneath this progression reads "The Evolution of Authority." A young and outspoken feminist, Hayley can tell you how the media manipulates images of women to emphasize their beauty and helplessness rather than their intelligence and leadership. She will speak angrily of the digital retouching of photos that causes young women to have unrealistic expectations of adult female bodies. She has been taught by her mother and other strong women in her life about the false formation that consumer culture offers her regarding her gender identity, and she has claimed these insights for herself. Yet, in painfully honest conversation with a group of close friends, she will share that when she looks in the mirror she thinks to herself: fat, bad skin, needs a haircut. Despite her personal confidence and her careful education about the formation of media culture, at some deep level, Hayley still assesses herself on the basis of criteria that she consciously knows are untrue and harmful to her well-being. She believes the story that consumer culture sells her even as she critiques it.

Hayley's story illustrates the difference between what we know cognitively and what we believe in our hearts, in the deep wellsprings of our desires, emotions, and aesthetic sensibilities. Both levels of knowing are powerful, but they can be in conflict with one another, as in the case of Hayley and her sense of what it means to be a woman. In seeking freedom for adolescents to live beyond the vocational scripts offered them by consumer culture, we must address more than their conscious awareness of the workings of consumer culture. The deeper kinds of knowing by which they evaluate themselves and their contexts must also be addressed. This deep knowing represents their faithful formation into the practices of consumer religion.

It's hard to find a young person who would consciously advocate consumerism as an adequate belief system. At a cognitive level, most religiously well-traditioned young persons have been warned about the dangers of materialism. They have heard the cultural wisdom sayings that have arisen in response to consumptive life practices: "Money isn't everything." "You can't buy happiness." "You can't take it with you." Yet young people's engagement in consumptive practices does not match their negative statements regarding this system. At the same time that they denounce the evils of consumerism in a conversation with their youth group, they make plans to go shopping with three of their friends. A cartoon from the *New Yorker* on the door to my office demonstrates this disparity. It shows a young person responding to an activist handing out leaflets on a street corner. The caption reads: "I totally agree with you about capitalism, neo-colonialism, and globalization, but you really come down too hard on shopping."[1] Knowing that patterns of consumption are problematic is quite different than changing the deeply held beliefs about "the way the world is" that the consumer system generates and the habitual ritual practices of consumption, like shopping.

Why talk about conversion?

The deep sense of "the way the world is" is where consumer culture has its strongest grip. The pervasive culture of consumer capitalism that is experienced by adolescents as a viable faith system engages the fullness of their understanding (emotional, bodily, spiritual, and

---

1. *New Yorker*, July 23, 2001.

cognitive). It is socially embedded in the institutions in which they regularly participate. They are deeply attracted to it and often find it a compelling object of their devotional attention. Participation in this culture of meaning distorts adolescent vocational imagination by (1) convincing young people that having enough money to buy certain branded goods is the critical task in human life, and (2) eclipsing other options for vocational self-definition with its sheer pervasiveness. This distortion makes adolescent participation in consumer culture particularly difficult to address.

In my search for an educational model to help address the issue of consumer culture and adolescent vocational imagination, I was initially quite attracted to the liberative educational philosophy of Paulo Freire. I wondered if the process of conscientization through communal political action might provide a helpful model for developing resistance to the social scripts of consumerism and for allowing alternative imaginings of human vocation. Freire focuses on establishing critical awareness, the ability of students to "read the world" in which they participate, to be able to name social and cultural dynamics that inform their unspoken assumptions about the world and how it works.[2] I imagined that raising critical awareness about the ways that consumer culture functions and its costs to the environment, workers, and our own desires would bring about transformation of individuals' participation in the system, if not social transformation of the system itself.

---

2. Henry Giroux is an excellent example of an educator addressing consumer culture who emphasizes increased agency to the near exclusion of enlivened imagination. When I have assigned students to read his text, they often appreciate his clear description of the situation, but they find themselves depressed and disheartened at the end of the text. While he does mention the need for a renewed language of social justice to inform resistance to consumer culture, he doesn't develop this language in a way that enlivens the imaginations of his readers. To be fair, the public educational context that Giroux addresses limits his capacity to advocate a specific religious tradition of social justice, and he does attempt to use the language of democracy and citizenship in inspiring ways. To assess his work for yourself, see Giroux, *Stealing Innocence.* For contrast, Maxine Greene is a secular educator who struggles to connect increased agency and enlivened imagination as a response to consumer formation in *Releasing the Imagination* (San Francisco: Jossey-Bass, 1995).

The difference in context between Freire's work with Brazilian peasants and my own work with middle-class American teenagers raises some critical issues for a strictly Freirian pedagogy. To state it briefly, Freire was able to assume that once participants in culture circles become able to name their own oppression, they would be motivated to resist this oppression through collective action.[3] However, in the case of participation in structures of meaning embodied in the cultural-economic system of consumer capitalism, awareness of our "caughtness" in this system through its shaping of our aesthetic sensibilities and desires often seems to engender feelings of guilt or powerlessness rather than motivation for resistance. We benefit from, enjoy, and are moved by the images of consumption by which we are surrounded. Simply knowing about how they work, knowing the cost of consumption to the environment and to the producers of the coffee and jeans we enjoy, does not provide adequate motivation for resistance. Persons may become disheartened when they recognize the complexity of their own loyalties, and feel confused about the residue of formation in consumer meaning systems and what to do with it. An alternative is that a person gets fired up about the issues and eagerly engages in resistance only to find that the effort is not quickly bringing about the needed changes, and they find themselves worn out and unable to continue the good fight.

Educational efforts to address faithful dependence on consumer culture often rely on prophetic calls for change to bring about transformation. Yet looked at more broadly within the experience of ongoing conversion, this prophetic call to change is but the first step in an extended pedagogical process to bring about transformation. This movement to a renewed sense of vocation requires a shift in more than just cognitive awareness. It requires a change in understandings and in commitments, in desires and loves, in impulse and imagination. This is the deep transformation of a person in conversion.

---

3. "Let me make it clear, then, that, in the domain of socioeconomic structures, the most critical knowledge of reality, which we acquire through the unveiling of that reality, does out of itself alone effect a change in reality." Paulo Freire, *Pedagogy of Hope* (New York: Continuum, 1992), 30.

The metaphor of ongoing conversion provides a helpful category for rethinking appropriate goals, methods, and approaches to religious educational efforts addressing the impact of consumer culture on vocational imagination. In these educational efforts, shifting the orienting pedagogical metaphor to conversion illumines several new aspects of the human as learner. Rather than thinking of learners as having inadequate information which can be corrected with increased data or perhaps more critical awareness of their current belief system, we come to understand them as faithful followers whose very security of self depends on the intactness of their consumer faith. Consumer culture provides the deeply held images that sort information and provide categories of meaning that are signposts for the direction and purpose of life. This faith is held largely beneath conscious awareness, and is supported by a myriad of social systems.

While my interest in conversion and my resources in discussing it emerge from the Christian tradition, the process of conversion stretches beyond the scope of traditional religious belief. The language of *religious* conversion involves the reordering of the self in response to major changes in objects of trust, communities of loyalty, or other primary sources of faith. While a new object of devotion that provides such a reordering might not be explicitly religious in content, it does serve the "religious" function of orienting the self in relationship to broader imaginations of the world. For example, young people may be deeply moved and convicted by a new ecological awareness of the interdependence of all living systems, which totally shifts their sense of how the world works, their personal values and commitments, and their relationship to the earth and its creatures.

In traditional theological language, the person in the midst of ongoing conversion is simultaneously old and new, sinful and full of grace, enslaved to sin and redeemed. A paradoxical quality to the self becomes evident in conversion. The process of conversion embraces the oppositions of a person in the midst of change: Hayley as committed feminist and Hayley who judges herself by distorted images of women's bodies. This self is not completed and static, but rather is fully immersed in the process of transformation. This paradoxical self in the midst of conversion can be particularly intense in adolescents and young adults, whose styles of making commitments and of participating in the world are often more fluid and provisional than those of more mature adults.[4] The self in conversion disturbs the notion of a static, completed self with integrated commitments and seamless loyalties.

Faith in consumer systems of meaning is not mere cognitive assent. It involves emotional attachment to our beliefs, and the experience of safety and rest in them. Adolescents don't wear name-brand clothing just because they know their friends think it's cool. They feel more confident and together when they wear it. The sense of safety and strength generated by the status-granting items transcends the mere awareness of what is cool and what is not. The love and trust afforded the objects is held deep; changing it involves the upheaval of a deep restructuring of the self.

Using the metaphor of ongoing conversion reminds us that it is faith rather than mere insight that is changing. So, a person not only encounters new information, but a new relation-, emotion-, and loyalty-laden belief system that encompasses both understanding and life practice.[5] To use biblical language, conversion involves transformation of the love that requires heart, soul, mind, and strength. The recognition of the difficulty of such a transformation introduces the need to have humility about the possibilities of change in deep faith

---

4. For a discussion of "probing commitment" and "pervasive ambiguity" as characteristic of young-adult meaning making, see Parks, *Big Questions, Worthy Dreams*, chap. 1.

5. This shift through Freirian pedagogy to a pedagogy of ongoing conversion mirrors that of religious educator Thomas Groome in his pedagogy for conation. In seeking to create a pedagogy that engaged the fullest being of the person and the "valuing" aspects of their knowing, Groome chose to employ the little-used English term "conation" to capture this broader understanding of the goal of education. Groome uses "conation" to describe the fullest wisdom of learners which shapes their identity and agency in the world — their cognition, their affections, and their behavior. Groome links his conative pedagogy to education for ongoing conversion because his pedagogy "functions in the lives of participants as a resource for lifelong nurture and renewal in Christian living." For Groome's full explanation of his use of this term, see Groome, *Sharing Faith* (San Francisco: HarperSanFrancisco, 1991), 26–29.

systems, awareness of the intentionality that will be required to make such a change, and awareness that the timeline for change may be quite extended, even lifelong. It's not enough to hear and understand that "it's what is on the inside that makes a person beautiful." Conversion occurs when an adolescent feels beautiful no matter what they look like or what they are wearing. This requires a different kind of education entirely.

A *deeper change*

Conversion, then, refers not just to a change in awareness and understanding, but to a change in both our intuitive sense of the way the world is (imagination) and our capacity to act in light of that intuitive sense (agency). Vocation can be defined as the lived expression of one's life (agency) in response to the call of larger meanings (imagination). Both agency and imagination are critical in any pedagogy addressing the development of alternative vocation in a consumer context.

Changing imagination

"Imagination" describes the larger concepts through which a person defines their sense of the world and their own participation in it. In lived experience, imagination resides in both conscious and unconscious awareness. It is a complex interweaving of emotion and cognition that often remains imagistic and unarticulated in words, even as it provides the criteria or emotiologic by which decisions and choices are made.[6] The world of imagination inevitably connects the

---

6. "Criteria" perhaps communicates a more cognitive and rational mode of decision making than what I am describing. Alison M. Jaggar discusses the way affective and cognitive elements combine to inform human behavior in emotion. She notes: "Emotions, then, are wrongly seen as necessarily passive or involuntary responses to the world. Rather, they are ways in which we engage actively and even construct the world. They have both 'mental' and 'physical' aspects, each of which conditions the other; in some respects, they are chosen, but in others they are involuntary; they presuppose language and a social order. Thus, they can be attributed only to what are sometimes called 'whole persons,' engaged in the ongoing activity of social

individual to a wider social realm because the images by which an individual makes sense of the world draw upon the linguistic, social, and environmental categories of the culture in which they are born.

Shifting deep images

An example of the function of these deep images occurred in my own life around perceptions of "good neighborhood." I grew up in largely white, upper-middle-class, suburban settings where the average neighborhood was quiet. Children played in their fenced backyards or in their homes. Adults spent recreation time in the evenings inside living rooms. Extended families rarely lived in the same neighborhoods, and neighbors did not socialize on front porches or in front yards with one another. As an adult, I purchased my first home in an urban, largely African American and working-class neighborhood. Here, the norms around neighborly interaction were quite different. Neighbors knew one another, and often socialized in front yards and on porches. Children regularly played in the streets and driveways since backyard spaces were smaller and not adequate for organized game playing. Car ownership was less universal, and public transportation was more widely used, which meant that people walked on the streets and sidewalks on a regular basis, greeting and chatting with one another throughout the day and evening hours.

When my husband and I first moved into the neighborhood, the noise level made me quite uneasy. I often stuck my head out to check on the neighbor children when I heard their play. I spent the better part of two years feeling a bit afraid. Some of this fear came from my own internal images around race that I was consciously trying to shift at the time. Some of this fear was realistic, as gang activity was common in the neighborhood and some neighbors dealt crack cocaine on my street. Mostly, my uneasiness arose from the fact that this particular neighborhood, which I liked very much in my rational thought,

---

life." In Alison M. Jaggar, "Love and Knowledge: Emotion in Feminist Epistemology," in *Feminist Social Thought: A Reader*, ed. Diana Tietjens Meyers (New York: Routledge, 1997), 391.

violated certain of my deeply held images about what neighborhoods should be like.

In the third year of our time in this neighborhood we visited my in-laws, who lived in a neighborhood very similar to the ones in which I had grown up. While walking my infant daughter in her stroller, my spouse and I were rather spooked by the seemingly deserted neighborhood. No humans could be seen, except when the occasional car would emerge from its garage and drive past. It was eerily quiet, despite the fact that it was a beautiful spring day. Where were all the people? It struck me as we talked about our uneasiness that my internal, preconscious image of a good neighborhood had finally shifted. Despite my conscious appreciation of our urban neighborhood from the very beginning, it had taken nearly three years of daily living for that preconscious image to shift. Only then did my new image of "good neighborhood" begin to inform the way I assessed new sensory input in novel situations. I was not consciously aware that this shift had occurred until I returned to a neighborhood that would have been familiar to me as a child. This kind of deep shift in imagination is one outcome of ongoing conversion.

Too often educational practitioners focus attention on a narrative-based, articulated form of understanding that is more readily communicable from person to person. Imagination includes a prearticulated form of understanding emerging from a more primal kind of knowing — often unarticulated — that is central to the human experience of faith. Fowler notes that this imagistic knowledge unites cognitive and affective information in a "vague, felt inner representation"[7] that is crucial to convictional knowing. Drawing on both left and right hemispheric patterning in the brain, images hold together conscious and unconscious knowing, both what we know and our feelings toward that knowledge.[8]

Fowler's descriptive work with images aligns with emerging neurological understandings of how the brain functions. As neurobiologist

---

7. Fowler, *Stages of Faith*, 26.

8. James W. Fowler, *Weaving the New Creation* (San Francisco: HarperSanFrancisco, 1991), 183.

Antonio Damasio states it: "Knowledge is embodied in dispositional representations,"[9] images constructed by our brains by a "complex neural machinery of perception, memory, and reasoning."[10] Image is a shorthand and phenomenological way of talking about the complex interweavings of the neural processes of the brain that allow for the sorting of reams of perceptual input into timely action and response. Hidden behind or beneath the insights that we can articulate are dispositional, imagistic understandings that deeply affect our choosing and action even though they are often inaccessible to conscious thought. They provide the shortcuts in sense making that allow us to avoid paralysis in the face of a constant barrage of novel sensory information. Images are the neural shortcuts that determined whether I assessed the neighborhood as good or not at an instinctual level without having to think consciously about what I saw around me.

These unarticulated images become a crucial element in educational efforts hoping to transform faith through ongoing conversion, which involves not only a shift in discursive, articulable understandings, but a shift in these underlying images that inform conscious understanding. This kind of primary shift is enormously difficult to achieve because the images function prior to conscious thought. They work before our conscious decision making or sense making of the world, and are difficult even to name, much less transform.

Faith as an expression of deep trust and loyalty rests primarily in dispositional, preconscious images that unite both our understandings and our emotional connections to those understandings. Ongoing conversion is partially about a change in imagination, a process that occurs slowly over time through a process of falling in love with newer, more adequate images that are able to integrate the fullness of individual experience in relation to broader realities. Eventually, these new images come to the place of sorting new sensory information and making sense of it prior to our conscious

---

9. Antonio Damasio, *Descartes' Error: Emotion, Reason, and the Human Brain* (New York: Grosset/Putnam, 1994), 104.
   10. Ibid., 97.

awareness of this work of faith, just as my changed image of "good neighborhood" eventually became the way by which I evaluated new surroundings.

Images and consumer culture

The function of images in the work of faith is particularly important to consider in light of the culture of consumer capitalism, which saturates its participants with images of a greater reality in which they participate through various forms of mass media. Michael Warren discusses the relationship between images, consumer capitalism, and religious belief in his book *Seeing through the Media*. Warren argues that the inner core of any cultural system is a system of images, both iconic and metaphoric. While Warren is concerned with the iconic or visual images and the often uncritical imitation that they inspire (think of Hayley and the mirror), he feels that the deeper issue arises from the metaphoric images. Metaphoric images are those images through which we see, the "analogies and metaphors by which to understand and name reality."[11] Warren argues that consumer culture is the primary dispenser of these metaphoric, dispositional, orienting metaphors in American culture.

The depth of these metaphoric or imaginal faith images and the fact that they are often unconscious makes their critique and transformation very difficult. However, movements to shift these kinds of primary images in individuals and even in societies have been historically successful. Warren cites the astute cultural action of the feminist movement as an example of this kind of shift in attempting to dismantle fundamental images of gender that were oppressive to women, such as the ideas that women were incapable of logical thought or didn't need equal pay to support their families.[12] Walter Wink also considers the capacity to imagine a different future as critical in generating change. He notes:

---

11. Warren, *Seeing through the Media*, 152.
12. Ibid., 156.

The message is clear: *history belongs to the intercessors, who believe the future into being.* This is not simply a religious state-ment. It is as true of communists or capitalists or anarchists as it is of Christians. The future belongs to whoever can envision in the manifold of its potentials a new and desirable possibility, which faith then fixes upon as inevitable.[13]

While the future may seem closed due to the cultural forces that predominate, Wink asserts that the future can be opened by small numbers of people who "fix their imaginations" on a new inevitabil-ity and call it into being.[14]

Sources of alternative imaginations

Where do these alternative images come from, and how do people come to be moved by them? Sharon Parks notes that religious men-toring communities are one source of these images. At their best, religious communities offer young adults alternative stories, symbols, and practices to live by and to anchor the meanings by which they make sense of their lives. She notes, "Even in a time between stories, if the great traditions offer their stories, symbols, and songs — less as dogma and more as gifts to the faithful imagination — then with crit-ical awareness they can be received as finite vessels to be treasured, reshaped, or cast aside according to their relative usefulness."[15] Parks asserts that the context of a community helps young adults to sort this wealth of imaginations with more discernment than picking and choosing among them individually. Hayley's story reminds us of the enormous time and effort required for those alternative images to become the foundational images from which meaning is made. We see this, too, in the repetition of our Christian story that is needed, Sunday by Sunday, for it to become one of the primary shapers of our imaginations.

---

13. Walter Wink, *Engaging the Powers* (Minneapolis: Fortress Press, 1992), 299.
14. Ibid.
15. Parks, *Big Questions, Worthy Dreams*, 203.

When educators focus on enlivening imagination as a means of resisting consumer formation, such as some of the recent focus on engaging Christian practices in contemporary youth ministry literature, they often work to form participants in an alternative Christian meaning narrative through increased participation in communal faith practices and/or deeper participation in the Christian narrative.[16] These efforts are designed to immerse persons into an alternative symbolic universe. Methods such as embodied storytelling, participation in traditional liturgical and spiritual discipline practices in community, and other efforts to vivify the Christian narrative in the individual imagination mark an attempt to shift the dominant meaning world which informs the imagination of the individual.

While these efforts correctly emphasize the social formation of the individual and the importance of the relational and symbolic contexts which form the milieu from which a person emerges, they often pay insufficient attention to the power of conflicting formation. If we remember back to the nearly three thousand discrete commercial messages bombarding adolescents every day, it is hard to imagine the volume of Christian formative practices necessary to even the score. Additionally, while the theorists are often more complex, particularly early church historian Margaret Miles with her constructive retrieval of the ancient Christian practices of asceticism, in practice this often seems to focus on "enrichment" Christian practices without an emphasis on self-critical practices to counter the formation in consumer worldviews. While alternative imagination is not sufficient to fully address the problem of consumer formation, it is a critical element of conversion worth further consideration. The need for self-critical practices in light of the overwhelming formative power of consumer culture turns us to the necessity of enlivening agency as well as changing imagination as we work with adolescents to resist that formation.

---

16. See Dorothy C. Bass and Don C. Richter, eds., *Way to Live: Christian Practices for Teens* (Nashville: Upper Room Books, 2002), for an example of this emerging body of literature.

Enlivening agency

A change in vocational understanding involves both a change in imagination and the capacity to act in light of that new imagination, or what is often called agency in educational theory. Agency is often emphasized in pedagogical approaches that have emerged to counter oppressive contexts. *Agency* refers to the capacity to make choices and to act in light of one's sense of what is meaningful. Agency values both the intentionality and the power to assert oneself actively in the world, often expressed as being the subject of one's own life and not the object of others' control. The capacity for agency connotes a life shaped, but not fully determined, by outside forces. Agency is something we learn. Liberative pedagogies in particular strive not only to create responsible adult actors within the power discourses of a certain community, but also to create agents who are able to choose to act outside of the most powerful discourses of that community. Therefore, agency in liberative pedagogy connotes the ability and power to act outside of the roles scripted by dominant discourses of power.

Examples of agency-based education for resistance to consumer culture include media education, sweatshop labor awareness, and organized political movement toward active resistance of consumer culture. Though these approaches may help people to name the ways in which advertising shapes their desires, they do not actually show how to transform those desires. Unless we offer an alternative meaning system to provide hope and structure in persons' lives, such education does not move beyond critique and resistance. The result is that participants are able to name the ways in which they are "caught" in this system of consumer meaning through its shaping of their aesthetic sensibilities and desires, yet have no alternative meaning system to inform a different life. This typically leaves them feeling guilty, powerless, or despairing.

Agency is not performed by solitary individuals who act as they choose. Rather, freedom emerges from an educational process that opens up other choices. Even after the economic structures that supported the ideology of the dominant groups toppled in Freire's Brazil for a short time during agricultural reform, he noted that the negative conditioning force of the ideology remained and continued to interfere with the peasants' exercise of agency. In such a situation, Freire felt that only radical revisions in human relationships and style of life could thwart the power of the old cultural scripts. Even with such changes, Freire was not sure that agency would be firmly established. By mere critical reflection, Freire asserts that the peasants are unable to reach a point at which they exercise agency. Freire notes, "Such a view is only possible when peasants actively participate in a political experience through a permanent mobilization."[17] For Freire, the development of agency comes through political action, through collective efforts in which participants act as if they already have agency. The educational process must provide opportunities for agentful action to take place. The role of the educator becomes decisive in this process of achieving agency. By being able to envision a different cultural script (more participatory and democratic structures of power, in Freire's case; forms of human life not dominated by consumer relationships in ours), the educator institutes practices in the very process of education that engage the learners as if they already are agents. In the dialogical process of education, participants become agents.

Enlivening agency is particularly crucial to nurturing the capacity for young people to choose paths outside of the proffered social scripts of consumer culture. The agency of young people is often muted by the institutions in which they participate. After the social movements of the civil rights and Vietnam War eras, the agency of young people became deeply distrusted in the United States. Work with young people often focuses on finding ways to contain their energy, mute their passions, and control their forms of expression. Thus, to focus on enlivening the agency of youth is a countercultural practice.[18]

---

17. Paulo Freire, *The Politics of Education* (South Hadley, MA: Bergin and Garvey, 1985), 32.

18. For more on the importance of enlivening agency in youth ministry, see Tim Van Meter and Katherine Turpin, "No Longer Guests: On the Dynamics of Agency

When insight is not enough

Often, educational practices assume the following equation of transformation: right understanding leads to right belief which leads to
right practice. If an educator can broaden or transform the cognitive understanding of the student through insight, they assume the
right belief system and life practices will inevitably flow from this
new understanding. This post-Enlightenment understanding of the
relationship between belief and practice depends on reason as the
primary change agent for life structure. However, pre-Enlightenment
theologians were not so confident that right belief always produced
right behavior. John Wesley addressed this issue in "On the Wedding
Garment," discussing the misrepresentation of trifling matters as necessary to salvation. One of these is having right opinions, about which
he commented, "But still a man may judge as accurately as the devil,
and yet be as wicked as he."[19] While he noted the close relationship of insight and practice, he also recognized that correct insight or
judgment does not guarantee righteous behavior.

Wesley's questioning of dominant assumptions about the relationship of insight and behavior finds corollaries in contemporary
discourse. In reflecting on the relationship between insight and
behavior, Margaret Miles describes how contemporary forms of
psychotherapy often embody the assumption that "change in behavior follows, rather than precedes, insight."[20] Thus, psychological
therapies often focus on reenvisioning the story of the patient's experience to encompass a more productive narrative that allows for the
revision of destructive behavior patterns. In short, therapy is about
improved insight of the patient's life story to alleviate suffering and
allow for different responses from the patient.

Miles contrasts this contemporary therapeutic model with ancient
Christian authors of devotional manuals who understood the religious self as an integration of thought and practice. For Miles, the

and Formation in Ministry with Older Adolescents," *Journal of Youth and Theology*
1, no. 2 (2002): 7–22.
    19. Wesley, *Sermons*, 563.
    20. Miles, *Practicing Christianity*, 89.

point of these authors is not that you get the mind right to change behavior. Rather, the reverse was true: "[I]t was the integration of thought and practice that defined the religious self. In contrast to twentieth-century consensus, most historical people thought it obvious that insight follows change; changed behavior — changed activities — produce insight."[21] For example, Athanasius noted that if one wanted to understand the insights of the saints, first one had to mimic their lives:

> Similarly, anyone who wishes to understand the mind of the sacred writers must first cleanse his own life, and approach the saints by copying their deeds. Thus united to them in the fellowship of life, he will both understand the things revealed to them by God....[22]

Miles notes that ancient manuals of instruction in the practice of Christianity often did not concern themselves with theological instruction or getting the mind right. Rather, they addressed needed changes in the behavior of their readers with the assumption that such a change in habits would lead to a change in insight.[23]

Ancient spiritual advisors knew that the key to transformation was not a change in thinking but a change in desires and actions. Changing desires or behaviors without providing a rationale for the change counters most contemporary educational practice. Even when I redirect my preschool-aged daughter's behavior, "Honey, offer your brother another toy instead of snatching yours out of his hands," I tell her the reason for my intervention in the hopes that the insight will sink in and affect future behaviors. "That way, he won't throw a screaming fit and make us all miserable." It feels repressive to call for changed behavior and desire when understanding has not been transformed. We may find it repressive, but to change understanding without changing desires is to create a miserable human being,

---

21. Ibid., 90.
22. St. Athanasius, *On the Incarnation*, St. Vladimir's Orthodox Theological Seminary Printing (Cambridge: Cambridge University Press, 1993), 96.
23. Miles, *Practicing Christianity*, 2.

caught between their changed insight and their characteristic patterns of knowing and being in the world. The ancient form of instruction may have been more compassionate and more attuned to the need to attend to agency as well as insight.

Philip Brickman, a social psychologist, explored this same relationship between insight and behavior through social-scientific study of commitment behaviors. Brickman asserted that consciously named commitments, such as a commitment to affordable housing for all, generally happens in retrospect after the behaviors which constitute the commitment have emerged in the life patterns of individuals, such as thinking you'd like to do something meaningful with your free time, volunteering with your young adult Sunday school class at a Habitat for Humanity build, and then forming relationships with persons who have suffered a lack of affordable housing. In other words, people experience a "progressive escalation of involvement through gradual and sometimes imperceptible steps"[24] that eventually leads to the conscious naming of a commitment attached to an already established sequence of behavior.[25] The establishment of commitment "implies transformations in the bases of both motivation and affect."[26] Commitments involve a blend of affect, motivation, understanding, and behavior patterns that is complex and interdependent, and their transformation requires attention to motivation, behaviors, affect, and cognitive understanding. These elements are not dealt with in sequence, but rather must all be attended to at the same time. According to Brickman's research, the conscious naming of the change in commitment is often the last, rather than the first, step.

The notion that changed understanding follows rather than precedes changed behavior is counterintuitive. We rely heavily on the notion that people's behavior arises from their thinking, the Cartesian "I think, therefore I am." We can learn from our ancestors, who lived

---

24. Philip Brickman, *Commitment, Conflict, and Caring*, ed. Camille B. Wortman and Richard Sorrentino (Englewood Cliffs, NJ: Prentice-Hall, 1987), 160.

25. Ibid., 161.

26. Ibid., 175.

with a much fuller and integrative understanding of the interweaving of emotion, desire, and insight in motivation for human behavior.

When willpower is not enough

The notion of will or willpower requires special consideration when talking about education to enliven agency. In general, scholars consider the will an outdated concept in psychological discourse. As a concept of the interior force required for volitional action, it was too vague a construct to survive in a behavioral science with quantitative measurements. Yet, laypersons talking about making a major change in their life still find the concept of will useful to describe their struggle to shift behavioral patterns. In common language people talk about making things happen "through sheer force of will," or about the "willpower" necessary to stay on a new diet or exercise regimen.

Often, assumptions about willpower, the unencumbered possibility of choice, are embedded in pedagogical models for transformation. For example, an educator will either directly or indirectly ask students to choose between an ingrained understanding and a novel one in a manner something like the following: "Here are two understandings of the theory of atonement. The first is the one you have always been taught to be true. Despite the fact that you have sung it in hymns and prayed it during the liturgy all of your life, it has the following flaws or inadequacies. The second understanding, which I have just explained to you, is more theoretically and historically adequate. Now, choose the second." The educator assumes that learners are freely able to shift their understanding based solely on new cognitive information. Is this possible? Under what conditions does the will function in the process of transformation?

In the story of the rich young man, when faced with the choice offered by Jesus between possessions and eternal life, the young man tragically finds himself unable to respond and walks away. Educational efforts that set up two meaning systems, Christian and consumer, as oppositional and ask adolescents to simply choose between the two deny the complexity and centrality of human meaning making to human behavior. Without mediational pedagogical

structures that might make the choice possible, this model of volitional choice often leads faithful adolescents to despair rather than to
the possibility for transformation. Careful attention to rich resources
of the Christian tradition in ongoing conversion points to the idea
that this kind of prophetic moment, what Wesley would call the
"call to awakening," is but the first moment in a long process of
transformation that requires much more pedagogical support.

Twelve-step programs for various forms of addiction address willpower almost immediately in their pedagogical design. The first step
of this program includes admitting powerlessness, that is, the inability of willpower to bring about a change in behavior. The second
step expresses the belief that a power greater than us could restore us
to sanity. Embedded in these first two steps is also an understanding
that the human will in isolation is not sufficient to bring about transformation. While the "powerlessness" language perhaps overstates
the inability for humans to be in partnership with God in their own
transformation, this model demands further consideration of the limitations of human effort and volition and their relationship to God's
intervention in the process of transformation.

In search of ongoing conversion

Many educators who write about resisting consumerism focus on
what, for a lack of a better term, I will call the "shock, inform, and
convert" pedagogy. For example, a teacher will introduce the session by stating that citizens of the United States use, on average,
twice the amount of the earth's resources per capita than are available per person for sustainable use. Then, combined with statistics
about the concentration of wealth present in the United States and
the amount of garbage we dispose of in any given year, the teacher
will invite participants to change their lifestyles to not be so greedy.
Some suggestions about recycling and controlling acquisition might
be offered to end the session, and participants may be asked to commit to changing their ways through involvement in a letter-writing
campaign.

The tone of these approaches tends to be prophetic and accusatory. Often, they are very appealing to adolescents, who are developmentally at a point where their antennae for responding to ideological arguments are quite finely tuned.[27] This kind of pedagogy assumes that if a person is exposed to a sufficiently compelling version of reality, they will desire more knowledge about that version of reality and subsequently change their behavior in response to this new knowledge. Such a pedagogical approach depends on a strong understanding of free will, and the ability to change behavior through volitional choice. In Christian religious terms, this pedagogy resembles the attempt to bring about an instantaneous conversion through scare tactics, such as a Halloween "hell house" or a revival event. However, as many studies on adolescent conversions demonstrate, these undoubtedly powerful experiences often lack the staying power to maintain a change in life habits and commitments over time.

So, what can one offer instead? In introducing the theological concept of conversion, I should note that I am working with a particular understanding of *lifelong* or *ongoing* conversion. Many times the word "conversion" conjures images of a dramatic switch from one religion or belief system to another. People describe conversion experiences as one-time events where there is a radical reordering of commitments and behaviors. These are important occurrences, and I do not intend to undercut their validity with my focus on ongoing conversion. However, the ongoing conversion I explore in this book is more indebted to Wesley's writings on sanctification and regeneration than to his dramatic experience of heartwarming at Aldersgate.[28]

---

27. Remember Erikson's assertion of the relationship between ideology and identity development in adolescence discussed in the first chapter.

28. Wesley has been used by scholars to defend both instantaneous and gradual conversion, and this argument is a small portion of a much wider scholarly debate about the true nature of conversion as either instant or gradual. Both instantaneous and gradual conversions have been documented in memoir and academic study, and Wesley himself believed that the experience of salvation included moments of both. He notes: "All experience, as well as Scripture, shows this salvation to be both instantaneous and gradual. It begins the moment we are justified, in the holy, humble, gentle, patient love of God and man. It gradually increases from that moment, as

Ongoing conversion captures the lifelong struggle to move toward increasing holiness even while we are surrounded by and participate in sin. Conversion is an accrual of events that show the gradual placement of trust and reliance in a different grounding, a different imagination of the world. As James Fowler defines conversion: "[B]y conversion I mean *an ongoing process* — with, of course, a series of important moments of perspective altering convictions and illuminations — *through which people (or a group) gradually bring the lived story of their lives in congruence with the core story of the Christian faith.*"[29] Ongoing conversion is the gradual shift of imagination and life practice from one object of devotion to another.

John Wesley used various theological terms to point to the process that I am calling ongoing conversion: way of salvation, regeneration, sanctification, and restoration of the image of God.[30] While there are careful theological distinctions between these terms and a theological heritage for each of them, Wesley used them rather broadly to point to the process of becoming increasingly steeped in the Christian life and experiencing greater power and freedom to live and love within it. Wesley scholar Randy Maddox notes:

---

a 'grain of mustard seed, which at first is the least of all seeds, but' gradually 'puts forth large branches', and becomes a great tree; till in another instant the heart is cleansed from all sin, and filled with pure love to God and man. But even that love increases more and more, till we 'grow up in all things into him that is our head', 'till we attain the measure of the stature of the fullness of Christ' " (Wesley, *Sermons,* 488–89).

29. Fowler, *Becoming Adult, Becoming Christian,* 115. Emphasis in original.

30. Is it appropriate to use Wesley in this way, when I understand salvation quite differently than Wesley did? In "The Scripture Way of Salvation," Wesley defines salvation not as the soul's going to paradise or an otherworldly blessing, but rather a present reality, "a blessing which, through the free mercy of God, ye are now in possession of.... So that the salvation which is here spoken of might be extended to the entire work of God, from the first dawning of grace in the soul till it is consummated in glory" (Wesley, *Sermons,* 372). Salvation in a "this-worldly" sense for Wesley meant a life fully immersed in the image of God, fully implicated by the demands and blessings of a Christian worldview. It is the dynamics of that slow transformation into a new imagination that I am interested in exploring. The freedom to live out a vocational path not fully determined by the meaning world of consumer capitalism would require a fundamental shift from that meaning system to another one, be it Christian or otherwise.

His typical definition of being "born again" or regenerated was quite broad; "being inwardly changed by the almighty operation of the Spirit of God; changed from sin to holiness; renewed in the image of him who created us." This definition makes regeneration nearly synonymous with Wesley's therapeutic understanding of salvation per se.[31]

Here I am employing Wesley's understanding of the process of working out one's own salvation as a kind of critical example of the process of ongoing change into a new subjectivity, a new grounding in a different faith system.

I am emphasizing the language of "conversion" rather than that of "change" or "transformation" to indicate the distinctly religious aspects involved in the transformation from reliance on consumer culture as a meaning system. The religious coding of the term and the use of "faith" language is meant to signify that this represents a change in loyalty and devotion as well as a change in knowledge and information. Using religious terminology also points to the social nature of consumer capitalism and the institutional support it enjoys. "Conversion" language illuminates the kind of deep change necessary within persons and communities. The language of religious conversion indicates change of the fullness of the person: his or her habits, beliefs, feelings, and disposition. Conversion is a dynamic process. It indicates movement from one self to another, and finding new integrity in a new system of organizing meaning. Conversion points to the fullness of transformation that occurs.

In contrast to the paradigm of instantaneous conversion and the pedagogies of prophesy, accusation, and call for immediate change that attend it, a paradigm of ongoing conversion informs alternative pedagogical possibilities for responding to an American context of consumer-driven vocational development. Theologians working with the concept of ongoing conversion have developed a unique understanding of the person in the process of change over time, which

---

31. Randy Maddox, *Responsible Grace* (Nashville: Kingswood Books, 1994), 159.

will be helpful to consider in thinking about pedagogical strategies to resist monodirectional formation into consumers. In addition, theologians have considered carefully how ongoing conversion begins, how communal contexts sustain it, and what powers the difficult and ongoing work in the person along the way. These topics provide helpful clues to a pedagogical strategy for helping adolescents in the process of conversion from commitment to the dominant life script provided by their consumerist context.

The outline of ongoing conversion

In the next four chapters, I draw upon John Wesley's explication of the *via salutis,* or the way of salvation, as a general outline to explore the pedagogical movements of ongoing conversion. To separate the movements is to risk reifying a dynamic process into artificial stages or progressive steps. Ongoing conversion does not necessarily progress in a linear fashion; it often moves forward and backward, building upon itself and revisiting old territory again in light of new experiences. However, separating out some phases of the process, even artificially, provides clarity in naming the kinds of movements and processes that constitute conversion.

The first movement in the process of salvation actually functions as the environment to allow for transformation. Wesley understood God to be the initiator and humans the responsive partner in the way of salvation. This conviction surfaces in Wesley's assertion that grace is a critical element in each stage of the process of salvation. For Wesley, salvation begins with preventing grace. Wesley understood the first desire to please God, the sense of being sinful, and the first sense of God's will for the believer to be signs of preventing or prevenient grace. He notes, "All these imply some tendency toward life, some degree of salvation, the beginning of a deliverance from a blind, unfeeling heart, quite insensible of God and the things of God."[32] I have linked this stage with another Wesleyan concept, the

---

32. Wesley, *Sermons,* 488.

call to awakening, a pedagogical effort which, in combination with prevenient grace, leads to the first awareness that change is needed.

The next stage in the way of salvation is marked by what Wesley calls convincing grace. This stage is a movement toward greater self-knowledge, which Wesley links to the scriptural term "repentance."[33] This movement involves persons becoming increasingly aware of their own implication in the consumer faith system that has been judged negatively in the call to awakening. The cognitive, emotional, and behavioral changes in this movement lead to a distancing of self from loyalty to consumer religious practices, as well as an increasing dissatisfaction with the meanings they generate.

A pedagogy informed by the dynamics of ongoing conversion highlights the balance of self-awareness generated through repentance and the gift of being grasped by a new vision of faith. While increasing self-knowledge of the ways in which we are entwined in consumer capitalism as a meaning system is central to transformation of our participation in that system, increased self-awareness can be debilitating if it is not accompanied by a beautiful alternative vision that lures a person into another way of moving about in the world.

This beautiful alternative vision Wesley named the "two grand branches" of salvation: justification and sanctification.[34] He notes: "By justification we are saved from the guilt of sin, and restored to the favour of God: by sanctification we are saved from the power and root of sin, and restored to the image of God."[35] For Wesley, justification is the moment in which persons recognize themselves to be saved from sin by the crucifixion and resurrection of Christ. In considering the function of justification in the conversion process of the believer, I have linked this movement with the experience of being grasped by a new set of meanings and symbols that reinterprets one's life in a fundamental way. While this linking broadens the meaning of justification to include meaning systems beyond the Christian one

---

33. Ibid., 488.
34. Ibid.
35. Ibid., 489.

explored by Wesley, it can be compatible with Wesley's understanding. In order for justification to be salvific, the new symbols must reinterpret the person's life graciously and in a way that elicits trust rather than terror or grief from the person.

Regeneration, alternately called sanctification and restoration to the image of God, is the gradual process of becoming more deeply steeped in the love of God. It is the movement toward increased holiness, a movement to bringing one's life more fully into rhythm with the desires of God. This movement evokes images for Wesley such as "renewal of our fallen nature,"[36] a spirit of adoption into the family of God,[37] and the gradual growth from childhood into adulthood.[38] Again, in thinking functionally about what this experience addresses, I have linked regeneration with the slow process of bringing one's life into congruence with the new faith system that has radically altered it in the process of conversion. Additionally, regeneration provides power and energy to sustain the work of ongoing conversion.

As evident in the above outline, Wesley was quite willing to be linear in his description of the way of salvation in his sermons and theological treatises. In the context of prevenient grace, a call to awakening brings about repentance, justification, and sanctification, in that order. At the same time, as a long-lived pastor, he came to understand that, for many persons, the process was neither orderly nor quick. Part of the genius of his leadership of the Methodist movement was his attention to the pedagogical structures and supports that allowed for the process of ongoing conversion to be sustained beyond the initial encounter in field preaching. These structures indicate that the process of conversion may not be as clearly delineated in the life of an individual person as described in his organized treatises. In a particular life, the process of conversion may occur in fits and starts; the timing, duration, and repeating of each of the movements is rather elastic.

---

36. Ibid., 336.
37. Ibid., 134–44.
38. Ibid., 343.

By attending to the various movements within the process of ongoing conversion, the following chapters provide a framework to assess the completeness of a pedagogical attempt to address the formation of consumer culture. In the movements of ongoing conversion we see the outlines of some critical elements for any pedagogy hoping to support a conversion from dependence on the meaning system of consumer capitalism.

Part two

Exploring the process and practices of ongoing conversion

Four

Awakening

Old faith fails to sustain

I can remember my youth leader standing in front of the group and saying, "Why do we always have to buy new clothes?" He pulled out the front of his well-worn shirt, and he pointed to the same old Converse tennis shoes he wore everywhere. "Clothes last a long time. Who says we need to keep up with changing styles? Who does that serve?" I realized that I had never asked these questions of myself. —Sara, recalling her adolescent self

Waking up

In the above vignette, Sara describes being invited by a mentor to question her assumptions about the dictates of fashion and the way they related to her buying practices. Sara, who as a young adult is still growing into her religious commitments to simple living, identifies this moment as a point where she began to become aware of her formation in the practices of consumer faith. The mentor, who embodied a different value system in his lifestyle choices, issued a gentle prophetic call for the young people in this gathering to reconsider their devotion to fashionable wear. The call was issued not to fault the youth for their gullibility in falling into the desires of marketers, but rather as a gracious invitation to unbind themselves from this formation.

Often teachers eager to reduce the participation of adolescents in consumer culture will intuitively start with a form of prophetic speech about the ill effects of consumption. These teachers note the failures of consumption by drawing attention to its inability to sustain meaning in the face of illness or death (e.g., you can't take it with you), its contribution to imminent ecological disaster, and its reliance on sweatshop labor to create affordable products sold in the United States. With these stories, mentors invite young people to pay attention to the underside of the meaning system in which they participate in an effort to produce "call to awakening" moments. They understand the call to awakening as an external prophetic call that is intended to jolt young people out of their normal way of perceiving and interacting with the world and to awaken them to other possibilities in the world.

The image of "awakening" evokes a person in an initial state without awareness. The metaphor addresses the sensation of suddenly understanding the world in such a different way that you wonder how you didn't see it that way before this moment. You wake up to a new reality. Consumer culture works as a faith or religious system by making itself "natural" or "normal," outside the realm of cognitive awareness. To awaken to its processes and to pay attention to the ways in which our lifestyles and choices respond to it disrupts this normalcy, and thus opens the space to begin to interrogate the meaning system.

While raising awareness has long been a part of movements for social change, awakening is also a metaphor that has its roots in understandings of religious conversion. In his sermon "Awake, Thou That Sleepest," John Wesley explores the image of sleeping to describe a person prior to the beginning of the process of salvation:

> The poor unawakened sinner, how much knowledge soever he may have as to other things, has no knowledge of himself. In this respect "he knoweth nothing yet as he ought to know.' . . . He sees no necessity for the "one things needful," even that inward universal change, that "birth from above" (figured out by baptism) which is the beginning of that total renovation, that sanctification of spirit, soul, and body, "without which no man shall see the Lord."[1]

1. Wesley, *Sermons*, 86.

Wesley valued self-knowledge, the awareness of sinfulness, and the awareness of the need for a new way of being in order to live in the image of God. This awakening is the starting point in the way of salvation. In contrast, a sleeper is a person contented to continue in her sinful ways or unaware of her own sinfulness and the dangers it generates.[2]

The call to awakening is basically a call for repentance that leads to the sleeper's awareness of the need for a different life. How does this awakening occur? Wesley thought that tragedies and natural disasters could bring about such awareness, or that sermons and conversations — like that of Sara and her youth leader — through which the Spirit could touch the heart of the sleeper, could lead to awakening.[3] The function of these awakening moments is to jolt people out of their apathy, to cause them to recognize that they were in error, and to convince them they have no ability to save themselves.[4] What Wesley named awareness of God's judgment generated through the call to awakening I would reframe as the revelation of the limitations of a faith system in organizing life meaning. While awakening can be provoked by external prophetic calls, it can also emerge through an internal sense of dissatisfaction or inadequacy that propels a person to search for more adequate means of making sense out of life. Either through external calls or internal sense, the old ways of making sense of the world become inadequate for continued salvation.

Old faith fails to sustain

The moment when the inadequacy of old faith is revealed becomes a first step in the transformation of faith commitments through ongoing conversion. The old way of making sense of the world becomes inadequate for coping with new information about the world or a new

2. Ibid., 87.
3. See John Wesley's sermon "The Spirit of Bondage and of Adoption" for a similar claim. Ibid., 137.
4. Maddox, *Responsible Grace*, 160.

problem that emerges. As Wesley indicated, this step can be precipitated by a calamitous event in the young person's life. For example, the serious illness of a friend may demonstrate the inability of consumer faith to provide answers and strength during a difficult time. Consumer therapy may fail to sustain a young person when his or her parents are divorcing or a parent is imprisoned. A layoff or change in policies may leave the children of working parents without health insurance, and the consumer method of health coverage is called into question.

Alternatively, the inadequacy of a consumer meaning system can begin to reveal itself in dissatisfaction or malaise. The children of professional parents may notice that their parents' lives have been devoted to maintaining economic prosperity at the expense of other valuable things. They notice that their parents don't have time to enjoy the nice things that their lucrative careers have allowed them to purchase, and they feel they are missing out on the connection and vitality of strong family life. Adolescents may begin to sense the emptiness of the Christmas season with its whirlwind of purchasing gifts, and wonder why everyone gets so worked up about buying things for each other. Or they may feel a tremendous letdown once the gifts are all opened; they have received the new items they had hoped for, and yet nothing miraculous seems to have happened.

Calls to awakening may also occur when an experience is challenged by the typical consumer culture's values. For example, in volunteering at a Habitat for Humanity work site, a young person meets a homeowner who has worked hard his/her entire life and yet cannot afford to purchase safe and decent housing for a family of four. This experience may call into question the young person's easy association of inaccessibility to the consumer system with individual moral failure or laziness. The adolescent who knows through his own family's life that poverty is not caused by laziness may be denied access to the symbols of shared meaning found in consumer culture because of his family's lack of economic resources. This adolescent's call to awakening may be nascent in the anger and frustration caused by his life experience being invalidated by the claims of the broader culture. In any of these ways and others, the inadequacy of the consumer system to organize life meaning becomes clear in the call-to-awakening moment.

Cultivating critical consciousness

The call to awakening as the beginning of a process of conversion has some similarity to the cultivation of critical consciousness in liberative educational theory. Consciousness raising has been a critical part of many movements for social change, such as the second-wave feminist movements of the 1960s and 1970s. However, similar to the process of ongoing conversion, the process of developing critical consciousness includes much more than a simple cognitive call to awakening. Critical consciousness is the ability of persons to "perceive critically the themes of their time, and thus to intervene actively in reality."[5] According to Paulo Freire, developing critical consciousness requires "an active, dialogical educational program concerned with social and political responsibility, and prepared to avoid the danger of massification."[6] In Freire's understanding, groups able to dialogue about their condition and to question the givenness of the social order move out of the uncritical acceptance of social values he names "massification." Through the process of dialogue, participants gain a sense of their own agency to name the world and become subjects rather than objects of history.

Coming to critical awareness is not merely a thinking experience for Freire. Truly transformative insight only comes in the context of political action to change the situation. For example, your understanding of the impact of factory runoff on streams is quite different if you've just heard a presentation in an environmental science class and if you've been involved in two years of work to get your neighborhood factory to change its wastewater practices. Through shared work for change, the person not only comes to different cognitive

---

5. Paulo Freire, *Education for Critical Consciousness* (New York: Continuum, 1998; orig. 1969), 7.
6. Ibid.,19.

awareness about an issue but also becomes committed to transformation of concrete situations in light of that awareness through shared work.[7]

Freire's educational theory was concretized through the establishment of cultural circles in which persons reflected on the nature of their context in order to clarify situations and to seek corporate action in response to their reflections.[8] The generative themes discussed by the circles were decided upon by the circles themselves, and actions taken were understood as crucial to gaining insight. The process of coming to awareness was part of a larger revolution of the self that involved a change in behavior and the relational support of a small community. We explore these kinds of mentoring groups with adolescents in chapters 8 and 9. For now, I note that the cultivation of critical consciousness was not merely a call to awakening, but also a movement into increased agency through communal political action. In other words, it involved a transformation of both agency and imagination. The behavioral practices of the cultural circles, the involvement in praxis as part of awareness, and the need for an alternative vision of the world makes the cultivation of critical consciousness more closely related to the entire process of ongoing conversion than to the call to awakening alone. However, there are clear connections between the desire to generate critical awareness and the moment of awakening that begins the process of ongoing conversion.

Educational practices of awakening

Educators approach the task of cultivating awakening from consumer faith through a variety of practices. In the sections below I offer some

---

7. "A more critical understanding of the situation of oppression does not yet liberate the oppressed. But the revelation is a step in the right direction. Now the person who has this new understanding can engage in a political struggle for the transformation of the concrete conditions in which the oppression prevails" (Freire, *Pedagogy of Hope,* 30).

8. Ibid., 42.

examples of awakening practices in the hope of stimulating your own imagination about how awakening begins.

Critical reflection on mass media

Mass-produced media is a key consumer institution involved in the formation of adolescent vocational imagination. Educator Maxine Greene describes the potentially destructive nature of this ongoing formation: "Little is done to counter media manipulation of the young into credulous and ardent consumers — of sensation, violence, criminality, things. They are instructed daily, and with few exceptions, that human worth depends on the possession of commodities, community status, a flippant way of talking, good looks."[9] Despite the fact that Greene is not a religious person, she is concerned with naming the values formed by media consumption and the way they inform youthful imagination about what is worthy in human existence. Thus, because of its power in formation, critical analysis of mass media becomes an important site for education that leads to calls to awakening.

Often religious education curricula using media invite young people to analyze the messages or themes contained within the content of the materials/programs. When I teach youth ministry classes, I ask students to watch/read/listen to four hours of mass media targeted to an adolescent audience. They do quite well at analyzing issues such as how the implicit moral messages in the material (particularly around sexuality and violence) relate to their understanding of Christian ethics. They name the parallels between *The Chronicles of Narnia: The Lion, The Witch, and the Wardrobe* and the passion narratives of the Gospels. Within the practice of religious education, there is a well-established discourse about attending to moral messages in movies and the symbolic themes contained in popular cultural offerings.

---

9. Maxine Greene, *Dialectic of Freedom* (New York: Teachers College Press, 1988), 12.

Fewer curricular resources attend to the dynamics of consumption embodied in its primary institution, the media. To root out these connections, it is perhaps more useful to begin to ask different kinds of questions, questions about the structural production and commitments of the media rather than the messages inherent in the content — questions such as: who produced the media, whose perspectives does it assume, whose interests are promoted, who is the audience it hopes to reach, whose experiences are ignored or ridiculed in the piece, and how are commercial messages embedded in the material push us to a different level of media analysis.[10]

One exercise I have found productive to generate critical awareness around consumer formation is engaging young people in critical reflection on advertising and television. After polling youth to find out what they like to watch, choose a two-hour block of television and record only the commercials during that block. Have the young people watch the commercials and analyze them as a team. I generally invite each youth to watch for a particular element of the commercials, with each youth given an individual assignment or working in pairs, depending on the size of the group. I assign the following tasks to youth, inviting them to keep notes as they watch the commercials so they can compare them in the discussion afterward:

1. Racial/ethnic analysis: Who was shown in the commercial? What were they doing? What kinds of products are targeted to different racial groups?

2. Gender analysis: same as above but focusing on gender.

3. Age analysis: same as above but focusing on age.

4. Class analysis: same as above but focusing on social class (usually requires some coaching in identifying social/economic class markers in the United States).

---

10. Michael Warren's book *Seeing through the Media: A Religious View of Communications and Cultural Analysis* is a great resource for analysis of media, particularly chap. 4, "Cultural Production as an Avenue to Cultural Analysis."

5. Sexual orientation analysis: same as above, but particularly noting who is engaged in romantic pairings.

6. Voiceover analysis: What kind of voices were used to sell what kind of products? (listening for regional and other kinds of accents, gender, perceived age or ethnicity, celebrity voices).

7. Keep track of the kinds of products offered in this time slot and the number of times certain commercials repeat.

8. Note how background music is used.

9. Note how jingles, catch phrases, and other forms of historical linking with ongoing advertising campaigns are used.

10. Note the values used to sell the products (speed, beauty, quality, affordability, sexual appeal). [I often assign multiple people to this task as they often name different values, and it is interesting to analyze who responded to what in the commercials.]

At the end of the commercials (about 40–45 minutes worth in a two-hour block, depending on when you start recording), I ask youth what they each noticed in their observational categories. Then we begin putting the observations together and naming the themes that emerge from their observations about what is valued, who is valued, and how commercials work to form consumer desire.

Many kinds of insights and conversations surface in this exercise, providing opportunities for awakening on a number of levels. The exercise invites youth into active rather than passive consumption of media, asking them to embody a questioning stance toward something they might normally let wash over them. The varied categories of analysis highlight the thousands of decisions that go into generating a thirty-second spot, and help them begin to name patterns across the variety of commercials. We ask why the producers of the commercials would make the choices we discern, and what those choices mean for the formation of values, desires, and social norms.

The exercise also becomes an opportunity to name the values that the makers of the commercials assume are important for their audience, and talk about how these values relate to the young people's stated values. The youth often note the difference between their assumption that all kinds of people are valuable in God's eyes, and the limited range of people who are featured in commercials. The youth begin to note the ways that racism, ageism, lookism, and sexism are embodied in the media, and how these values are made natural by repetition. The exercise disrupts the practice of passively consuming commercials, and calls for being awake to their purposes, methods, and cumulative formative effects.

Often religious educators want to introduce particularly meaning-ful forms of media that do not get much publicity. Helping young people identify alternative media streams is a worthy educational venture in its own right. For analysis purposes, I find it best to use the most popular forms of media out there. The high-volume, highly popular media tend to be the ones that are speaking the cultural vernacular of consumption most effectively and most blatantly. By using pieces that your youth would actually consume if you weren't with them, even if you find the material obnoxious, you are eliminat-ing distinctions between media they should attend to carefully and media that is merely entertaining. For example, when teaching about the formation about ideas of gender in the media, I took a group of young people to see *Batman Begins* simply because it was the most popular movie in release at the time. When they identified that only two women had speaking roles in the movie (the mother and the romantic interest), the popularity of the piece became an indictment of a purportedly neutral entertainment experience that privileges the experiences and stories of men over women.

Since engaging in media entertainment is a fairly normal mode of interaction in church youth groups and family settings, this is not a difficult place to start eliciting awakening moments. This kind of media analysis may come more naturally for persons whose lives are rarely represented positively in the mainstream of consumer culture, either because of their racial/ethnic or class background. For young people who are white and middle class, the recognition that their reality predominates in media channels may be more of a sobering wake-up call.

Remarkably useful media resources analyzing the role of the media in consumer culture have become available in recent years. Films such as the PBS *Frontline* special *The Merchants of Cool* directly address the relationships between adolescents, media, and consumer culture. This special exposes MTV's market-research techniques, the cooptation of adolescent cultural expressions by global media conglomerates, and the circular cross-promotions within mega-corporations that control multiple streams of media. While this particular special is now several years old, the marketing processes described are still relevant, making it an effective tool to watch with young people to begin to ask questions about media formation.

Field trips around town

One of the benefits of addressing a system as pervasive as consumer culture is the ease of engaging in experiential education through field trips without much expense or planning. Opportunities to observe the consumer system in action are as close as the neighborhood grocery store or the local landfill. The more normal and everyday the setting seems to the young people, the more important the critical engagement with it becomes.

This summer I went on a field trip to Target (a popular affordable department store) with a group of adolescent girls involved in a residential theological program. They were quite excited when we announced the field trip and also quite suspicious about our motives. Would they be allowed to buy anything? What were they going to do? Why would this be an appropriate field trip for a religious educational event? Similar to the commercial-watching exercise, we prepared a list of questions for the youth to explore, gave them clipboards and pens, and sent them off into the store.[11] The focus of this learning

---

11. Because of the general suspicions against young people in American culture, it is important to remind the youth not to disrupt other shoppers or to be particularly obvious in their tasks if they don't want to be asked to leave the store. This is particularly important if participants are young persons of color, who are more likely to be targeted by store employees as potential troublemakers. This can be an occasion to have an important conversation with youth about their own disenfranchisement

event was to discover how consumer culture shapes gender identity, so we had them looking in the toy aisles (which are conveniently gendered at Target) and clothing departments to find what kinds of items were marketed to boys and to girls and what these items indicated it means to be male or female. In order to raise more general consumption questions, I included questions such as:

How many distinct kinds of toothpaste can a person choose from?

In what countries are the clothes offered made?

What is the ratio of packaging to product in the kids' food aisles?

What percentage of products would you assume are designed to be replaced or rebought in the next few years?

Who is shopping in this store, and what kinds of things are they buying?

Again, have the youth take notes on what they observe, and use those notes for a group conversation after the trip.

Turning the youth into investigative reporters appeals to their desire to sniff out hypocrisy and to take ownership in the insights they generate. They are also likely to name things about consumption patterns in the store that will not seem obvious to you but that are critical to their own interaction with the system. In inviting them to construct the knowledge about consumption present in the store, you indicate your confidence that they know something about the world and are able to make sense of it. At the same time, you are embodying the process of getting them to ask questions about common practices that they normally would not question, such as buying toothpaste. A word of warning: with both this activity and the media analysis you will be accused by the youth of setting out to ruin activities that they find enjoyable and satisfying. In a sense, they are right. By asking them to engage critically in the activities, it will be hard for

---

within the broader culture. Strategically lending adult support and visibility with the youth in the store is critical for the completion of these tasks.

them to engage uncritically the next time, and much of the pleasure in engaging these activities lies in their unthinking acceptance.

In addition to these more mundane field trips, there may be opportunities in your community to visit the corporate headquarters of some popular brand of consumer product. Often, the corporate headquarters has some sort of visitors' center or community relations person who would be willing to talk to your group. You may also follow connections in your congregation to see where you have contacts in local sites intimately related to consumer culture. You might be surprised to discover you have people with access to local television or radio stations who could talk about how their programming and advertising relate. If you have contacts in government or sanitation services, a field trip to a local landfill or a conversation with a city manager could serve as a call to awakening about the issues of overconsumption, waste disposal, and the effect of nonrenewable resources on the living environment of a community.

In field trips with young people it is helpful to have a local informant, particularly if that person is able to talk candidly about how the marketing process works for their product, or how their faith life relates to their work with the company. For some companies, this means meeting off the premises of the corporation in order to have candid conversation. I ask the young people to be good guests, utterly polite but deeply inquisitive about what is going on at the company. How do they generate consumer interest in their product? Who decides what is news and what isn't for the community? What criteria do they use to make these kinds of decisions? Having a real person involved in the work present shifts the youth's perspective of these corporations and institutions from faceless realities to human constructions. For example, I can remember the shock on the faces of young people when a producer for Headline News answered quite frankly the question about what criteria makes something newsworthy: "It's important news if I decide it is." Young people who were discerning enough to know that CNN might be a better source of news than some other sources were shocked to discover that behind the huge brand and reputation was this one guy who made choices every hour about what received headline status. This demystifies the power of the brand in important ways.

When I lived in Atlanta, both the World of Coca-Cola Museum and the CNN headquarters were accessible to the community. The World of Coke was a particularly fine pilgrimage destination for consumption, as it has both an opening film that celebrates the product's global domination and a room where you can watch fifty years of television commercials made for Coca-Cola. After some initial conversation about consumer culture and how it functions, this field trip sent adolescents with whom I was working through the roof about the company's aggressive practices of generating desire. If you don't have access to this kind of site physically, you can go on a virtual tour. For example, at *www.cocacola.com* or *www.pepsi.com,* you can view the latest commercials for these products, and read all of the company's public relations material about their understanding of their role in the United States and the world. Often, the crass and universal claims made by these companies shock young people, and provide space to talk about the ways in which branding and consumer loyalty impact identity formation in consumer culture.

Young people often feel that they are already savvy to marketing techniques and media manipulation, and they may resent any insinuation that they are influenced by these processes. Youth are subjected to an enormous amount of educational effort that tells them to value "being their own person" and not to be duped by advertising. Indeed, a level of healthy cynicism about marketing is present in young people, but they often need opportunities to push beyond the layer of "of course they want everyone to drink soda instead of water, that's how they make money" to a deeper level of understanding about the impact and influence of this formation on themselves and the culture as a whole. In order to move beyond the first level of "knowingness" to really become awake to these issues, I find that exercises that invite young people into carefully naming the processes in detail and their own concerns with them are a good first step.

Study about the consumer culture and its impacts

Often young people are engaging economics and environmental science in school but are not given the space to consider the religious and ethical implications of this academic study. Young people are often aware of controversies surrounding the study of evolution and religious faith, but they can also be invited to think about the religious implications of economic theories and policies and the environmental impacts of consumer culture. While youth cultures and individual interest around academic life vary, for many youth academic pursuits are a high priority. This interest is not often honored in religious communities.

Those young people who have had opportunity to study environmental or economic issues can serve as peer resources in a conversation about the impacts of consumer culture in these two areas. By asking around to discover what they are learning and what they are concerned about, you may identify what they can share with their peers. In other school environments, students are not exposed to either of these areas of study, and may need more encouragement to dip into these important questions. Here you may need to seek out resources in your community, persons passionate about these issues who can invite young people into considering them as conversation partners. In either case, an individual with whom young people have a relationship becomes the avenue to engage bigger issues that may initially seem uninteresting or unimportant to the youth.

Often we are shy about inviting youth to use the fullest gifts of their intellect in matters of faith. However, many young people chafe at the sense that their religious life is not big enough to handle the hardest questions they face. As leaders and teachers of young people, we feel most comfortable inviting youth into the questions that we have answered already for ourselves. We often forget to invite youth into wrestling with our hardest unanswered questions, or the questions about which we know very little. For most of us, environmental and economic questions seem too big and too complex to begin to address. At the same time, they fundamentally shape our experience as human beings and the experience of those who suffer because of the policies and practices that we participate in as consumers. For this reason, making the effort to chip away at understanding these issues is critical. It may be easiest to choose one trajectory within these topics related to concern for the poor — say, food production or unemployment rates — as a beginning point. As you look toward the big picture of these systems, it is important to help youth make connections down to the situations of persons they know or daily practices in which they engage. In doing this kind of serious analytical work, you are inviting youth into a new skill of critique of systemic structures in addition to their more familiar skill of responding to individual human suffering. Both are important to mature faithful living.

Contrasting consumer and Christian meaning systems

I recently taught a session about spiritual disciplines to a group of Jewish and Christian parents and named "household economics" as a spiritual practice. The group was utterly puzzled by this statement. What did I mean by that term? How was it a spiritual practice? As I began to describe the ways in which the decisions we make about the use of our resources form us spiritually and indicate our values and commitments, the group began to become a bit clearer about the connection. However, their initial blankness made it clear that this line of thinking was pretty foreign to them. How they used their money and what they bought seemed unrelated to their spiritual life. Disrupting this unthinking consumer religious practice and inviting more considered relationships between religious meaning making and consumption become important goals of religious education toward ongoing conversion.

In analyses of consumer practice and policy, you are inviting youth to uncover and to describe the meaning claims of consumer faith. In each case, these claims can be placed into conversation with Christian theological claims. By helping youth notice the places where consumer and Christian meaning systems do not easily merge, you may create enough cognitive dissonance to generate initial suspicion of consumer claims and curiosity to look deeper into how they are embodied in culture. Here are some examples of consumer meaning claims that conflict with Christian theological claims:

Brand acquisition provides meaning in life (Coke is life? Coke is it? Make it real?)

Human value lies in imago dei vs. human value lies in youth, beauty, and celebrity

Care for creation vs. convenience and disposability

Concern for the poor vs. concern to imitate the rich

Local news mantra "Be scared of your neighbor" vs. loving your neighbor

Together with your youth, you can generate a much more complete list of the conflicts. The goal is to highlight the ways in which consumer culture rises to the level of values and norms that people actually believe and around which they shape their life practice. It is likewise the goal to begin to question the adequacy of that meaning system. If achieved, the cognitive dissonance will not transform life practice, but it can serve as a call to awakening.

Mission trips

The mission trips and service-learning experiences offered to many youth in communities of faith have the disruption of consumer faith as part of their intended educational outcome, although often as an implicit or unnamed goal. Groups market these experiences in terms of giving youth an opportunity to put their faith into action or to engage in hands-on acts of ministry. Adolescents respond well to the opportunity to serve others in a concrete manner. These experiences meet an adolescent developmental need to demonstrate competence and to make a difference in the world. The opportunity to contribute constructively to the world comes in opposition to other contexts where young people are in a holding pattern until they can get through education and get onto the real work of adulthood. Mission trips can be a positive group-building activity for youth groups, where fun and fellowship can be combined with opportunities to love and serve the neighbor.

Mission trips also offer a subtler curriculum around consumption, poverty, and wealth. Sometimes parents and churches send their children into situations of poverty so that they will see how privileged they are within the consumer system and will be more grateful for what they have (often interpreted as being thankful for God's blessings). Even if parents don't have this as a learning goal, the first response of youth when exposed to situations of poverty can be to interpret the experience in terms of their consumer meaning categories. In reflection times after their service experiences, youth will report in wonder: "Those people had no money, and they were still so happy." This comment reflects a genuine point of confusion and surprise because the experience violates the consumer tenet that increased possessions bring increased happiness. Or they start to ask questions during the service experience such as "Why does Mr. Smith work two jobs, and his family still lives in that scary, run-down neighborhood?" These questions provide evidence that belief in the system of consumer meanings is being disrupted in the understanding of the young persons.

When young people are invited to be in service to persons on the underside of consumer culture, the encounter may also lead to greater self-knowledge about their reliance on consumer culture as a faith system. Young people may begin to critique their own living situation and familial values in light of the ways in which the people they serve are living. Upon returning home, they may view their homes and possessions in a different light. This kind of dislocation can generate familial resistance: "What did you do to my kid on that trip?" Parents who just wanted their children to do something less self-centered with their time find their children questioning the commitments of the family and the church to consumption and their lack of sharing with those who have less access to consumer goods.

For all these reasons, mission trips can serve as an opportunity for calls to awakening to occur around consumer culture. However, these insights and questions don't arise automatically for the youth.

Moments of awakening can be encouraged with intentionality about learning goals and opportunities for preparation prior to and reflection after the event. To move beyond interpreting the experience out of the old consumer faith mode requires modeling of alternative faith systems to understand the event.

Additionally, some young people live in situations not far removed from poverty and lack of access to the consumer system. For these youth, mission opportunities may not serve as a call to awakening in quite the same way. I once took a youth group from a downtown church in Atlanta to serve with an established mission agency in the Appalachian region. The youth attended church each week in the same building where four hundred homeless persons ate lunch in the church's soup kitchen. Some of the young people came from families whose economic situations were tentative at best. Most of the other youth participating in the weeklong mission experience came from more suburban kinds of churches. At the first evening reflection, several of the young people from other churches responded with shock and dismay at the living conditions of the people whose homes were being repaired. The youth from the downtown church wondered about the response of the other youth present. Why were they crying? What was going on with them? We had to explain that many young people were removed from the daily experiences of poverty through class-segregated living, and that situations of poverty are not often represented in media. The experience of a call to awakening about poverty and its impact on real human lives was clearly affecting the other youth. Through watching the reactions of the other youth, our young people were given an opportunity to consider the ways in which they understood the world quite differently than their peers. This interaction helped them to name in new ways the dynamics of media formation and class living. Additionally, the opportunity to spend a week in service with one family offered an opportunity for our youth to live into understandings of solidarity with the poor in ways that their weekly experiences had not.

This anecdote points to the ways in which service experiences can support many stages in ongoing conversion beyond the call to awakening. In addition to providing opportunities to disrupt consumer faith, mission trips embody a lived theology that directly counters consumer tenets. Service without desire for reciprocity is a theological motif that directly contradicts the consumer precept of assured return for investment. While consumer faith teaches us that the purpose of a religious life is personal satisfaction and enrichment, service opportunities provide a connection to the social responsibilities of a life of faith and an opportunity to deepen religious understanding beyond personal salvation and satisfaction. Concrete practices of compassion can move youth into an increased awareness of God's call to solidarity with those who find themselves on the underside of consumer culture. All of these are opportunities for justification, to be discussed further in chapter 6.

Unfortunately, mission trips can also use people who are poor to provide an opportunity for more privileged youth to learn gratitude for their good fortune, to feel good about themselves as sometime servants, and an opportunity to "collect" experiences to "sell oneself" on a college resume. If done without careful reflection about structural issues, they can reinforce stereotypes about poverty such as poor people are lazy, happy being poor, or poor because of bad individual life choices. Careful reflection and attentiveness to power dynamics are required for mission trips to serve as a call to awakening without unduly exploiting those served. Given the serious dangers of service-learning experiences, their potential benefits in the actual physical work completed, relationships established, and potential for learning together nonetheless make them valuable, if engaged in cautiously and keenly aware of the possibility of exploitation.

My own awareness about consumer culture was awakened in the experiences of service learning that I had as an adolescent and young adult, and I believe they can serve powerfully as calls to awakening despite their potentially exploitative dynamics. An important call to awakening occurred for me at age nineteen, when I participated in a service-learning trip to Juiz de Fora, Brazil. The trip combined service in a local mission agency with learning opportunities of various kinds. One evening during the trip we met with several Brazilian college students to engage in conversation and mutual learning. One of the students we met was the son of an American missionary who was familiar with both American and Brazilian culture. During the conversation, he began to challenge some of the American students about our understanding of what we were doing in college. In America, he noted, college students assume that they "own" their education as a private good. Higher education is all about what will get you as an individual into a higher-paying job so that you can own more things and take care of your personal families. He contrasted this to the understanding of education that he felt predominates in Brazil. He noted that very few people get to go to university, particularly out of the rural villages and other underresourced communities. If you go, you know exactly who in your village is picking up the slack for your absence and what it cost the village to allow you the privilege of attending school. Thus, many Brazilian students are clear that the education belongs not to the individual who attends university but rather to the whole village. What you are learning is for the benefit of the community, not solely for personal gain.

I can remember being utterly floored by this conversation. He was right. I had never thought of *my* education as belonging to anyone but me. Not even my parents, who had financed parts of that education, had I given any authority to tell me what to study or what to do with what I studied. It was an utterly new concept for me to think of myself, my vocational phase as student, or my college education as communally owned. I had never thought of myself as responsible to anyone else in my studies, other than a vague sense of wanting to please my parents by doing well. This was my awakening to the ways in which consumer assumptions utterly defined the experience of higher education for me. This conversation began a long path of rethinking educational goals in light of the broader communities to which I was connected and the responsibilities of being privileged enough to engage in higher education. To be honest, the lure of consuming a trip to Brazil informed my desire to engage in the service-learning experience. Fortunately, a call to awakening can happen in the midst of bad motives and misdirected desires.

Always in the context of grace

In the first chapter of this book I shared the story of Michael and his sermonette on the virtues of proper consumption that was a catalyst for my own consideration of this topic. When I first reflected on this incident in a public setting, including an extensive theoretical explanation of the dynamics of the formative situation in which Michael found himself, somebody asked me a rather startling question for an academic lecture hall. The audience member challenged: "You're an educator. What would you have done if you were Michael's parent?" It was a question I had not yet asked myself, pushing me to concretize in practice what I was addressing theoretically.

After a long and rather awkward pause, I said the first thing that came to mind: that Michael needed a response of grace. Even as I said the words, I was surprised by them. Upon further reflection, I am more convinced that my instinctive response was correct. Instead of a rant about how material things were not what was important in life, and how he shouldn't want them, Michael needed a word of compassionate understanding about the forces that had shaped his belief in proper forms of consumption. To condemn him for his consumer commitments would be blaming the victim of an entire system of formation well beyond his control. He needed noncondescending understanding in the face of the very real sanctions that not purchasing the ritual icons of this belief system would cause in his school setting. To place him in the space between two belief systems without any support for choosing the one that doesn't have currency in our culture would be unfair at best.

An atmosphere of grace is required for the courage to hear and respond to a prophetic call. Wesley had a term for the grace that allows a response to calls to awakening in the life of the individual believer. "Prevenient" or "preventing" grace intercedes to generate a person's ability to hear and respond to the call to awakening.

Responding to calls to awakening requires that our ears be opened by something larger than ourselves through personal experiences, historical circumstance, or God's gracious nudging. Fear of judgment or accusation does not generate an atmosphere in which hearing hard truths can happen.

The initial word of grace would not be followed by a sanctioned endorsement of the religion of consumption. I would not suggest providing Michael with all of the consumer goods he needs to fully participate in the posturing of middle-school environments. The difference between offering grace and legitimation of consumer culture as a viable faith system is that the word of grace contains an invitation to awakening and the full process of ongoing conversion. This invitation to conversion from consumer faith is offered not with a tone of judgment, but rather with a gracious anticipation of liberation, salvation, and wholeness offered by other kinds of religious systems. Prophetic calls coupled with derision for the person rather than gracious desire for their movement toward greater wholeness can generate defensiveness and resistance to the possibility of transformation rather than readiness for conversion.

Often, in the heat of the moment of consumer struggle, parents react to their consumerly faithful youth in ways that are meant to serve as calls to awakening but instead become prophetic calls outside of a sense of grace. One young adult remembers as follows a typical conversation with his parents about consumption:

> I can remember as a teenager trying to make a case for my parents to buy me a popular brand of expensive running shoes. My parents' response to this was to declare that it was bad to let other people tell me what kind of taste to have. They said, "They're your feet." I replied, "I want my feet to have the best!" Later, this reasoning didn't apply to my father as he chose to "reward" himself with a luxury vehicle.

In the face of blatant responses to relentless targeted marketing, it can be a struggle to remember that youth can only respond to calls to awakening when they occur in the context of grace. While inciting youthful anger at the ways in which advertisers try to manipulate them can be a moment of a call to awakening, it can backfire if we communicate a smidgen of lack of respect or compassion for the very real formation that this marketing has generated. Recognition of the ways in which we, too, are attached to this formation can encourage a shared sense of compassion and make extending grace much easier.

The limits of the external prophetic call

Even within the context of grace, prophetic calls to awakening can lead to guilt and despair if used in isolation as an educational method. In the beginning of his life as an evangelical preacher, John Wesley believed strongly in the pedagogical effects of awakening sermons.[12] He was, after all, involved in a revival movement with field preaching. Early in his career, Wesley thought one should only preach the law as an awakening event. He thought it was good to increase the anxiety and discomfort of his listeners to no end, because he believed that, once they came into belief, they would be filled with immediate assurance of their pardon and connection to God.[13] Over the years of experience in the movement, Wesley became less confident that immediate assurance occurred at the moment of acceptance of justification in Christ. He also changed in his understanding of the function of sermons that were calls to awakening. In later years he recognized

---

12. See Albert Outler's introductory comment to John Wesley's sermon "Justification by Faith": "There is no mistaking the threatening tone and spirit of Wesley's university sermons in the late 1730s and 1740s; they measure his move from pious don to itinerant evangelist" (Outler in Wesley, *Sermons,* 111).

13. In a helpful discussion of Wesley and the pedagogical function of awakening sermons, Randy Maddox notes: "During the first years of the revival Wesley did indeed stress fear of punishment and reward of heaven as primary motives for salvation. Of course, he also assumed at that time that conversion brought immediate deliverance from all fear. As he increasingly recognized the possibility of justifying relationship with God prior to full assurance, fear ceased to be merely a goad to salvation.... This is not to say he stopped preaching awakening sermons, or on the subjects of death and hell. He could still do so on occasion, when he encountered an audience that he believed needed to be awakened, but no longer with the same severity or the consuming purpose of driving them to despair" (Maddox, *Responsible Grace,* 160–61).

that this moment of awakening should include both preaching of the law (for conviction) and proclamation of the gospel (for assurance). Emphasis entirely placed on conviction or accusation could prolong despair rather than encourage movement toward salvation.

One of my students shared the example of a sermon that she had preached several times about consumption and the environment. She jokingly called it her "Stop it, you gluttonous pigs" sermon. Part of the worship service she had designed to surround the sermon involved an "ecological footprint" exercise that allowed congregants to see how much of the earth's resources they use in their current lifestyle. One evening, during a retreat in which she was to preach the ecological awareness sermon, she did the "ecological footprint" exercise that she had assigned to her participants for the next day's discussion.[14] Despite her commitment to sustainable living and recycling, she discovered, much to her horror, that she was using a disproportionately large amount of resources within the global context, several times the amount that each global citizen is allotted for equitable sharing. She told me that she cried for an hour, and then felt like a fraud. Although she now is seeking a more graceful way to invite herself and others into further reflection on these issues, this anecdote shows an example of both the nature and impact of the prophetic call to awakening. While crucial in stimulating to self-reflection and awareness, calls to awakening can sometimes lead to grief and despair rather than action and redirected commitment.

Calls to awakening are a crucial part of the process of ongoing conversion. Without them, we would not be aware of our need for transformation from consumerism or the extent to which we participate in consumer culture as a faith system. At the same time, calls to

---

14. An ecological footprint calculates how many acres of the earth's resources your lifestyle consumes. When I complete the quiz, I consume about five times what is available for each citizen. For a sample ecological footprint quiz, go to *www.redefiningprogress.org/footprint/*. There are also versions of the quiz that can calculate a community's ecological footprint, which might be an interesting task for a youth group.

awakening in isolation are not an adequate pedagogy of transformation for ongoing conversion. Coming to awareness can lead to denial,
repression, or other unhelpful responses counter to the intentions of
the one who issues the call to awakening. A pedagogy that relies
solely on the call to awakening addresses the lack of self-awareness,
but it does not address the deep change aspects of the faithing self,
who depends on the existing meaning system for making sense of life.
This step requires a fuller pedagogy of conversion, which we continue
to explore in the next chapter.

Five

Repentance

*Seeking self-knowledge
and disrupting "old" faith*

Rediscovering repentance

A teenaged girl runs out on stage barefoot and dressed in ragged overalls, blond hair ratted out and flying wildly, pointing and spitting at the audience: "You sons of snakes." Passionate and over the top, the girl brings the role of John the Baptist to startling life in a youth group performance of the musical *The Cotton Patch Gospels*. She calls for the audience to change their hearts or to risk the fury coming down on them. Youthful members of the audience titter at her boldness, perhaps marveling at her courage to step out and play the role with such abandon. If they are like me, they imagine themselves into playing that role and assess whether or not they have the guts to do it. We never identify ourselves as the persons in need of repentance.

After the youth group I served attended this performance, a reenactment of the "sons of snakes" scene became a running joke for months to come, sure to elicit a knowing laugh from those who had attended the performance. The youth toyed with the dramatic power of the moment, but the call to repentance remained firmly placed as an exotic experience distinct from their daily lives. Repentance was for crazy street preachers and criminals on death row, not for nice kids who try hard in school. It belongs to John the Baptist in the wilderness, and maybe to the teenager who injures his friends driving unsafely, but not to the marching band member and honor student.

We have a seriously truncated notion of repentance. The Christian tradition is rooted in rich practices of repentance and confession that are all but lost to us and our young people, particularly in Protestant congregations. Repentance is commonly understood as the dramatic moment of turnaround reserved for only the worst of sinners rather than as the subtle daily process of discovering and weeding out our commitments to things that separate us from living our lives in God. The relegation of repentance to extreme forms of sinful behavior reduces its capacity to assist young people on the road to ongoing conversion. It is time to reform our notions of repentance.

In the process of ongoing conversion, the awareness that begins in the call to awakening continues in the process of repentance. After the initial discovery of the inadequacy of the consumer faith system to sustain meaning making, a more regular process of developing awareness of our implication in the consumer system is necessary. During this process, our reliance on the consumer system of meaning as an organizing faith system continues to be disrupted, now with our knowledge and assistance. Through repentance we can come to greater awareness of the ways in which we are involved in the consumer system of meaning and the impact this involvement has on our lives and others. Rediscovering repentance is central to educational efforts to generate resistance to consumer culture.

"Repentance" may be too loaded a term to be recovered for use with young people. Just as language about sinfulness and corruption sounds antiquated and laden with shame, language of repentance may be forever handed over to street preachers. However, the educational process of repentance is so central to being freed from bondage to consumer culture that I am willing to risk reclaiming the term and redefining it for the purposes of our understanding, even if we decide we need to come up with different terms when we describe the process to youth.

Repentance is hard work!

The call to awakening helps us to know "Consumerism is bad" in a more general way. Repentance helps us to know "Consumerism is bad, and here are all of the particular ways I am still utterly committed to being a consumer." This is no small task. The difficulty of moving to repentance from the call to awakening is that being awake does not transform our sincere investment in the idea that owning the right things will make us happy, safe, and whole. Consumer culture makes a beautiful, compelling, and repetitive case for its fittingness as an object of devotion. Our shared rituals of consumer faith cement in our imaginations a latent vision of "the way the world is." We have faith in consumer culture at a deep level that is difficult to uncover and dislodge, making repentance tough work.

Another difficulty in engaging the work of repentance is that we try desperately to protect our sense of ourselves as basically good people. If we know at some cognitive level that "consumerism is bad," then it's hard to face up to the fact that we might still be deeply invested in it. As scholar of Christian formation Brian Mahan writes: "We humbly confess ourselves sinners and resolutely deny all the particulars. It's the same with our attachment to wealth, fame, power, and the rest. We know our lives are scripted and that the scripts have to do with such things, but we'd rather leave it at that."[1] So we engage in vigorous and effective self-deception to maintain our sense of ourselves as basically good. The repentance that is most difficult is not about seeking forgiveness and rehabilitation after dramatic and obvious sin. The hardest repentance requires uncovering those valued objects of devotion such as looking fashionable or being respected in certain circles, unconscious but deeply rooted, that we secretly believe can truly make everything okay. Mahan calls these secret hopes "our closely guarded and cleverly concealed 'programs for happiness.'"[2] These programs express our deepest trusts and inform our sense of well-being at such a basic level that to question them seems potentially disruptive of our very selves and our ability to be happy.

Adolescents have a sensitive detection system for the hypocrisy of others. However, seeing the ways in which they are compromised

---

1. Mahan, *Forgetting Ourselves on Purpose*, 97.
2. Ibid., 100.

and conflicted in their personal commitments is much more difficult. Part of this arises from the reality that adolescents' commitments and sense of identity are not yet firmly established. Adult identity is rooted in commitments that are not easily reversed (taking on significant educational debt, mortgages, having children, partnering with another human being, etc.). Young people often haven't yet made many commitments that are difficult to reverse.

As an adolescent, I can remember people encouraging me to be true to myself. My internal response was always twofold: Yes, that's important. And, Who is that, exactly? Because adolescents don't have much control over the environments in which they find themselves (family, school, neighborhood are all "givens"), they haven't had an opportunity to discern who they will be when those constraints of their contexts of origin are lifted. At the same time, young people can begin to take some agency in the ways in which they interact with those "givens," and can start to name the identity-forming values, beliefs, and practices inculcated by this original context. This naming is but the beginning of a lifelong process of understanding who we are within the full spectrum of human identities. In adolescence, when identity feels particularly fluid and unsettled, interrogating oneself for inconsistencies and seeking out our hidden programs for happiness become even more difficult tasks.

Repentance, rightly understood

Repentance has not always been reserved for the moment of dramatic turnaround in the lives of the worst sinners. Voices within the Christian theological tradition indicate that recognition of the ways that we participate in sin is crucial to the task of increasing holiness for all believers. For example, John Wesley notes:

> Hence may appear the extreme mischievousness of that seemingly innocent opinion that "there is no sin in a believer; that all sin is destroyed, root and branch, the moment a man is justified." By totally preventing that repentance it quite blocks up

the way to sanctification. There is no place for repentance in him who believes there is no sin either in his life or heart. Consequently there is no place for his being "perfected in love," to which that repentance is indispensably necessary.[3]

Wesley includes "repentance, rightly understood" in a list with the practice of all good works of piety and mercy as "in some sense necessary to sanctification."[4] Wesley explains that "repentance, rightly understood" means repentance without guilt, fear of the wrath of God, or sense of condemnation. It is repentance with assurance of the favor of God, repentance in the gracious context of our acceptance by God as we are.

Repentance rightly understood takes into account our paradoxical and conflicted nature as both justified and not yet perfected in love. We participate in sin that still remains, though it doesn't reign, in our hearts.[5] An atmosphere of gracious acceptance allows for the seeking out of those places where sin still remains with the recognition that finding them doesn't indicate shameful failure. Rather, identifying the ways in which we are still committed to consumer culture facilitates movement toward our fuller reflection of the love of God. We can only undertake repentance, rightly understood, when we are free from an undue sense of shame and guilt about our attachment to consumer culture. The work of repentance is best understood as an adventure in partnership with God, an educational process that assists the Holy Spirit in helping us move toward a life that more fully expresses the love of God.

Repentance as self-knowledge

The simple definition that Wesley most often used for repentance was "self-knowledge."[6] The desired self-knowledge is awareness of the

---

3. Wesley, *Sermons*, 378.
4. Ibid., 377.
5. Ibid.
6. Ibid., 128.

"corruption" of the inner nature, in this case the ways in which we love consumption with all of our heart, soul, mind, and strength. Self-knowledge for Wesley went beyond cognitive awareness to include "every faculty of the soul": eye of understanding, knowledge, will, affections, and passions.[7] Repentance was about recognizing with all of your capacities the distortion of the entirety of the inner nature, the soul.

You may notice that Wesley follows the early church fathers in talking about sin as "corruption" of the soul rather than individual acts of wrongdoing. When Wesley discusses the ongoing repentance that leads to sanctification, he is concerned about the corruption of the soul generated by original sin. Original sin lost favor as a theological doctrine because of the unfortunate historical interpretations that linked it to human sexuality in misogynistic ways. However, revisiting the doctrine of original sin allows us to consider an initial state of faith that requires transformation because of its attachment to unworthy objects, such as consumer culture. This faith is programmed into young people prior to their capacity to make choices. It is "original" in that it is a "given" operating in their lives because they were born into this culture of consumption.

What would it mean to consider reliance on consumer capitalism as a faith system as part of original sin in the American way of life? In her book *The Fall to Violence,* process theologian Marjorie Suchocki rethinks original sin for a modern context. Suchocki understands original sin to be expressed in a trifold structure of genetic endowment toward violence, the social interdependence of all humans, and "the unique structures of intersubjectivity that mediate the values of one generation to the next."[8] She notes that the particular forms of sin

---

7. Ibid., 128. The language that Wesley uses here is quite fascinating. Knowledge includes the fullness of desire and emotional life for Wesley: "Thy affections are alienated from God, and scattered abroad over the earth. All thy passions, both thy desires and aversions, thy joys and sorrows, thy hopes and fears, are out of frame, are either undue in their degree, or placed on undue objects" (128).

8. Marjorie Suchocki, *The Fall to Violence* (New York: Continuum, 1995), 129.

that take form in society's institutions deeply influence the structures of awareness and conscience of the next generation.

Along these lines, the narratives of meaning that support the institutions of consumer capitalism are hardwired into the awareness and conscience of persons growing up in American culture. For example, from the moment of birth, American children are steeped in the values of buying and selling. Corporations such as McDonald's target with their advertising children as young as eighteen months in order to affect parental purchases. The typical American child recognizes some five hundred brands by the age of five. Public educational efforts on a national level emphasize the study of math and science for children across the age spectrum because these skills will allow them to "compete in a global marketplace."[9] Liberal arts education and other forms of education that emphasize broad human development are becoming increasingly challenged as economic utility drives the educational marketplace. In hundreds of ways, human beings born into the culture of the United States are socialized into an understanding of their function as consumers and participants in a global capitalism.[10] When talking about repentance, then, we are talking about working against individual formation into sinful social structures as

---

9. "Goals 2000: The Educate America Act" was legislated into federal law and set forth national goals for the next five years in education. One of the seven stated goals of this act was that "all students in the academic disciplines should meet world-class standards and rank 'first in the world in science and math achievement' " (Greene, *Releasing the Imagination*, 17). Math and science were singled out because they are most closely related to participation in a largely technocentric global economy.

10. By making this connection between consumer capitalist structures of meaning in American culture and Suchocki's understanding of original sin, I do not intend to suggest that consumer capitalism is the only sin in American corporate meaning making that passes from one generation to the next. Of course, narratives of racism, sexism, violent resolution to conflict, etc., are passed down from one generation to the next as well. They, too, require ongoing conversion. But this emphasis on buying and selling goods as fundamentally crucial to the good life is particularly damaging to the vocational imagination of adolescents, particularly when the only criterion for deciding a life path becomes "what could make me the most money while utilizing the unique skills and interests that I have."

a form of original sin. The "corruption" of the soul occurs through the daily reality of living within consumer culture.

Repentance as dehabituation

One strategy to generate self-knowledge is dehabituation. Dehabituation includes any practice that disrupts our current imagination and patterns of living, opening the soul, mind, and body to the possibility of other ways of organizing meaning. Dehabituation is critical to adolescent and young adult identity formation. For example, leaving home for short or extended periods allows adolescents to gain perspective on the formative markers of their identity in relationship to other possibilities. The practices of dehabituation allow the believer to see herself and her belief system in a new light, a form of repentance that increases self-knowledge and fuels ongoing conversion.

Pilgrimage

One example of ancient Christian practices of dehabituation is pilgrimage. Although pilgrimage eventually became spiritualized and shifted to a purely imaginative experience, in its earliest form it involved literal travel, often with great risk, to places of spiritual significance. The inspiring destination was only one element of the important formative experience. Historian of Christian spirituality Margaret Miles notes that disrupting regular patterns of experience was equally important: "Removing the context and habits of daily living results in the revivification of experience: altered physical conditions produce an altered — a more alert and sensitive — consciousness."[11] Mary Elizabeth Moore also explores the power of sacred journeys and pilgrimages in contemporary religious life, noting their potential to introduce people to alternative worlds, to disrupt normal social structures, and to disrupt the hierarchies of normal church life.[12] By changing the physical details and routines of daily

---

11. Miles, *Practicing Christianity*, 51.
12. Mary Elizabeth Moore, *Ministering with the Earth* (St. Louis: Chalice Press, 1998), 113.

experience, a new attentiveness to the patterns and commitments of daily life can be achieved. Pilgrimages offer dehabituation by removing or altering daily habits for the sake of increased awareness of their significance.

Many youth groups regularly engage in pilgrimage, albeit in a much different fashion than their ancient Christian forebears. Weekend retreats or camping experience without access to mass media, weeklong revival events where the community is gathered for worship every evening, or a service-learning trip to an economically challenged area all can serve to interrupt the context and daily habits of consumption. Any of these events dehabituate the young person's regular engagement in the ritual practices of consumer faith. This dehabituation becomes particularly meaningful when coupled with a context of interpretation that offers other organizing meaning systems and metaphors for life.

Pilgrimage can also function outside of religious contexts. For example, residential environmental programs allow participants to gain distance on consumer culture and to begin to imagine the world more systemically and interdependently through extended stays at organic farms or other sustainable living sites. In these summer or school-term programs, young people live in intentional community, engage in study about environmental issues, and often live and work on a sustainable farm. Participants abstain from electronic technology and other forms of mass media merchandising, particularly television consumption. Additionally, they throw themselves into the rhythms and work of organic farming, often at hours of the day that they never see in their "normal" lives. They become immersed in a small community that embodies the values of sustainability and interdependence. This experience both disrupts the consumer meaning system and provides an alternative vision for the way life could be.

Within Christian circles, many adolescents participate in regular pilgrimage to summer camps as participants or even working on staff as junior counselors. The camp can become a sacred site for young people, a place where they have a sense that they can be their most authentic selves. The experience is so powerful it defies explanation for some young people; when pressed they eventually just say you had to be there. They are right: the power of the experience is in being there rather than in their regular environment. A camp environment takes away access to shopping experiences (except perhaps the evening canteen). As young staffers, participants are not often earning enough money to spend anyway. Access to media is limited by the camping setting. Camp provides intense forms of communal interaction and living together in small spaces that is quite different from daily life. If serving as staff, the shared work of leading younger campers, engaging in challenging activities, and taking on the administrative work of the camp evokes the feeling of contributing significantly to the lives of others. Opportunities for group worship and individual communing with creation inform a different imagination about how the world can be. Camp can provide a powerful dehabituating experience from consumer faith even as it offers opportunities for participants to understand themselves in different ways.

Physical pilgrimage has always been a costly venture. Unfortunately, without significant intervention it may not be available or possible at all for economically less-privileged youth. Often, communities question the use of resources for travel when similar kinds of formative activities could be engaged in the local community. However, this kind of disruption of daily routines and engagement in a different community and daily practice provides a powerful experience in dehabituation. The dehabituation fuels self-knowledge, providing powerful energy for the work of ongoing conversion.

Ascetic withdrawal

As pilgrimage can be expensive, a more economical option for dehabituation is ascetic withdrawal from sites of consumption. While careful to critique the bodily harm that was at times self-inflicted in historical forms of ascetical practice, Miles asserts that it can be reclaimed as a useful tradition.[13] Present in many different cultures,

---

13. Although Miles finds the practices of asceticism useful and needed, she finds that the term "asceticism" itself is not: "Individual and communal practices of self-discipline based on self-knowledge must name themselves differently if Christianity

religious belief systems, and historical periods, Miles defines asceticism generally as "the practical observation that an alteration of physical conditions produces a changed condition of the psyche."[14] Ascetical disciplines as dehabituating exercises were assigned to address the idiosyncratic destructive behaviors and thought patterns exhibited by an individual. Ascetical practices work out of the assumption that since the body was socially conditioned into certain subjectivities (characteristic ways of experiencing the world as a self), the body can be reconditioned to a new organizing center or self that is religiously based through a different form of social conditioning. Miles notes:

> In ascetic practice, the body, conditioned in every culture to find gratification in objects specified by the culture, becomes the ally of the religious self, a tool for breaking mechanical attraction to the objects that gratify the social self and for reorienting desire and gratification. The *same* energy that originally organized the person's pursuit of sex, power, and possessions can be removed from the socially conditioned self and relocated in the religious self.[15]

By relying on the intimate connection of body and soul, practices that break down the conditioning on the body exacted by the broader culture can provide space for a new organizing center with different desires and practices.[16]

The ascetical practice most often introduced to contemporary adolescents is the practice of abstinence from sexual activity before marriage. Unfortunately, the rationale behind introducing this practice often has more to do with our fears about the expressions of adolescent sexuality and its potential dangers than about the space

---

is not to perpetuate its popular caricature as body denying and world rejecting" (Miles, *Practicing Christianity*, 104).

14. Ibid., 95.
15. Ibid., 96.
16. Ibid.

such abstinence might create for other kinds of significant relationship and connection. Appeals for sexual abstinence are shrouded in all kinds of conflicted messages about sex being sinful, dangerous, and unholy. The purpose of abstinence is not punitive withdrawal from attractive things. Neither is it about abstaining from things that are dangerous or harmful. Rather, saying no to certain things allows us to make space to say yes to other things that are valued.

Withdrawal from media

One option engaged in by many families interested in resisting the culture of consumption is the ascetic withdrawal from mass media. Some parents remove televisions from their homes and work to reduce the impact of other kinds of mass media marketing on family members. Other parents choose certain days or times to restrict television viewing, Internet surfing, instant messaging, listening to the radio, and other interactions with media. While it may not seem directly related to bodily religious practice, the ritual effect on subjectivity created through sitting in front of a television set for the forty hours a week that is average for many American teenagers could certainly be considered a practice of formation in the religious subjectivity of consumption. To drastically reduce the occurrence of this bodily habit is a radical change in attention and bodily experience that may elicit change in subjectivity. Newly reclaimed time, once devoted to television watching, also generates space for other kinds of interaction within the family. This space may provide opportunities to embody and practice other values such as care for one another, musical and creative expression, and community service. The purpose of ascetic withdrawal is not the abstinence itself, but rather the space generated by withdrawal for other kinds of immersion and formation.

In recent years I've been interviewing many older adolescents about their sense of vocation and where it has developed. One young woman, "Lydia," clearly articulated a vocational path constructed in resistance to consumer values. Lydia noted in the interview that she uses a form of asceticism to help nurture her clarity about her alternative commitments. When I asked Lydia how she dealt with conflicting messages from her family, her school, her church, and broader American culture about what it means to have a successful life, Lydia immediately named her coping mechanism as isolating herself as much as possible from mainstream American culture: "I think that I do as much as I can to separate myself from American culture. I don't watch TV. I don't drive a car. . . . I mean . . . I just try to block it out." Her withdrawal from television consumption has been a lifelong practice initiated by her parents and now continued on her own authority. She felt that this withdrawal had cost her in terms of social relationship throughout her life:

> In middle school, not watching TV definitely cut out a part of the social scene when people would come in class and be like: "Oh, did you watch *Dawson's Creek?*" and they'd start this whole debate about who looked better, and I'd be like — "What? How is this relevant?" So, I think I made the choice. When I was little I watched *Sesame Street* and *Mr. Rogers* and *Reading Rainbow.* And then I stopped that and since then when people were talking about *Teenage Mutant Ninja Turtles* I was left out and when people were talking about . . . you know, on up the age progression of TV shows, I was just out of it. It wasn't something I envied about other kids.[17]

At the same time, Lydia notes that she didn't feel like she was missing out on something fundamentally significant in not watching television. Without bitterness, Lydia simply noted the ways in which commercial television dominated the conversation topics of her peers.

Lydia found rather disturbing what her peers talked about in terms of television. For example, her thoughts on the then-popular reality television show *Survivor* during her interview point to the ways in

---

17. Lydia's connection between the culture of children and youth and the shows and commodities they consume is quite striking. Her familiarity with the names of shows and their general content despite her parents' decision not to allow her to watch them points to a frustration shared by many parents who attempt to limit their children's access to media-driven "children's" culture. This observation of the commodification of children's culture is explored in Warren, *Seeing through the Media,* and in Giroux, *Stealing Innocence.*

which she assessed these shows based on core values established elsewhere: "I never watched it because I didn't want to. It just seemed so disgusting, you know? I mean, deciding which of the people around you was worth less than everyone else? What kind of a life is that [laughs]?" Although her parents and sister had recently started watching a show that Lydia found less objectionable, she reported that she had decided she wouldn't watch television on principle and excused herself from their weekly ritual of watching it together.[18] Now she feels like the decision to abstain from television is totally her own.

Withdrawal from consumptive entertainment

Lydia also found that consumption dominated the entertainment sought by her peers at school. She noted: "Peers are shopping on the weekends; they go see movies. It seems like a good criteria for how much fun you're having is how much money you're spending among those people." Lydia felt that her parents have helped her to understand that recreation and consumption don't have to be linked, and she has occasionally tried to teach her friends this same value: "So, sometimes I try to distract peers and friends from doing those kinds of consumer-oriented entertainment things that would be a 'normal' part of a good life, and sometimes I just go my own way, and sometimes I really try to start a discussion, but that's rare, 'cause I'm too shy for that [laughs]." Lydia was quite clear that her critique of consumption and her attempt to live out different values from mainstream consumer culture isolated her from her peers at times. However, the supportive communities that she encountered in

---

18. The ritual of watching television together (which provides an opportunity for critical appraisal of what is being consumed) is also a countercultural practice in the United States. The Kaiser Family Foundation study on children's media usage noted that only half of American households have any rules about television viewing, and by the time children reach the third grade the likelihood of there being family rules drops off rapidly. The study also notes that half of all children and two-thirds of older children have their own television, often located in their own rooms. For more on this phenomenon, see Roberts and Foehr, *Kids & Media in America*, 199–200.

her family and other environments and her own clearly articulated counter-value system had helped her to sustain these choices.

Many youth groups struggle with the pull of consumptive forms of entertainment. Because of the structure of our culture, it seems normal to engage with young people in fun activities that are "prepackaged" forms of entertainment: miniature golf, movies, amusement parks, rafting trips. There is nothing inherently bad about any of these experiences. However, to routinely choose them for recreation communicates that the group cannot make its own fun without paying for an entertainment commodity. As Lydia notes, the cultural norm at work here is "you have more fun the more money you spend."

I had the privilege of working with a youth group that had made a self-conscious commitment on behalf of its less economically resourced members not to engage regularly in recreational activities that cost lots of money. The actual guidelines adopted by the youth council were that the group would engage in one recreational event outside of youth group each month, and every other month that activity would have to be free. On the alternate months, the activity had to cost less than five dollars per person. The gift of this commitment was that the members of the group knew how to make their own fun. They invited each other into their homes to have board game parties. We played basketball and kickball in public parks. We had lock-ins at the church where we played equipment-free games such as sardines and ghosts in the graveyard. We played Wiffle ball in the church sanctuary (our parking lot had too much broken glass to play safely), and we played elaborate made-up simulation games that involved lots of running around in open spaces. The youth had to call on their own creativity to come up with activities they enjoyed doing together that cost nothing, but when they did, they often found that these kinds of activities allowed space for communal interaction in ways that consumer forms of entertainment often do not. The constraints of the commitment to abstain from consumption evoked renewed relationship.

Communities of faith often secretly fear that entertainment is all that is keeping youth present and active. While young people do value fun and camaraderie in all that they do, fun does not have to be manufactured and sold to young people. Given the challenge and some space to create, they find imaginative ways to bring energy and fun to otherwise boring and repetitive tasks. The participants of one youth program I evaluated named the day they spent gleaning spinach as their favorite part of a three-week program packed with all kinds of learning and recreational activities. On that particular day, the youth picked spinach for about fifteen minutes in the field and then spent the entire rest of the day washing and rewashing the spinach so that it could be frozen and distributed to people who struggled to put food on the table. In fact, the young people canceled their afternoon free time to put in the extra two hours needed to finish packaging all of the spinach they had picked. The youth had enormous fun singing the two songs they could find that most of them knew, generating contests in speed-washing spinach, and talking to one another as they worked in a cramped kitchen.

The youth felt particularly fond of this event for two reasons. The first was that they knew that their efforts would make a concrete difference in the lives of others. The second was that they found out they could really enjoy one another even in the midst of unexciting activities. If young people sense that they are engaging in an activity that ultimately has some significance, they will find a way to make it energized and joyful.

Withdrawing in order to engage the world

Avoidance of mass media, trips to the mall, and other consumer forms of recreation represent a kind of ascetic withdrawal from the formative practices of consumer culture. The ascetic withdrawal can open up the opportunity to encounter a new faith system, or be embraced by another form of meaning making. Margaret Miles discusses the value of this kind of asceticism in generating awareness about the downside of U.S. patterns of consumption:

> From a global perspective, Americans who possess and use a greatly disproportionate amount of the world's wealth have a

similarly disproportionate responsibility for the lack of food and other resources in the so-called Third World. Temporary or permanent renunciation of some of the consumer "goods" we find essential to our lives might begin to sensitize us, both to the conditions of hunger and want in which most of the world's inhabitants live and to our common conditioning as a society to expect and require consumer goods.[19]

While we often think about asceticism as withdrawal from the world, Miles describes the ways in which ascetical practice is more about changing our physical practice in order to change our engagement with the world. For example, Lydia's ascetic withdrawal from television viewing allowed her to question the ethics that were expressed by the characters in the shows that her peers were viewing in light of other values offered by her religious communities and her family.

Asceticism is not always about removing inherently unhelpful things from our lives. For example, engaging in fasting does not indicate that eating is wrong.[20] I have a friend, "Susan," who serves as a juvenile court judge. All day long she hears the stories of children who suffer from inadequate relational and economic resources. I once asked Susan how she dealt with the burden of hearing those stories day in and day out. She noted that she went for a long walk each morning, and she used to bring her headphones so she could listen to the news on National Public Radio while she was walking. Eventually she found that she could not bear to hear both the hurts of the world through the radio and to hear the hurts of the immediate young people that she dealt with all day. So she gave up listening to the news each morning and instead used that time for meditation and centering prayer. Withdrawing from the global news allowed her the space to engage with the immediate hurts that she had the power to alleviate. While being aware of world events is a mark of a learned person, in Susan's case she found it prevented her ability to generate

---

19. Miles, *Practicing Christianity*, 103.
20. This is actually a perversion of the Christian practice more akin to eating disorders than spiritual discipline.

compassion and response in the venues where she has more direct power. Her discovery and response to the practice of listening to the radio demonstrates the function of repentance in the facilitation of living out the vocations to which we are called.

In addition to individual practices such as Lydia's and Susan's withdrawal from mass media, youth groups often participate in short-term forms of ascetical experience such as the Thirty-Hour Famine that could be reinterpreted to draw attention to the impact of American forms of food production and consumption on hunger in other world communities. Many church communities participate in alternative giving during Advent, or choose this time to encourage their congregations to find other ways to celebrate Christmas than participation in consumer frenzy. A youth group might also decide together to, for a year, only engage in practices of recreation as a group that do not require consumption. Many forms of ascetic withdrawal are available to groups of adolescents that open up the possibility of entering into alternative imaginations about their relationship to the broader world.

Simple living

In some ecologically sustainable or organic farming communities, another form of ascetical practice is living simply and sharing resources rather than buying into the idea that each single consumer must own individually every item that is needed to maintain a lifestyle. Simple living often shuns expensive and rapidly obsoletizing technologies and consumer products, reducing the need for outside income. Another simple ascetical method involves sharing items of occasional use (e.g., lawn mowers) with several other families, and thus abstaining from purchasing those items that can be shared communally or reused by others. While adolescents do not have the authority to make these decisions for their own families, it is important to enliven their imaginations with the possibilities of simple living before they establish independent living situations. Once those not-easily-reversed commitments are made, such as taking on a great deal of consumer credit debt during college, it is much more difficult to live into commitments to simplicity.

The simplicity movement is essentially an ascetical movement addressing the purchasing habits of consumer capitalism. Scott Savage, editor of *The Plain Reader,* tells this story:

> When we married, Mary Ann and I had a combined income of about $65,000 (in 1998 money) plus health benefits. That amount seems like a small fortune to us now. Eight years and four children later, our family of six now achieves the basics of life with a salary of about one-third of what we started with. But I was about $16,000 in debt back then, all since repaid. Today we have nicer, handmade clothes. We eat better food. All of these things feel to us like upward mobility, where the *upward* has some true meaning.
>
> It has all come about because our family is beginning to learn the art of sharing with our neighbors and friends. With the help of community, we are slowly leaving more and more of the global economy out of our private accounting. By letting go of all that we once thought we could not live without, Mary Ann and I have discovered there is an unexpected gift waiting. We haven't just left the global economy; we aren't heroic individualists going it alone. We have, instead, come into the economy of loving and mutual obligation.[21]

Savage's tale points to the ways in which the dehabituation of ascetical living — in his case, by reducing participation in consumer economic systems — opens up the possibility of a new life in mutual obligation with neighbor. In the introduction to his book, Savage calls the shift to living plain "a revolution of hearts," linking this practice to an experience of conversion to a different meaning system. But,

---

21. Scott Savage, ed., *The Plain Reader* (New York: Ballantine, 1998), 89. There is a burgeoning literature on simple living, and it is largely a movement of the disaffected white middle class. However, many people have lived simply historically due to material constraints posed by forms of economic and social oppression or due to religious commitments.

only through the practice of dehabituation achieved by letting go of the regular income was the dependence on the consumer system of meaning disrupted and increasing self-knowledge about the person's dependence on it revealed. At the same time, the opportunity to understand the world through the experience of the gift of mutual obligation marked the replacement of an old system of meaning with a new one, an experience explored further in the next chapter.

Finding the hidden gardens of the heart

A key part of the practice of repentance is naming the particular ways in which we get caught up in consumer culture. Another way of describing this process is discovering what Brian Mahan calls the "hidden fountains and gardens of the heart." In his book *Forgetting Ourselves on Purpose*, Mahan shares the story of teaching a class in which he encouraged students to name the images that generated their own insensitivity to others. In the process of hearing a student talk about her jealousy at the fountain owned by an old friend who had come into wealth, Mahan became powerfully aware of his attachment to the tastefully hidden gardens of the wealthy blue-book Bostonians of his youth. Even though he would more likely share stories of rough-edged Irish Catholic heroes that inform his sense of identity and heritage, he recognized that a secret part of him aspired to owning a beautiful and tasteful garden of his own just off Beacon Hill. This repressed imagery has a powerful though hard-to-recognize effect on his life: "I think it's the images that we don't talk about, don't catch, don't echo and inspect that are likely to have a hold on us, to dictate our decisions, determine our moods, and desensitize us to our daily recruitment by neighbors near and far and by God as well. The hidden fountains and gardens of the heart are the deeper wellsprings of our striving and longing."[22] Naming these hidden images that represent the ways in which we believe, truly believe, in the beauty and power of consumption is a central part of repentance from consumer belief.

---

22. Mahan, *Forgetting Ourselves on Purpose*, 106.

Turning to a youth context, how do we help young people begin to notice the particular ways that they get sucked in by consumer culture? In order to do this, adolescents must first be able to name for themselves the ways in which they are individually caught up in consumer culture. Perhaps they may be hooked by lookism, and they may spend lots of time being dissatisfied with the way they look and coping with the internalized messages that pop up into their head. They may be committed to branding, and feel more confidence when they possess the correct kinds of clothing and retail items. They may get hooked by acquisition, and find that they have an insatiable desire to acquire CDs, shoes and clothes, toys, beauty products, or other kinds of goods. Perhaps their particular connection is with celebrity, and they begin to note how their sympathy and energy is elicited by the lives and trials of famous persons. Within each of these broad categories, young people will find their particular hidden gardens with which they must contend.

Call-to-awakening moments may be helpful in beginning to cultivate that personal awareness. In the last chapter, I named one call-to-awakening moment that had to do with the way I understood my college education in a consumer meaning frame. I could probably name forty other call-to-awakening moments around the particular ways that I am attached to the consumer system, from compulsively acquiring more books than I could ever possibly read to the sense that I *had* to have a station wagon once I had given birth to my first child. We all have a large task in identifying the hidden gardens of our hearts. Repentance is such a demanding and ongoing task because our formation into the consumer meaning system is so varied and thorough.

Once we have begun to name the hidden gardens of our heart, the trick becomes how to become eager to catch ourselves when we are motivated by those hidden gardens. Let me tell you a story to show you what I mean. Once upon a time, there was a youth group full of members who liked playful humor, but who didn't always know where the line between playfulness and harmful teasing should be drawn. Often, angry outbursts occurred between members because someone had crossed that line into hurtful territory. Eventually, the youth grew tired of the fights and named the problem for themselves: How do you tell someone that they are about to hurt your feelings without appearing to be overly sensitive or getting angry and defensive? The youth came up with an ingenious solution: Blart! "Blart," by dictionary definition, is the sound a cow makes when it moos. In our youth group, the word functioned as the lighthearted signal that something serious was about to occur. When somebody was being teased and wanted to say, "Back off, you're getting into tender territory" without really having to say it, the group decided to use the word "blart" as a face-saving shorthand. The sheer goofy randomness of the word kept the tone light, but it functioned effectively to bring to mind the whole discussion about teasing and communicate what needed to be communicated. The group decided that when somebody blarted, the direction of the conversation would turn without further ado or discussion. No guilt, no accusation. Just blart. They were all committed to a hurt-free but playful environment, and found the "blart" mechanism perfect to remind themselves when that environment was endangered.

Besides the fact that the discovery of "blart" was probably one of my finest moments as a youth minister, I tell this story because the dynamics of "blart" in intergroup relationship feels similar to the appropriate dynamics of paying attention internally to our commitments to consumer culture. What you're hoping for in the adolescent is a neutral, perhaps humorous, internal response that pops up when they recognize that they are being motivated by their consumer training. The internal voice should not sound like an inner nag, but rather like the gracious and accepting voice of God. While each young person would have to find the appropriate words to describe their own particular way of getting hooked by consumer culture, you would want it to be something in the tone of: "Silly human, there you go again." A gentle reminder, graceful and guilt-free, but attentive to the fact that they are acting out of their consumer formation rather than out of the values in which they truly believe.

Cultivating self-knowledge

If we ascribe to multiple intelligence theory, we know that different youth will have different levels of ability with what Howard Gardner calls "intrapersonal intelligence," or the ability to be internally reflective about one's motivations, fears, feelings, and commitments.[23] Whatever their innate ability, many young people may not have had much practice in this form of self-awareness and reflection. The formation of the young in a contemporary religious context is often more about internalizing the voices of external authorities than about cultivating young people's ability to discern their own internal "state of the soul." Self-knowledge may be a skill that has to be cultivated more vigorously. It can take a long time to develop, and it may never fully develop in some people. Inviting young people into self-knowledge, describing and modeling it for them, is critical in the task of repentance for ongoing conversion.

One way of cultivating this kind of awareness is to find in poetry and fiction adolescent voices that model self-reflection and to share them with young people. Sometimes less self-reflective youth can "borrow" the skills and insights of a more self-reflective peer as a starting point. They recognize themselves in the words and reflections of another young person, and are invited into their own practices of reflection. Many resources exist to share with young people, and identifying useful ones for the issues of your particular young people can be a large task. One example is the utterly self-revealing poetry and essays of young women in *Ophelia Speaks*. For example, Charlotte Cooper talks about her struggle to contend with images of a perfect self in response to the media despite her awareness of how they function: "Because no matter what I say in class about images, I truly

---

23. Howard Gardner, *Frames of Mind: The Theory of Multiple Intelligence* (New York: Basic Books, 1983), 239. He notes: "In its most primitive form, the intrapersonal intelligence amounts to little more than the capacity to distinguish a feeling of pleasure from one of pain, and on the basis of such discrimination, to become more involved or withdrawn from a situation. At its most advanced level, intrapersonal knowledge allows one to detect and to symbolize complex and highly differentiated sets of feelings."

believe that it is my own fault that I don't look like a model. I feel that I don't deserve anything when I look in the mirror." Later, she notes that even though she really knows that anorexia and bulimia are deadly and destructive diseases, at some level she wants to sign up for them in order to have the body that is acceptable.[24] Cooper models beautifully the distinction between cognitive awareness about an issue (in this case, the media's effect on girls' body images) and the effect of her personal formation into the belief system.

Other youth may need more regular conversation partners and groups to whom to be accountable in the work of repentance. Beyond the examples of call-to-awakening education in the previous chapter, persons hoping to increase self-awareness about attachment to consumer meaning systems may engage in discussion of their spending habits, keeping a spending journal in which they also note what they wanted to buy but didn't. They may also work together on media literacy, body image efforts, and other experiences designed to call into question their current patterns of behavior and understanding around consumer culture. What marks the move to repentance is the difference between looking at these elements as phenomena of the general culture and looking at their personal places of attachment to that culture. Again, moving from critique of consumption in general to self-knowledge about the myriad of personal attachments to it takes time. An interpersonal setting makes an atmosphere of grace even more important, especially for adolescents who are particularly sensitive to the judgment of their peers. I describe further in chapters 8 and 9 the role of small pedagogical communities in supporting ongoing conversion.

Repentance, an ongoing task

Because consumer culture and its formation are constant, the need for processes of repentance and increased self-knowledge also never goes

---

24. Charlotte Cooper in *Ophelia Speaks: Adolescent Girls Write about Their Search for Self,* ed. Sara Shandler (New York: Harper Perennial, 1999), 8.

away. Even after we begin to be grasped by other objects worthy of our devotion, we continue to be connected to and committed to consumer faith. We are multifaithful, both Christian and consumer. For Wesley, the process of salvation requires repentance at every stage, from the first whispers of prevenient grace to the ongoing process of sanctification. While the repentance is especially necessary to set the stage for receiving the kingdom of God, the need for repentance continues after the moment of justification as well.[25] After justification, the believer's relationship to sin is different: "Yet we cannot allow that he does not *feel* it within: it does not *reign*, but it does *remain*. And a conviction of the sin which *remains* in our heart is one great branch of the repentance we are now speaking of."[26] Wesley noted that even "true believers" were likely to find themselves tempted by pride, idolatry, and other evidence of excessive love of the world. One of the ways Wesley exemplifies this postjustification need for repentance relates directly to consumer culture:

> If he does not keep himself every moment he will again feel "the desire of the eye," the desire of gratifying his imagination with something great, or beautiful, or uncommon. In how many ways does this desire assault the soul! Perhaps with regard to the poorest trifles, such as dress, or furniture — things never designed to satisfy the appetite of an immortal spirit. Yet how natural it is for us, even after we "have tasted of the powers of the world to come," to sink again into these foolish, low desires of things that perish in the using![27]

Attentive believers note that sin not only remains in their hearts, but it also "cleaves to our words and actions."[28] Despite the abundance of God's grace in the process of salvation, Wesley acknowledged that sin could never be fully exterminated in the person of faith.

---

25. Wesley, *Sermons*, 406.
26. Ibid., 407 (emphasis original).
27. Ibid., 408.
28. Ibid., 409.

Wesley's response to the situation of perpetual sinfulness and the resultant need for constant repentance to continue in the way of salvation demonstrates his pastoral sensibilities. He encouraged believers not to despair in the face of this reality, but to "be content, as well as we can, to remain full of sin until death."[29] Wesley understood this to be possible because of the balance of the gift of faith in response to increasing self-knowledge in repentance. He noted:

> Thus it is that in the children of God repentance and faith exactly answer each other. By repentance we feel the sin remaining in our hearts, and cleaving to our words and actions. By faith we receive the power of God in Christ, purifying our hearts and cleansing our hands.[30]

The balance of the gift of faith and increasing self-knowledge critical to Wesley's understanding of how believers can continue to deal with the reality of sin throughout their lifetime provides critical insight into educational practices designed to increase self-awareness about participation in consumer culture. If those practices of self-awareness are not balanced out by a "gift of faith," the educational efforts are likely to end in despair rather than in increased agency. The need for the powerful renewal offered by a renewed imagination stirred by an alternative faith system is critical to allow the tough work of repentance to occur. We now turn to the nature of that gift of faith that fuels repentance.

---

29. Ibid., 412.
30. Ibid., 414.

Six

Justification

Grasped by objects more worthy of worship

Our mentors in the youth group were not anticapitalist, but pro-community. They lived together in community near the college. They told great stories about the community meals they held together and about the ways that they made their own fun with limited resources. They were just pretty countercultural. They modeled a way of being together and having fun not only outside of buying stuff, but also without alcohol, drugs, and other options we were offered as teenagers. In college, simple living became more politicized for me (anticapitalist, etc.) and I took on more of the guilt about overconsumption, sweatshops, and the environment. I'm not sure that was such a good thing. With my mentors it wasn't about naming what was bad and wrong in the world. They offered up a really good thing in the ways they lived together. If you offer up a good thing, people will choose it.   — Sara, remembering her adolescent self

Choosing a good thing

Sara is on to something in the recounting of her experience of conversion to simple living. The motivation for her movement away from consumption and toward simple living was not brought about by guilt about her participation in materialism, by careful teaching of her Quaker tradition, or by increased awareness of the impact of capitalism on vulnerable persons and resources, although all of these became a part of the process later on. She was initially moved by a

vision of another way of living offered to her by young adults that
she respected. In her words, these mentors "offered up a good thing,"
and she chose it.

Sara describes in this vignette the core of the experience of justification for the believer. Justification is about the gasp of wonder, the
moment of "that's awesome" in response to the fundamental sense
that something is so right it is worth staking your life on. We become
justified when we find something that's beautiful enough and powerful enough to make sense of all that we are and that we hope for in
life. This "gift of faith" allows us the freedom to imagine ourselves
differently, and thus to live differently in light of this new imagination.

Adolescents (and adults) are not best motivated by guilt. Children's
author and Anglican poet Madeleine L'Engle once wrote: "We do not
draw people to Christ by discrediting what they believe, by telling
them how wrong they are and how right we are, but by showing
them a light that is so lovely that they want with all their hearts
to know the source of it."[1] In revelation we are apprehended by a
new reality that grasps us and becomes irresistibly arresting in its
beauty and rightness. These images offer a new object of devotion, an
organizing image of meaning upon which we can depend, an image so
compelling as to feel salvific. For example, in the earlier description of
Scott Savage in the simplicity movement, the gift of mutual obligation
to neighbor became a life-giving new image of the way life could
be organized as a substitute for individual consumption of goods.
Adolescents are enlivened by passion, a particular charism of youth.[2]

---

1. Madeleine L'Engle, *Madeleine L'Engle Herself: Reflections on a Writing Life*
(Colorado Springs, CO: Water Brook Press, 2001), 123.

2. "Much popular youth ministry encourages the notion that energy, vitality,
faith, and life must be pumped into young people — requiring that we create spectacles and enormous amounts of our money and energy. In reality, young people
in partnership with the Spirit can provide enormous energy for the healing of the
world." David F. White, *Practicing Discernment with Youth: A Transformative
Youth Ministry Approach* (Cleveland: Pilgrim Press, 2005), 9–10. For more about
cultivating the gift of passion in adolescents, see also Kenda Creasy Dean, *Practicing Passion: Youth and the Quest for a Passionate Church* (Grand Rapids: Wm. B.
Eerdmans, 2004).

When they get a vision for a way of life that just seems right to them, they are moved to respond with energy and enthusiasm.

The gift of faith

If we take seriously the idea that consumer culture serves as a faith system and not just cognitive assent to economic practices, calling that faith system into question through awakening and repentance can leave persons stranded without an organizing system of meaning, or without the ritual support of the practices of their earlier belief system. The move toward a renewed sense of wholeness and safety requires a replacement of the old images from consumer systems with new images of beauty and goodness, new objects of "worship" to sustain a changed lifestyle. This is a process of falling in love, of being wooed by the new images that make sense of our lives in a broader context. I relate this experience of being fully claimed by a new meaning system, a new revelation of the divine, to the theological concept of justification in the process of ongoing conversion.

The Christian theological tradition defines justification as the legal removal of the guilt of sin by the sacrifice of Jesus on the cross. In the experience of the individual on the path of salvation, justification is the personal moment of recognition that this has happened. Wesley describes the drama of this moment in his sermon "The Spirit of Bondage and of Adoption": "His eyes are opened in quite another manner than before, even to see a loving, gracious God.... Overpowered with the sight, his whole soul cries out, 'My Lord, and my God!' "[3] In these brief sentences, Wesley captures the experience of being grasped and transformed by a vision of loveliness that causes the whole soul to respond. The sermon title also points to the primal shift that Wesley believed occurs at the point of justification: the person moves from feeling enslaved to a master to feeling adopted by a loving parent. This event brings an end to both

---

3. Wesley, *Sermons*, 140.

"remorse and sorrow of heart" and the "bondage unto fear."[4] In traditional theological language, the believer is moved from a moment of the awareness of her sin in the face of a judging God to a moment in which she is grasped and renewed by the love and pardon of a forgiving God.

Wesley's refined language may make this experience seem far removed from the experience of contemporary teenagers. What might justification look like for adolescents? A youth group with whom I worked loved a practice they dubbed "fried-chicken talk." Fried-chicken talk had its humble beginnings on a youth mission trip where we stayed in a mobile home and cooked our own food. "Joyce," a parent who had volunteered to come along as chaperone and chief cook, stayed up late one evening to bread and fry chicken for lunch the following day. She invited the youth to keep her company while she worked. I wasn't actually present for this inaugural talk, but it became the stuff of legend in our group's life. Many deeply personal stories and concerns were shared in the space opened by this wise woman when she indicated to the youth that she valued their company and conversation. Fried-chicken talk became the group's name for any conversation where they could be real with each other, sharing the hurts and struggles of daily life in a place where they knew they would be heard with respect.

An example of the stories shared is that of "Jordan," a middle-schooler who had struggled with being bullied by peers at school. During this initial conversation, Jordan had shared with great vulnerability his stories of feeling devalued and out of place at school. The other youth, who themselves were often annoyed by Jordan's immature acts as a younger member of the group, were able to hear the pain of his story and respond with concern and gracious naming of his value to the group. Jordan found in the space of conversation a place where he could drop the masks that most teenagers have to wear in peer company, share his story of deep pain that would be shameful if revealed in other contexts, and encounter God's love and

---

4. Ibid., 141.

affirmation embodied through a loving community of peers. Fried-chicken talk became an undisputed place of holy ground, a justifying encounter with the gracious love of God.

This gracious space of conversation and acceptance "just as you are" is a common descriptor of why many church camps and youth groups are such powerful and meaningful contexts for young people. This atmosphere of welcoming and valuing flawed humans counters the lookism, branding, and the sense of constantly being judged and found wanting so common to the adolescent experience in the broader culture. Fried-chicken talk was an embodiment of grace, a moment of justifying encounter with a different way of being in the world. The youth longed for the space for fried-chicken talk because it represented something much bigger: the grace of unconditional acceptance and embodied love in the midst of one's own sense of unloveliness.[5]

Likewise, Sara's experiences with her mentors offered her a vision of the divine that gave her a renewed sense of the possibilities and joys of interconnectedness in simple, intentional living. She shared that there was great coherency in the experience offered her at youth group. There was a richness of relationality modeled on all levels. Her mentors communicated the idea that a devotional life was about being real in relationship with God, "hanging out" with God. This divine relationship of simple living in joyous relationship was mirrored in the relationships between youth and mentors. They could also link the commitment of simple living to the historic Quaker tradition. This good thing, this lovely light was offered to the young people in a vibrant and immediate fashion, and they wanted with all their hearts to know its source.

In the last chapter we learned from John Wesley that the journey of the way of salvation is sustained by a balance of repentance and the gift of faith. Similarly, H. Richard Niebuhr believed that all revelation contains both judgment and a vision of God's goodness.

---

5. Dori Grinenko Baker captures the power of this kind of holy conversation in *Doing Girlfriend Theology: God-Talk with Young Women* (Cleveland: Pilgrim Press, 2005).

Revelation begins in awareness of God's judgment, through which we become aware of our limitations and the limitations of the idols to which we have shown our loyalty. However, this is only the first half of divine revelation. Niebuhr adapted from Jonathan Edwards an understanding that the second half of revelation serves to evoke a constructive response to the beauty of God. James Fowler reflects on Niebuhr's understanding of this aesthetic revolution: "It must be a response of the self or the community, bereft of its idols, to a new vision of the beauty, power, love, and comprehensive oneness of the source and ground of all being and value."[6] Fried-chicken talk and relational community became more than individual events in the life of these young people. They are moments of revelation, times where the beauty of God is demonstrated in a compelling way that is life-transforming. This gift of faith provides the energy and the endurance to continue the work of repentance and resistance to consumer culture.

The education of the intellect alone cannot generate the energy and transformation required for ongoing conversion; rather, a revolution of the fuller self is required. This revolution is generated by aesthetic means; we are transformed by finding something better worth our worshiping. Grace is found in our apprehension by revelatory images that give us devastatingly attractive alternatives to our current means of understanding reality. Niebuhr relies on the symbols of cross and resurrection as being the key to this kind of transformation, but the symbolic imagery of the new object of worship and beauty could be widened to include other things. In Sara's case, it was a vision of simple living grounded in an understanding of relationship with God and community. For Jordan, it was a vision of gracious acceptance rather than attack at the point of showing one's vulnerable self. The gift of faith presents itself in a variety of disguises with a range of intensity. In whatever manner it appears, it is essential to fueling ongoing conversion of faith in consumer culture.

---

6. James Fowler, *To See the Kingdom: The Theological Vision of H. Richard Niebuhr* (Lanham, MD, and New York: University Press of America, 1974), 111.

Being grasped

The experience of justification can be described as feeling apprehended or grasped by an external reality that shakes you to the core.
The experience doesn't feel like a self-aware commitment, but rather
feels like a revelation that reorders you by its very existence. Young
people do not self-author the justifying encounter. This is not about
making a personal decision to give yourself over to a new object
of faith. Faith development theory would tell us that self-conscious
choices about belief come later in the process. At this point, young
people are at the moment of being "grasped" by objects more worthy
of worship than consumer culture.[7]

We often equate the experience of being swept away by idealistic visions as a characteristically adolescent experience, but even for
adults, justification is an experience of being grabbed by a new sense
of the whole. Niebuhr rejected the idea that transformation of fidelity
from one object to another could happen through sheer effort of
will (willpower). Niebuhr believed that the will is always committed to some object, and efforts by the will to change the will result
only in increased devotion to the current object of devotion. Niebuhr
explained that loyalties shift when one object of devotion fails to
support and maintain the integrated self. This may occur through
a traumatic event or because we find we must cut out parts of our
experience in order for the object of loyalty to generate a meaningful
narrative. In a moment of grace, we are grasped or apprehended by a
compelling image that holds a powerful alternative for the possibility
of our lives. Thus, we gain a new object of faith when we encounter
a compellingly attractive new reality that reorients our entire lives.

---

7. James Fowler's faith development theory puts most adolescents at the point
of synthetic-conventional faith. This doesn't mean that the content of their beliefs
is conventional, but rather that they are constructing a unique amalgamation of
the beliefs offered to them by the significant people and cultural forces in their lives.
Sara's sense that in college her beliefs became more politicized and more critical indicates movement into Fowler's next stage: individual-reflective faith. This movement
generally happens at young adulthood and beyond, and is unusual in adolescents.
For a full description of Fowler's faith development theory, see Fowler, *Becoming
Adult, Becoming Christian.*

Another common religious term for this kind of experience is an epiphany. Brian Mahan uses the phrase "epiphanies of recruitment" to describe this kind of encounter: "Some experiences come to stand for others — who knows why? They emblazon themselves on our consciousness. They wound and claim us. We are never quite the same, for despite all our attempts to marginalize or redefine them, we find that it is we who have been redefined."[8] These epiphanies are not the end of the story, but rather "an invitation to a different kind of life."[9] They call us to a different way of being and doing in the world. They leave us justified, transformed in wonder, and at times, confused.

The way I am describing the gift of faith makes it sound like one dramatic moment in time. This description causes fear and trepidation in me, recalling my own adolescent self who lived in fear that she was not a "real" Christian because she could not tell a conversion story like her devout Southern Baptist peers. I find Mahan's "epiphanies" language helpful because it indicates that these experiences are not once-for-all-time. They may occur multiple times, and our response to them may be a slower transformation. The drama of the moment is less important than the constructive, beautiful vision of the divine that is made available, whether slowly or quickly. In order to become more faithful in response to God and neighbor, believers must seek these fitting images to inform their reasoning. Niebuhr notes, "[The heart] cannot make a choice between reason and imagination but only between reasoning on the basis of adequate images and thinking with the aid of evil imaginations."[10] Revelation provides these more adequate images from which we reason and come to understand the nature of our reality by offering new images of beauty and grace that more adequately integrate the meaning world of the believer.

---

8. Mahan, *Forgetting Ourselves on Purpose*, 134.
9. Ibid., 135.
10. Niebuhr, *The Meaning of Revelation*, 79–80.

Beautiful visions

For traditional Christian theologians like Niebuhr and Wesley, the shift in commitment or object of devotion found in the moment of justification meant a shift to belief in Jesus Christ. While such a shift *is* a viable way to reduce reliance on consumer capitalism as a meaning system, Jesus Christ is not the only possible replacement object of faith in a conversion from consumer meaning systems. I am using justification as a metaphor for the moment of being grasped by a new and gracious reality that allows us to reimagine our lives and relationships to neighbor and world. This new faith system might be renewed gospel fidelity in the Christian tradition, as is explored by Michael Warren.[11] In the movement on many college campuses to end sweatshop labor, the new reality that starts a revolution of meaning making in the self may be an awareness of solidarity with the persons who produce the jeans and iPods we purchase. Environmental awareness of the interdependence of all systems in the natural world may also bring about change by relativizing the importance of human life in the midst of broader systems.

In each of these examples, it is not only the convicting awareness of the downfalls of the consumer system that causes transformation. Calls to awakening and repentance are not enough to generate lasting conversion from consumer faith. A new and beautiful way of understanding the world and our relationship to it enlivens agency and imagination with a new image of reality even as it critiques the consumer system of meaning. Let's explore some of these beautiful visions that have grabbed young people and fueled their ongoing conversion from consumer faith.

Community

You may remember Lydia from the last chapter. Lydia was very articulate about alternative visions that grabbed her and challenged the cultural faith in consumption. Community was a key element of

---

11. Michael Warren, *At This Time, in This Place* (Harrisburg, PA: Trinity Press, 2000).

Lydia's vision of the world and an integral part of sustaining her vocational imagination. "Community" was one of the core values of the Friends school that she attended: "Part of the philosophy is realizing the interconnectedness of people within a school community, and then wider and wider and wider communities. I've been taught that since I was so young that it kind of stuck with me really well." When I asked Lydia if she felt that everyone emerged from the school with the same value of community that she held, she noted that many of the other students did not take it as seriously until they left the school: "They go to college, and then things are really competitive and individually oriented." Only in this different environment do they fully recognize the ways in which their commitments have been shaped by the vision of community embodied in their school experience.

One of the reasons Lydia is interested in attending college is the opportunity to live in a community of peers in a similar way to her powerful experience of intentional community at the residential environmental education program:

> I lived with eight other girls in a cabin for four months, and when I moved home I was just kind of thrown off, I was in shock because I wasn't used to living with nobody my own age, and I really missed it a lot. I don't expect college to be quite that tight of a community, but there's something to be said for the support of peers all living close, and I'm interested in that.

For Lydia, living in community is an opportunity to practice her calling to respect other persons and "to make an effort to find what is good in them and what they have to bring, even if it's not on the surface." This understanding of community is an important part of her vocational self-definition. She feels that living in community forces you to search beyond a person's exterior to discover what you have to learn from him or her. This provides a powerful counternarrative to the obsessive attention given to image and appearance in consumer meaning systems.

Lydia plans to live simply as an organic farmer as an adult. When I asked Lydia if she ever felt responsible to her future children, her potential spouse, or herself as a retired person as she thought about entering the occupation of organic farming, she indicated that she did worry about what she would do when she got too old to continue farming. Her plan was to depend on the care of community: "Hopefully I will have been in a stable community for long enough and be in a stable place where people will take care of me because I've taken care of them for a long time." This vision of interdependent care had a quality of beauty and fittingness that would qualify it as religious faith for H. Richard Niebuhr. This vision of community stands against the individual competition, overwork, and connection through status symbols offered by consumer culture.

Sustainability/care for creation

Another vision that inspired Lydia in her resistance to consumer culture was an understanding of sustainability and care for the earth. Lydia had hands-on mentoring in organic gardening at both her school and her semester residential program, and she had also initiated a garden for her own family's food supply. When I asked her who had contributed to her imagination of herself as an organic farmer, she named her gardening teachers at both schools as critical to her development in this direction. Not only had they offered her the space to do a lot of reading about environmental concerns such as freshwater depletion, but they had helped her to really desire to learn how to "make the earth a good place to live." In other words, the teachers had fostered both her critical awareness and an alternative faithful vision of "the way the world is."

Lydia noted that her teachers weren't dogmatic about their positions on environmental issues, but they pushed the students to really investigate the issues and come to their own conclusions. Her imagination was enlarged by fiction that provided utopian and dystopian visions of interconnection and sustainability. In this challenging and supportive process, Lydia forged her own beliefs about environmental issues: "I don't know what conclusions others made, but I figured that I had strong feelings about how food should be provided to the country, and they didn't match up with Monsanto and other big food corporations." The vision of providing enough food for everyone through sustainable means fueled her decision to become an organic farmer.

Solidarity with the poor

In the earlier discussion of mission trips, I hinted that bonds of solidarity with persons on the underside of capitalism can provide revelations that function as a gift of faith. When young people feel truly connected in a real way to real people who suffer because of the economic system, they can be moved to resistance of its central tenets. I spoke of the young people who attended a downtown church and were confused by the reaction of their suburban peers to persons in poverty. Let me share with you the story of these young people and the shoe ministry that initially formed these bonds of solidarity with persons on the underside of capitalism.

In addition to worshiping with guests from the soup kitchen each Sunday, once a quarter the young people would set up a shoe ministry in a room off the hallway where guests were exiting the soup kitchen. Most of the guests of the soup kitchen lived on the street, a lifestyle that requires an enormous amount of walking from place to place to find food, bathrooms, and places of rest. Decent shoes are critical to avoid foot pain and great discomfort. The rule of the shoe ministry was that you had to trade in your shoes to receive another pair. This was to be sure that people did not acquire shoes if they did not truly need them, as the supply was limited by the donations we could gather. Guests would come in, and the youth would ask them what kind of shoes they were looking for and what size they needed. Then they would go into the closet where the available shoes were sorted, try to find a pair of shoes that fit the needs of the person, and bring them out for fitting.

The shoe ministry was smelly, frustrating work. The kinds of shoes that the guests needed, comfortable walking shoes and work boots, were not often donated by our more well-off patrons. We had seemingly endless supplies of uncomfortable dress shoes, but few patrons needed these kinds of shoes. The youth struggled to please their guests, who often were also uncomfortable taking off their shoes because their feet smelled from the Atlanta heat and lack of access to showers.

The youth often began as younger teens enjoying playacting as shoe salespeople, and trying on their best manners and/or charming personas for the guests. As they hosted the shoe ministry multiple times over the years, they began to share the frustrations of the guests that we did not have the right kinds of shoes. They struggled to take on the perspectives and desires of the guests and to find ways of making them feel honored in the midst of these potentially degrading circumstances. They found ways to connect and laugh with them in the moment, and grew increasingly angry with their circumstances in our debriefing sessions. This identification with the guests provided critical formation in solidarity that was transformational for their attitudes toward those without access to the consumer system. Rather than being contemptuous or fearful of the poor, they formed relational bonds that engendered empathy. This revelation of connection and meaning was an epiphany of recruitment that fundamentally shifted their perspectives about consumer values.

Directly countering the consumer meaning system

The above stories contain visions that fueled resistance to consumer culture because they directly counter the beliefs of that system. For example, ecological commitments provide a concrete alternative vision of interdependence of limited and fragile resources that specifically contradicts consumer values. Traditional religious belief *can* provide a vibrant, self-critical alternative symbol system that speaks directly to consumer reality, but often this directness is lacking in the worship lives of faith communities. For example, Christian theology about care for creation and an appropriate theological understanding of creaturehood could provide a vision to live into as well as a basis for critique of consumer culture. Likewise, the Christian theological tradition of love for neighbor and care for those who are economically at risk (widows and orphans in the biblical literature) could provide an alternative vision that concretely addresses the pitfalls of consumer culture as a meaning system.

However, as millions of American Christians demonstrate, belief in the saving power of Jesus Christ can live alongside or even reinforce consumer meaning systems. Religious alternatives to consumer faith that don't provide images of belief constructed in direct contradiction to consumer culture fall short of this requirement. This oppositional characteristic allows practices informed by positive engagement in alternative meaning systems to also violate tenets of consumer religion. For instance, practices of charitable giving (investment without thought of return), of valuing nonbought and even nonmaterial things, of repairing and handmaking the goods we use are practices suggested by alternative value systems that directly contradict the central beliefs and concrete practices of consumer culture.

Made lively and immediate

It is important with youth not only to name the clear ways in which the Christian message stands over/against consumptive values, but also to find devotional and liturgical expressions that embody these alternative claims. Adolescents don't just think faith. They sing, pray, live, and relate faith. The occasional young person may find their way intellectually, but for most youth transformation of faith is a full-bodied, relationally based experience.

In the history of Christian experience, we have had many figures who understood that new theological understandings required new liturgical practices. The birth of the Church of England became embodied in Thomas Cranmer's prayer book. The great hymns of the social gospel movement embody Christian faith response to industrialization. Even the antiwar protest folk songs from the Vietnam era powerfully embodied a faith stance that many youth groups were singing long after the war ended. Drawing upon the historic Christian tradition and generating new hymns and prayers that embody alternative visions is critical.

When Lydia was asked to describe her vision of her life at age thirty-five, she expressed an alternative vision of beauty characterized by simplicity and small scale: "Simple life — living with another family or working under someone who has been a farmer for a long time. Small house, small family. I really love the mountains and being outdoors. Composting toilet...things made out of recycled materials." Her experience of living for four months in a small, sustainably designed cabin with eight other persons during the residential environmental education program had clearly informed this vision for her. The practice of living reinforced a new symbol system about care for the earth. This image of controlled consumption had also been emphasized by her parents, whom Lydia characterized as understanding a successful life as one in which you have "all of what you need and a portion of what you want."

Think of Lydia rapturously "getting her hands in the dirt" while organic farming, living in a cabin with eight other young women, and going to a school that focused on community rather than competition as a core value. Remember the youth "selling" shoes in an act of smelly but sacramental service. Being grasped by a vision often requires these kind of embodied, social, devotional moments, not just thinking or hearing about them. Youth need to live into their new faith just as they lived into their consumer faith: mind, body, and soul.

It all makes sense now

When Sara talked about her conversion to simple living, she noted that part of the capacity for change came from her early experiences of backyard gardening and shopping in thrift stores when her parents were in their early hippie days. The vision of simple living allowed her to reincorporate these long-forgotten aspects of herself in light of a new worldview. One mark of adequately revelatory images for Niebuhr is that they serve to integrate every event we remember from our past into a meaningful, coherent unity. He notes: "There is no part of that past that can be ignored or regarded as beyond possibility of redemption from meaninglessness."[12] For Niebuhr one purpose of revelation is to understand the meaning of our own experience in its fullest context, so that we are not completely determined by the vagaries of our limited concrete experience. Truly divine revelations don't cause us to cut off parts of ourselves. They provide space for us to understand all that we are in light of more adequate visions of the divine.

When I was an adolescent, my family moved into the Deep South, and I quickly became best friends with a young woman who was a profoundly committed evangelical Christian. This friendship led me into regular Bible study and into a struggle to form a personal relationship with Jesus Christ that would assure my eternity in heaven through a regular devotional life. My journals from that period are full of anguished appeals to Jesus to help me in this struggle even as I was unsure how this understanding of Christianity related to the rest of my religious formation to that point.

During the same period, I was participating in a youth group in my own United Methodist church that went on an annual mission trip to rural Appalachia. I went along on the trip because I was assured by my peers that it was the most fun we would have all year, despite the fact that I was utterly unclear how working outside in the summer on people's homes with strangers would be fun. In true adolescent fashion, that week was a jumble of highs and lows, of connection and undoing that took many years for me to sort out. It was fun to spend a week with my friends and to engage in the recreation and worship in the evenings. I formed my first romantic relationship that week and began to explore who I might be in a dating relationship. Finally, I encountered a revelation of the divine that was big enough to pull together disparate elements of my life and move me forward into a new set of commitments and beliefs. Let me tell you that strand of the story.

The first day of service, my small group was sent out to help clean a home that, to this day, represents the worst situation of poverty

---

12. Niebuhr, *Meaning of Revelation*, 82–83.

and neglect that I have ever seen in the United States. Because of mental health issues combined with physical and mental disabilities, the elderly couple who lived in the home with their adult son were unable to keep up with even the most basic daily maintenance needs. We spent the entire day cleaning the house, killing cockroaches and flies, and trying to deal with our horror that people could be forced by poverty and lack of adequate medical care to live in these kinds of conditions in a wealthy nation. The two adults accompanying our group helped us to name this difficult work in terms of two gospel stories: Jesus washing the feet of the disciples and the admonition that by serving the least of God's children we were serving Jesus himself.

This experience was a moment of revelation that drew together many elements of my religious belief left untouched by my best friend's understanding of Christianity. My childhood religious formation had taught me that Jesus loved the little children of the world and I was called to do the same. (Unfortunately, I had learned little more in fourteen years of Sunday school, but that's not a bad place to start!) In the poverty of the region, I came to understand more fully the stories of my own parents, who had grown up in similar conditions in the mountains of western North Carolina and north Georgia. Despite the desperate conditions of the persons we were serving, there was something intensely beautiful about the ways in which our chaperones were able to connect with them and serve graciously and without condescension. I remember feeling much more awkward in my attempts, but still moved by this understanding of God's love to give my best in the situation and love this family the best that I could in that moment.

This event was an epiphany of recruitment in the truest sense of that phrase, and it took me a long time to sort out why it was so powerful for me. One critical element was that it did not require me to relinquish my own familial history and my early understandings of God as a loving parent who wants the best for everyone, but rather provided integration of these childhood understandings in a more critical way. Unlike the theologies offered by my evangelical peers, it honored my intuitive sense that salvation was about more than where we spend the afterlife. This family was "saved" in that sense, but their devotion had not changed the material conditions that were causing them so much suffering. The fuller understanding of salvation embodied by the act of offering care and grounded in the stories shared by my adult companions made sense to me in some deeply integrated way that was lacking in the other forms of Christianity with which I had been wrestling.

Returning to repentance

This story raises for me an example of why a linear model of ongoing conversion (call to awakening → repentance → justification → regeneration) utterly breaks down. While repentance may or may not precede justification, repentance almost always follows the experience of justification. The gift of faith fuels ongoing repentance. When we have a renewed vision of what is true and beautiful in the world, it truly challenges and causes us to rethink what we had believed and how we live our lives in light of those beliefs.

When I returned home from this experience of service, I returned to my normal routines of school and gymnastics. In that period of my life, I was a committed gymnast who spent nearly twenty hours a week in the gym practicing. Gymnastics defined my identity in one sense; it scheduled all of my free time outside of school and many of my weekends. For the first time that fall, I recognized that my family was committing enormous resources of time and money to an activity that, in the end, only benefited me. I began to recognize that I would not spend the rest of my life doing gymnastics, and I began to question the allocation of my family's resources to this activity given that it didn't serve anyone besides me. This was a moment of repentance caused by the experience of revelation in the act of service. To be fair, the experience of service was only one of many elements that brought about this experience of self-examination of commitments (the new boyfriend, troubles with my coach, and many other factors were also critical), but it was the reason that felt most compelling and "right." My vision of a God who was committed to the "least of these" and called me to join in their service caused me to look at my sporting life in a completely different light and led me to leave it within a few months.

Being grasped by a new and beautiful object of devotion involves a new sense of a coherent whole and of one's place in it. It provides new imaginations of the "way things are" and renewed agency. For Niebuhr, the new imagery and new agency must work together for the reasoning heart to use revelation to understand life's meaning. Revelation renews the imagination by providing a fuller, more adequate image from which we make sense of all parts of our history and our understanding of the world:

> By reasoning on the basis of revelation the heart not only understands what it remembers but is enabled and driven to remember what it had forgotten. When we use insufficient and evil images of the personal or social self we drop out of our consciousness or suppress those memories which do not fit in with the picture of the self we cherish.[13]

For Niebuhr, the revelation of a fuller image is not enough. The reasoning heart must then use that image to interpret, apprehend, and reconstruct the soul in light of the new imagination.[14] For Niebuhr, this must include understanding our selves in light of the whole of the human past, even the darkest moments of oppression in which we are implicated.[15] In other words, the work of repentance is continued with the gift of the broader imagination that comes in revelation at the moment of justification. In dealing with consumer meanings, this process of reconstructing the soul in light of the full human experience could take the form of understanding ourselves as related to those outside the economic prosperity of the United States, especially those whose labor allows for the easy consumption of cheap products.

---

13. Ibid., 113.
14. Ibid., 116. Here again, Niebuhr and Wesley emphasize similarly the balance of repentance and the gift of faith.
15. Ibid., 117.

However, Niebuhr warns us that this examination of the self and
our social history is not easy, as has been demonstrated in recent years
with the struggles to negotiate and reconstruct history in light of the
subversive memory of oppressed peoples. This process demands our
confession and repentance:

> It demands and permits that we bring into the light of attention
> our betrayals and denials, our follies and sins. There is nothing
> in our lives, in our autobiographies and our social histories, that
> does not fit in. In the personal inner life revelation requires the
> heart to recall the sins of the self and to confess fully what it
> shuddered to remember.[16]

Because this work is demanding and difficult, the work of *metanoia*
in the light of ongoing revelation is never completed, and, in some
cases, is never even started.[17] However, without the gift of revelation
to the faithful imagination, this work of critical apprehension of self
and communal awareness would not be possible.

A slow and difficult process

I've been talking about the immediacy and power of being grasped
externally, but the shift from one object of worship to another can
be a slow and painstaking process. Generally, we cannot leave one
organizing faith system without having another in which to place our
hearts and trust. This concept is echoed in social psychologist Philip
Brickman's discussion of the dissolution of commitment. He investigates the relationship between new and old objects of loyalty in
changes of commitments. In his research, Brickman found that making alternative commitments was a critical piece in the dissolution of
old commitments.

Brickman describes a process by which new commitments supplant
old ones in five stages. In the first stage, the original commitment is

---

16. Ibid., 84.
17. Ibid.

"gradually, often imperceptibly eroded" by "a series of actions that are increasingly discrepant with the nature of the commitment."[18] This leads to the second stage in which there is a great deal of ambivalence and emotional turmoil about the commitment, which often leads to renewed investment in the old commitment as an attempt to ward off the impending loss. In the third stage, any remaining sense of the goodness of the original commitment is lost, and a stable anticommitment is developed: "a strong and coherent negative orientation to the former object of commitment."[19] In the fourth stage, this emotional anticommitment wanes as it struggles with the residue of attachment to the old commitment.[20] His description of the emotional aspects of this stage echoes the language of the loss of an object of faith:

> Much of the terror and loneliness that characterize this stage in the loss of a major life commitment derive from the fact that the person has lost a major source of meaning and value in his or her life and hence must cope not only with inner feelings of ambivalence about and grief for the loss, but also with a sense of inner emptiness that makes the beginning of a search for alternatives all the more difficult.[21]

Eventually, in the final stages, the original commitment fades in importance as the person's attention is occupied by new or alternative commitments. Brickman notes that recovery from the loss or change of a vital commitment is never complete, but the strength and vitality of new commitments is critical in the fading away of the old commitment.[22]

This description of the long process of changing commitments calls into question an understanding that the gift of faith, an adequate

---

18. Brickman, *Commitment, Conflict, and Caring*, 200.
19. Ibid., 201. Notice the lack of continual progress toward commitment to the new object hinted at in the second stage of Brickman's process. This relates to my earlier claim that conversion is rarely a linear process of transformation.
20. Ibid., 202.
21. Ibid., 202.
22. Ibid., 208.

revelation, can bring about immediate changes in consumer faith. Brian Mahan addresses this concern when he talks about the pain that people feel "at the memory of epiphanies of recruitment now grown cold."[23] The hard part for Mahan is continuing to remember those epiphanies in a way that is life-giving, where people don't feel set up for failure. They may have been moved by inspiration and ready to change the world multiple times only to find out that the very things that kept them from living out of that vision the last time are still powerfully in place. For those of us who have seen many young people recruited and then left without the resources to sustain their new commitments, the intensity of being grasped can be disconcerting. These kinds of experiences in our own lives and in the lives of the young people we accompany can leave us muttering about overly idealistic young people. This is an appropriate caution about epiphanies of recruitment, but I believe that in the long term we are not left bereft by our visions of loveliness. However, trying to live faithfully in the light of new revelations can be discouraging. This highlights the importance of regeneration, to which we now turn.

---

23. Mahan, *Forgetting Ourselves on Purpose*, 31.

Seven

Regeneration

New life for continued resistance

There are a lot of things that I feel like I should be speaking out for, but school is such a big part of my life that it just *becomes* my life during the school year. That is really depressing to me because I can't stand for the things I want to stand for. But, one good example is right now I'm really working for environmental things.... A lot of places are so far behind what can be happening that it's something that's not too hard to bring awareness about.

— Lydia, reflecting on her current sense of vocation

After Lydia experienced conversion to interdependence and sustainability during her time at the environmental residential program, she returned to regular high school and became a bit discouraged by the constraints that school placed on her life. Within the time limits created by her busy time at school, she was still finding space to live out of her newfound ecological commitments. Despite the challenges created by the return to her regular environment, Lydia felt energized to speak out for care for the earth, to witness to this new vision that she had embraced. This new image gave her new life for continued resistance to the disposable culture supported by consumer faith.

Regeneration: More than new information, it's new birth

As evidenced in Lydia's reflections, the renewed agency and imagination arising from the gift of justification is sustained by the process of regeneration. In the process of conversion, an object of worship not only gives a new comprehensive image of the world, it provides increased energy for agency and participation in the alternative faith system. The person is both reshaped and renewed by the new belief system. In traditional theological terms, this phase in the process of conversion is labeled "regeneration," literally rebirth. Wesley understood this rebirth to transmit divine energy to the person on the way of salvation: "We are inwardly renewed by the power of God."[1] The person finds his or her life increasingly implicated with the new belief system, and finds this intertwining energizing rather than debilitating.

The full integration of new objects of faith discovered in revelation is an ongoing project. Niebuhr describes this process as the "progressive validation" of new revelations:

> The more apparent it becomes that the past can be understood, recovered and integrated by means of a reasoning starting with revelation, the more contemporary experience is enlightened and response to new situations aptly guided by this imagination of the heart, the more a prophecy based on this truth is fulfilled, the surer our conviction of its reality becomes.[2]

Niebuhr describes a slow building of trust in the new object of faith as it shows itself worthy of devotion by being able to sustain meaning making. This dialectic of revelation does not move forward in the sense of simple historical progression. Rather, there is a constant reinterpretation and reconstruction of life situations, past and present.[3] This reconstruction involves a consistent movement back and forth from experience to revelation (as interpreted by the reasoning heart) in which the meaning of the revelation becomes progressively clearer and richer as it comes into conversation and mutual correction with God's action in present reality.[4] This describes the ongoing work of

---

1. Wesley, *Sermons*, 373.
2. Niebuhr, *The Meaning of Revelation*, 97.
3. Ibid., 99.
4. Ibid., 100.

regeneration, as the person becomes increasingly confident in and connected to the newly revealed object of faith.

The importance of the energy provided by the new faith system cannot be understated. One of the pitfalls in sustaining work for social justice is, as ethicist Sharon Welch has named it, cultured despair, a failure of the moral imagination leading to weariness in the face of persistent injustice. The danger of despair makes the enlivening of the imagination, the renewing of the mind, and the increased energy offered in regeneration vitally important to sustaining social change. Welch discusses the inadequacy of some imaginative systems to sustain work for justice. This critique highlights the ways in which some symbol systems are unable to provide the energy and vigor of regeneration for their faithful adherents:

> Middle-class people can sustain work for justice when empowered by love for those who are oppressed. Such love is far more energizing than guilt, duty, or self-sacrifice. Love for others leads us to accept accountability (in contrast to feeling guilt) and motivates our search for ways to end our complicity with structures of oppression. Solidarity does not require self-sacrifice but an enlargement of the self to include community with others.[5]

Welch expresses a practical concern about working out of an image of self-sacrifice rather than an image of love: self-sacrifice is not an adequate image of faith able to offer regeneration in the resistance to injustice. The renewal and power offered by a new, positive system of love that understands the self in relationship to a much broader community is much more able to sustain. Its worthiness as an object of devotion is indicated to Welch by the power that it generates for persistent resistance.

Sharon Welch's insight about the difference between love and duty as adequate motivating factors for sustained work on justice indicates that any new object of faith offered as an alternative to consumer

---

5. Sharon Welch, *A Feminist Ethic of Risk*, rev. ed. (Minneapolis: Fortress Press, 2000), 162.

belief must both specifically counter consumer belief and be winsome enough to delight adherents. In addition to bringing about new imaginations of "the way the world is," the beauty of this new symbol system must be enough to sustain believers' consequential processes of regeneration. One criterion for judging the adequacy of a new object of faith to which young people turn from consumer faith is whether or not it provides energy, vitality, and direction for their lives.

Richness and depth of encounter with a new symbol system

If we take Sharon Welch seriously on the need to find wellsprings of joy to fund resistance and persistence in an alternative imagination, we recognize that increased opportunities for constructive dreaming into a new meaning system assists in the process of regeneration. For example, Lydia's initial conversion experience was funded by her joy in organic gardening and in living in sustainable intentional community. Her love of working the earth and living with peers in close quarters was arguably a form of worship within the new symbol system of ecological interdependence. Leaving this situation and getting mired in the ongoing work and rhythms of school left her feeling temporarily unable to continue her desired witness around ecological issues. Another source of imagination and dreaming had come from reading literature about environmental issues that was poetic and metaphorically evocative. Lydia drew on the symbols of this literature in explaining her own commitments. However, she was experiencing fewer opportunities for the kind of renewal of imagination required to sustain her alternative commitments.

An important characteristic of residential environmental educational programs is involvement in the ongoing practice of a community informed by an alternative faith system.[6] One of the

---

6. This characteristic relates directly to Wesley's understanding of participation in small, accountable communities as a means of grace. It has also been a theme in contemporary religious education, particularly the work of C. Ellis Nelson (*Congregations: Their Power to Form and Transform*), Charles Foster (*Educating*

central practices in a residential environmental education program is the ongoing work of environmental stewardship. Participants in these programs are invited into the practice of maintaining a sustainable homestead. They often raise and prepare their own food, manage woodcutting for heating or other kinds of tasks, and live in buildings that use passive solar heat and composting toilets. These practices embody a care for resources that runs counter to dominant paradigms of exploiting nonrenewable resources for convenience in contemporary U.S. consumer culture. To use the language of Paulo Freire, participants are engaging in an ecological praxis that is formative of an alternative vision of the world. By living in a sustainable community, they are living into an alternative insight about the way they participate as agents in the world.

Also, the vision of interdependent communal living that Lydia experienced in the values of her Quaker school and the daily life in a cabin with eight other young women embodies an alternative understanding of relationship that directly contradicts understandings of the human as an individual consumer of goods. This understanding of interdependent relationality was not only verbalized, but lived out in the bodies of participants through living together in small groups, regular meetings to deal with the conflicts of close community living, and practices of community service. Living in community generates the insight of human interdependence. This vision of connection provides an alternative to the shared consumer icons offered by the broader culture.

Dreaming a new self and world can occur constructively through expressive arts, prayer practices, even creative projects or works of ecological justice shared with good friends. Exposure to poetry and fiction that imagines the world in ways that resonate with the young person's new vision of the world can renew their own imaginations. Young people can be invited to meditate on segments of these texts or

---

Congregations), Maria Harris (*Fashion Me a People*), and Michael Warren (*At This Time, in This Place*).

biblical verses, perhaps while drawing meditatively with chalk pastels or watercolors. They can work together on a permanent image for their communal space, a mural or sculpture or wall hanging that captures their shared visions of themselves in the world as something other than consumers of goods. Opportunities to cultivate the imagination through worship that evokes alternative images of world and self are of vital importance in sustaining an alternative vocational path. Duty and critical awareness are not enough to sustain; the experience of conversion is most often fueled by the exquisite joy of being embraced by a new vision both bodily and imaginatively. Shared experiences of immersion within the new symbol system are critical to its ability to provide renewing energies.

Creating awareness of the process of ongoing conversion

Helping adolescents to develop an awareness of the process of conversion can also be a critical aid to the process of regeneration. Young people need to explore the possibility that setbacks and conflict in commitments are a normal part of the process of ongoing conversion. While attending to the setbacks is important, it needn't be demoralizing. They can better understand the way consumer culture operates as a faith system and continue to discern their own ritual commitment to it. They can claim a need for a community of discernment to support their ongoing conversion and to share in the living out or praxis of alternative action. They can be helped in the process of seeking practices that enliven their alternative imagination and that will give them resources to deal with the ambiguity of their own experience.

An increased awareness of the continued process of conversion is helpful for adolescents on its path. Young people generally assume the static and completed nature of their commitments, which limits their capacity to wrestle with important questions, such as questions about attending college and concerns for their financial well-being in the future. In particular, adolescents raised in communities with a rhetoric of strong commitment need further opportunities to sort out the contradictory loyalties embodied in their own families and faith communities. Being familiar with each of the steps of ongoing conversion allows youth greater agency in participating in their own conversion.

John Wesley often preached on the process of salvation as well as topical sermons about various elements in the process, such as the continued presence of sin in believers after justification. He did this because he hoped to create a theologically and pedagogically informed laity that was better equipped to move on toward salvation. By recognizing the movements of sanctification, believers would be better able to understand the state of their own souls. For Wesley's followers and for adolescents struggling to transform their commitments to consumer capitalism, knowing about the process of conversion may help them to make better sense of their own commitments and state of the soul. Also, awareness of the process may help adolescents make better choices of pedagogical communities, circles of grace that help them to continue on the path of ongoing conversion.

One way to help adolescents understand the process of ongoing conversion is to have an elder who is able to speak honestly about his or her own struggles to be faithful to commitments that contradict consumer culture. Brian Mahan tells the story of Marilyn, who is a good example of someone who can speak with great honesty about the struggle to live up to a revelatory encounter with a different vision for her vocation. Marilyn was a peace brigade volunteer who had gone to Sri Lanka to act as a human barrier for a woman whose life was threatened by the government. In the process of this act of service, Marilyn felt fully alive, directed, and committed in a way she had not experienced before. Mahan had invited Marilyn to his classroom to share with his students about her experiences. In her sharing of the stories about the work and the character of her calling, Marilyn also shared her confusion about what to do with this call when she returned home. Once she was back in her home environment, she was frustrated, confused, and even a bit angry about what to do with her newfound calling in the midst of her old responsibilities. She was even concerned that she might be misguiding the class. Mahan notes: "Marilyn's presentation implied something truly unexpected: you were allowed to speak about a powerful moment of recruitment with passion and in detail even though you really had no idea what to do about it at the moment."[7] This insight was met with great joy and relief in the classroom as the members of the class realized that setbacks and confusion are part and parcel of the experience of commitment and vocational discernment.

In many ways, awareness of the process of ongoing conversion may require more maturity and lived experience with their own failures to sustain commitments in any pure way. Teaching young persons to be their own "soul monitors" is difficult because their own sense of authority is not yet fully internalized, and most settings (schools, family, etc.) are working to keep it external for young people's "protection" and control (e.g., the old "as long as you are under my roof you will do things my way" argument). This kind of self-awareness is an invitation into greater maturity, creating a zone of proximal development into which young people can grow.

Mentors who understand multifaithfulness

This awareness of the dynamics of ongoing conversion would also help mentors better understand multifaithfulness (the continued commitment to consumer faith in the midst of emerging alternative faith) and help interpret it to young people. Many teenagers are quite attuned to ideology and respond with passion to calls for ideological purity. Paradoxically, multifaithfulness may be more pronounced in adolescents because of their developmental stage and life experience. Many adolescents have not yet made close-to-permanent commitments (having children, spending ten years in school preparing for a career); the grooves of their selfhood are not as deeply worn. Often they express inconsistencies without noticing them. For example, psychologist Niobe Way completed an ethnographic study of urban

---

7. Mahan, *Forgetting Ourselves on Purpose*, 132.

teenagers. She notes this multiplicity in many of her subjects, using the story of Malcolm as an example:

> Malcolm speaks about fearing an early death and about having hope for the future; he speaks about being responsible and about being arrested for being in a stolen car; he speaks about being lazy and about being on the honorable mention list at school; he says he does not want a committed relationship with a girl and claims that the closest relationship he has right now is with his girlfriend. Malcolm seems caring and reflective and, at other times, tentative and disengaged. His presentation of himself and his life in his freshman and sophomore years is typical of the adolescents we interviewed. While there were a few students who presented themselves as one-dimensional (e.g., those who were seemingly the most depressed), the stories of the majority of students were three-dimensional, alive, and filled with ambiguities, contradictions, and discontinuities.[8]

Adolescents on the path of conversion need mentors who recognize this inconsistency as typical, but who also know how to graciously point them to greater integrity and emerging coherence. This would involve pointing out inconsistencies not as judgments, but rather as puzzlements or things to consider. Calls to integrity are important, but adolescents are not only struggling to get "it" together, they are trying to figure out who "it" might be anyway. They are just beginning the process of emergence into vocation, into developing a sense of themselves in the context of their many roles and in light of larger meanings that are important to them. At times adolescents seem so confident and together; at times they seem unreflective and inconsistent. Effective mentoring requires patience with this multi-faithfulness, and the ability to help young people understand their

---

8. Niobe Way, *Everyday Courage: The Lives and Stories of Urban Teenagers* (New York: New York University Press, 1998), 63.

multifaithfulness as movement toward increasing integrity rather than failure or hypocrisy.[9]

Repentance, yet again

Regeneration also requires the continual recognition of divided loyalties and the long journey to reintegrate both bodily practice and new imagination into the new faith system. This "restoration to the image of God" is a gradual process, a journey full of detours and paths that circle back upon themselves. Wesley wrote quite a bit on the persistence of sin in believers over the course of his lifetime. These writings addressed the experience of persons who had a dramatic conversion moment and thought that they were completely transformed by their faith in God. Eventually, they discovered that temptations and sin returned to their lives. He notes:

> They now feel two principles in themselves, plainly contrary to each other: "the flesh lusting against the spirit," nature opposing the grace of God. They cannot deny that although they still feel power to believe in Christ and to love God, and although his "Spirit" still "witnesses with" their "spirits that" they "are the children of God"; yet they feel in themselves, sometimes pride or self-will, sometimes anger or unbelief.[10]

Wesley understood the work of sanctification to be a gradual process. The process of conversion to perfect love was not a linear progression. There are moments where we recognize split loyalties, multifaithfulness, movement toward increased integrity that may never be complete. He advised waiting for entire sanctification, or for "a full salvation from all our sins,"[11] by participating in the means of grace.[12]

---

9. For the full discussion on multifaithfulness as an indication of movement toward fuller conversion, see chap. 2 of this work.

10. Wesley, *Sermons*, 374.

11. Ibid.

12. The means of grace were a topic of conversation that spanned Wesley's entire life, and he shifted subtly in examples in each list. Wesley scholar Randy Maddox

Only in naming the ways in which we are continually drawn into making sense of the world through consumer categories do we understand the degree to which consumer culture continues to powerfully dominate our meaning making. An important part of gaining critical awareness may involve opportunities to reengage with dominant U.S. culture after a time of immersion in a community embodying different values. Lydia's comment about her friends who don't understand the emphasis on community in her Quaker schools until they go to college illuminates the value of moving back into mainstream culture and seeing it with "new eyes" after an immersion experience. My own example from an earlier chapter about going back to a suburban neighborhood after having chosen to live in an urban neighborhood for many years also points to the ways in which returning to the original environment allows one to see the critical awareness that one has cultivated. Thus, praxis and engagement outside of the primary community of formation may support regeneration, as this ability to gauge the extent of change in imagination can often be a source of increased agency and further commitment to an alternative value system.

Paying attention to the small voices

Regeneration is finally about the inherent power of an object of faith to sustain and enliven its worshipers. However, within the Christian tradition, we believe that humans partner with God in the work of ongoing conversion. One practice that humans can cultivate to assist regeneration is the practice of paying attention. In moments when adolescents find themselves in the position of having two conflicting impulses held in the mind, attention becomes a key element to the faithful life, particularly if they hope to respond to the less strong of the two ideas. Philosopher and early psychologist of religion William

---

notes about his lists of the means of grace: "The items included in these lists range from such universal Christian practices as fasting, prayer, eucharist, and devotional readings to more distinctively Methodist practices like class meetings, love feasts, and special rules of holy living" (Maddox, *Responsible Grace*, 192).

James believed that we are not able to supplant one idea for another and make ourselves act accordingly, but only to hold the nascent idea fast so it can strengthen and make the body respond accordingly.[13] James describes the dynamic of affirming a moral, if small, voice in light of other options: "The strong-willed man, however, is the man who hears the still small voice unflinchingly, and who, when the death-bringing consideration comes, looks at its face, consents to its presence, clings to it, affirms it, and holds it fast, in spite of the clamoring host of mental images which rise in revolt against it and would expel it from the mind."[14] Thus, habits of attention formation and the sheer stock of the ideas furnished to students are what can be offered to enable the work of the regeneration in light of the new faith system. Even with this, our acts of voluntary attention are but an occasional and brief part of our life, but James names them "nevertheless momentous and critical, determining us, as they do, to higher or lower destinies."[15]

Practices of attention are particularly important in a cultural situation in which human attention is the most valuable commodity. Advertisers compete mightily for the attention of young people, and helping young people attend to and remember the "less strong voice" is a critical practice. Our more socially conservative Christian brothers and sisters are aware of the importance of paying attention to the less powerful voice, which is what was behind the WWJD (What would Jesus do?) bracelets of some years back, and now the "true love waits" rings of the Christian purity movement. Both of these concrete reminders of a particular kind of Christian commitment have become completely intertwined with consumptive practices. However, the idea of having a material reminder, a touchstone that evokes the initial beautiful vision that grasped the young person, is not a bad idea. It may be that the young person creates a personal icon that represents the vision of faith, or creates a breath prayer practice

---

13. William James, *Essays in Psychology: The Works of William James Edition*, ed. Frederick H. Burkhardt (Cambridge, MA: Harvard University Press, 1983), 226.
14. Ibid., 227.
15. Ibid., 111.

that captures the heart of that vision, such as "enough for all God's sheep."[16] Whether visual or oral, the reminder calls to the forefront of attention what really matters most to the young person.

In a recent testimony about what sustains her on the life of faith, a colleague of mine, church historian Jean Miller Schmidt, shared a story about being an adolescent in a denominational camping program. After a culminating gathering in which many of the young people made commitments to a life of Christian service, Jean remembers that the young people were invited to go back to their cabins to write a letter to themselves about these newfound commitments. The letter was then mailed to them six months later so they could remember the moment of vision and be renewed by it. Forty-plus years later, Jean still remembers this event and how it encouraged her own commitments to be of service to God, even though at the time she had no idea what form that service would take as a young woman who didn't want to be a missionary and couldn't be ordained. What is central in this story is that the vision of commitment was understood to be located in the young people, and they were encouraged to begin a practice of reminding themselves of their epiphany in ways that were encouraging and not guilt-invoking. These critical moments of remembering what we understand to be the deepest truth we have encountered pair with the ongoing processes of self-awareness to sustain and revitalize the newfound faith.

We begin to answer the complicated question of how pedagogical designs might respond to the assumption that God is working

---

16. This prayer is based on Ezekiel 34:17–19: "As for you, my flock, thus says the Lord GOD: I shall judge between sheep and sheep, between rams and goats: Is it not enough for you to feed on the good pasture, but you must tread down with your feet the rest of your pasture? When you drink of clear water, must you foul the rest with your feet? And must my sheep eat what you have trodden with your feet, and drink what you have fouled with your feet?" This text (and the larger text in which it is embedded) reminds me that God desires for all of God's children to share in the available resources rather than the more powerful dominating the resources of all. The short prayer, "enough for all God's sheep," calls to mind the sense that the earth's resources are for all.

in partnership with humans in the process of conversion. Cultivating practices of attention will increase the possibility of attending to smaller, alternative narratives of meaning that one finds to be more adequately integrated with faith perspectives. Practices of attention may also help a person to recognize and respond to the divine gift of revelation, visions of more beautiful ways of relating to one another and the world. In addition, educators can offer gifts to the faithful imagination from religious traditions that increase the sheer stock of ideas and generate the conflicting impulse situation in which the will operates. The gifts may become sources of revelation for students, places where they meet the divine in partnership and begin the journey of conversion. Finally, these gifts may open students to a wider reality that holds the possibility of meeting the Spirit about her work in the world in novel and enlivening ways.

Communities of support for the "not yet"

Finally, adolescents need help to develop strategies for sustaining communal support, praxis, and alternative imagination despite the lack of broader "victory" of the beautiful visions that have grasped them. In working against a dominant culture, a crisis can occur when young persons realize that they may never bring about broader societal change around consumption. A healthy attitude of developing realistic communities of relative support can go a long way in supporting regeneration within the new belief system. For example, Lydia expressed modest utopian hope that the ecological values she wanted to work for would some day be embraced more broadly, but she recognized that her sources of support would be smaller at first.

Finding more modest expectations of support and success in sustaining an alternative imagination and praxis is particularly important to address with young people, who are often quite zealous in their belief, energetic in their action, and demanding of the shared commitment of others. Sharon Welch addresses the importance of these modest hopes:

Rather than a hope for eventual victory, for a world without injustice or serious conflict, I describe the power of having a more modest hope, a hope for resilience, a hope for company along the way. Rather than expect that at some time major social problems will be solved and not replaced by other challenges, I discuss what it means to hope for resilience in the face of ongoing and new challenges. I explore the paradox that seemingly lowered expectations for social change provide staying power and effectiveness.[17]

Welch indicates that staying power emerges from a source of joy grounded in alternative imagination: "What is the wellspring of courage, transformation, and persistence? Acts of respect, of courage, of resistance and transformation spring from a deep reservoir of vitality and joy."[18] In my own categories, this deep vitality and joy come from a faith system that has captured loyalty with its beautiful way of characterizing the world and relationship within it. Finding and participating in communities of celebration that embody this new faith will be critical for sustaining the alternative imagination. While Welch emphasizes the need to be aware of the difficulty of social transformation and even entertains the notion of its impossibility, she recognizes the necessity of finding companions of shared imagination to celebrate moments of resistance, resilience, and courage along the way. We now turn our attention to how to cultivate these communities of support and challenge.

---

17. Welch, *Sweet Dreams in America*, xvi.
18. Ibid., 134.

Part three

Nurturing contexts for adolescent ongoing conversion

Eight

Forming the underground

The power of small groups
to nurture ongoing conversion

As an adult who works with young people and who wants to help them as they journey on the path of conversion from consumer faith, you may be thinking ongoing conversion is nearly impossible to support. The formative power of consumer culture is pervasive and alluring to young people, and we often don't feel we have much control over their formative environments. At the start of this book I confessed that it was born out of my own puzzling work with young people around these issues. I shared with you the story of Michael, a young man who, despite intentional formation into alternative commitments shared by his family and his faith community, parroted consumer tenets gleaned from the broader culture. He was frustrated that his mom wanted to buy him off-brand shoes and clothing, and he extolled the virtues of being a proper consumer, willing to spend money to purchase the right goods.

I caught up with Michael and his parents last year, and I'm happy to report that Michael no longer preaches sermonettes on proper consumption. As a graduating college student, Michael hopes to complete his doctorate in literature and currently lives the ascetical life of a graduate student. His current commitments around consumption as a young adult are much more reflective of the nurturing environment of his family and church than they were as a fourteen-year-old. I was delighted to reconnect with Michael for many reasons, most of which had to do with the intriguing person he has become in the years we have been apart. This visit encouraged me on two counts. First, I was reminded that the self an adolescent performs at fourteen often differs markedly from who they will be as an adult or even a young adult. While we know this at some gut level because we remember ourselves as teenagers, it is an insight we can forget in the moment of working with young people. I worked with Michael when he was struggling to fit into the artifices of the high school environment and to wrestle with the broader culture's understandings of "the meaning of life" that differed so radically from those he was receiving in his family and in his church. He was trying on imaginations of himself offered by those two environments, and they were most prominent in his younger self. Second, I realized that all of the counter-consumer formation offered Michael in the embodied communities of family and church was not offered in vain. In fact, it nurtured his conversion from consumer faith in powerful ways that were beginning to show fruit.

In the previous chapters I have explored the dynamics of ongoing conversion as a pedagogical process and named some of the key movements in the process. This was largely a description of the process of conversion and its impact on individual adolescents. In this chapter, I turn to small communities as structures that support the process of conversion in individuals, but that also serve as a source of social conversion on a broader level. In the next two chapters I use two images to describe small pedagogical contexts that nurture ongoing conversion in adolescents: the underground and circles of grace. Both images are offered to encourage you in your work with adolescents on the path of conversion from faith in consumer culture.

Exploring the underground

Undergrounds are groups that operate underneath the cultural radar. When referring to music or social scenes they generally indicate emerging alternatives to mainstream culture, experimental and avant-garde groups that challenge the establishment. When referring to political movements, undergrounds are groups agitating for social change but trying to stay out of the light of public scrutiny during the time that they are building solidarity and momentum for change. Both of these common meanings inform my understanding of the small groups that support adolescents as they struggle with consumer faith. Small groups can offer emerging alternatives to mainstream consumer culture for their youth participants. They can be a place where young people find like-minded companions who share their dreams for a different world.

At the same time, the term "underground" suggests that the alternative faith commitments being explored and tested may remain "underground" in the adolescent, rather like Michael's nonconsumer commitments did in his early adolescence. The present lack of visibility of alternative commitments may, in the end, have little to do with their long-term power in formation for young people.

This double sense of "underground" highlights the two related functions of forming a small group that support the process of ongoing conversion in its members: the individual educative function that attends to the formation and transformation of the imagination of participating members in an alternative meaning system, and the political function of a small body as a base for collaborative action toward social change. Both functions are critical for the transformation of faith in its broadest sense.

Communities of critical engagement

While ongoing conversion is ultimately an individual change in subjectivity and commitment, it is an ancient pedagogical strategy to set up communities of alternative consciousness to encourage participation, support, and accountability in the process of transformation. Because formation of religious identity and vocation draws upon social categories and relationships, the transformation of identity and vocation best occurs in social settings as well. In *The Meaning of Revelation*, H. Richard Niebuhr asserts that we only come to believe as we become aware of the faith of those we trust and with whom we live in communion:

Nothing happens without the participation of our bodies, but the affections of the soul come to us through and in our social body almost as much as in our individual structure. We suffer with and in our community and there we also rejoice. With joys and sorrows, fears, hopes, loves, hates, pride, humility, and anger combine. And none of these affections remains uninterpreted.[1]

This theological insight is affirmed by studies of human development. Participation in a community is crucial for the development of dispositions and discernment. Participation in a social body with others who share a commitment to an alternative meaning system generates more full integration of a new faithful imagination. The need for a social context in which to explore these commitments is intensified in adolescents, who developmentally are in a stage where they value peer relationships enormously.

Some persons form a small community with a distinctive subculture in order to create a community of retreat that functions largely outside the bounds of broader culture.[2] However, if a group has the goal of transforming the broader culture as well as forming its participants, the linkages between these smaller formative groups and the larger culture become more complex: They must be communities of critical engagement rather than communities of retreat. To retreat from the broader culture risks the necessary connection with the larger culture that they hope to transform. An important goal of these small groups is to support the ongoing process of individual transformation into a new vocational path, but this is not the only goal of small pedagogical communities. They also serve as a home base for persons who are working for the transformation of a wider world.

Social ethicist Nancy Fraser explores the function of small alternative communities created in response to the strength of a dominant

---

1. Niebuhr, *The Meaning of Revelation*, 98.
2. Parker J. Palmer, *The Company of Strangers: Christians and the Renewal of America's Public Life* (New York: Crossroad, 1996), 120.

culture in an essay reworking the notion of public sphere to include the history of subordinated social groups. Fraser describes the ways in which these groups have found it beneficial to create alternative spaces in which to articulate their own interpretations of their identities, interests, and agendas.[3] Fraser labels these entities "subaltern counterpublics" and notes that they have a double function:

> On the one hand, they function as spaces of withdrawal and regroupment; on the other hand, they also function as bases and training grounds for agitational activities directed toward wider publics. It is precisely in the dialectic between these two functions that their emancipatory potential resides.[4]

The pedagogical strategy of setting up small communities for support and political action discussed in this chapter is not a full-scale "subaltern counterpublic" in Fraser's description. In her concept of counterpublic, Fraser points to large constituent groups that can provide a viable cultural alternative to the dominant power. While the smaller pedagogical communities I am describing represent a more modest scale, they can still provide an alternative space for support and a critical mass for action and engagement in the broader culture.

A postmodern underground

Before I get into describing the nature of these underground groups, a small caveat is in order. For adolescents and young adults, these groups are much more fluid entities than the stable forms of community often harkened to in youth ministry literature extolling the virtues of communal connection. For example, communal contact was Lydia's key strategy for sustaining the unique path of becoming an organic farmer. When I asked her how she would find sources of

---

3. Fraser points to women, workers, peoples of color, and gay and lesbian persons as examples of this phenomenon. Nancy Fraser, "Rethinking the Public Sphere," in *Justice Interruptus: Critical Reflections on the "Postsocialist" Condition* (New York: Routledge, 1997), 81.

4. Ibid., 82.

support for living out her countercultural understandings, she noted: "Community is one of the key things. Right now, family, and built community that supports what you want to do. Ideally culture and society will someday support it too. And I have some communities I could pop in on and they'd say, 'Awesome! You go be that organic farmer.'" Lydia understood that maintaining these connections would be crucial to helping her sustain her recently claimed vision of becoming an organic farmer. In the face of lack of support from the broader culture for her chosen vocational direction, Lydia knew there were communities she could "drop in on" that would validate her visions through their own lifestyles and work. She named this her "built community."

Lydia has generated an ecological version of Ruether's "women-church," a temporary alternative space with visions of the identity of participants that counter a dominant paradigm of consumption. It is interesting to note that these are mentoring communities for Lydia, but not ones in which she is a full, participating member. As an emerging young adult, she has not yet settled into a lifestyle where she has made lasting commitments to a particular community. However, this does not diminish the importance of her knowing that such communities exist and that she can connect with them peripherally in order to sustain her emerging vision.

Lydia's insight about her own need for mentoring communities points to the importance of maintaining an ecology of support for young people on the path of conversion, particularly as they venture out of the original setting of claiming a new faith system and into other communities. Whether this happens through college chaplaincy and university fellowship communities, or through a mentor family found in a new community when they move (such as the family that Lydia was searching for to begin her apprenticeship as an organic farmer), or extended friend networks or other communities of shared faith, there is a need to find way stations along the path that help maintain vision, that stimulate further imagination and possibility, and that reaffirm the critique of consumer values. This shifting milieu of support may be more realistic than the stable, historic, more structured communities that I describe in the next section. Envision for yourself a postmodern underground ... fluid, shifting, but critical to sustaining alternative faith commitments.

Functions of small pedagogical communities

Small pedagogical communities perform two functions simultaneously: formation and support for continued work of personal transformation in an alternative culture, and collaborative action for the transformation of the broader culture. In this section, I break these two overarching functions into four smaller functions:

1. engaging formation into a new faithful imagination and alternative culture

2. providing individual support and accountability for this ongoing process of transformation

3. generating a critical perspective on the broader culture and commitment to work for its transformation

4. embodying a viable alternative for the witness and transformation of the broader culture

All four functions are important for a community to generate the kind of critical engagement with the broader culture that encourages both the journey of individual conversion and incremental social change. For each of the functions, I explore a historical and a contemporary example of its embodiment.

Formation into a new faithful imagination and alternative culture: The example of ascetical and monastic groups

Monastic and ascetical communities in the Christian tradition demonstrate how intentional small communities actively form persons into a new faithful imagination informed by an alternative culture. Margaret Miles indicates that historical monastic communities structured experience in such a way as to form a new person with new understandings: "Monastic practices were based on the possibility of a coordination of effects — sexual abstinence, ascetic practices, diet — that, together with a communal rhetoric and mutual reinforcement, created experiential knowledge."[5] The communal rhetoric provided images and justifications that gave meaning to the daily practices of the community, and doing the practices together provided support and reinforcement for the individual's transformation. The practices of the community both create the space for new religious experiences to occur and generate a lifestyle that reinforces their meaning for the individual.[6]

Ascetic communities both ancient and modern have as their goal the creation of persons whose subjectivity is grounded in a culture and symbol system alternate to the culturally dominant meaning system. Contemporary scholar of asceticism Richard Valantasis advances the following definition of asceticism: "Asceticism may be defined as performances designed to inaugurate an alternative culture, to enable different social relations, and to create a new identity."[7] Performances of certain acts (fasting, for example) become naturalized through repetition and carry specific significance within the meaning world in which they are performed. However, the intention of the performance is more than mere imitation of behavior. The behavior points to a larger world of meanings that opens up "an alternative culture and the potential of a new subjectivity."[8] These new cultural performances within the ascetic community are designed to break down the dominant culture and establish a new culture created through the patterning of basic behaviors and relations.

In this process, the presence and reinforcement of relationships with other persons for whom the alternative culture is already naturalized is critical to the process of transformation for new members. Through the practices and relationships that the community provides,

---

5. Miles, *Practicing Christianity*, 90.

6. Ibid., 91.

7. Richard Valantasis, "A Theory of the Social Function of Asceticism," in *Asceticism*, ed. Vincent L. Wimbush and Richard Valantasis (New York: Oxford University Press, 1995), 548.

8. Ibid.

the often theoretically complex ascetic culture gets translated from concepts into patterns of behavior that the person can apprehend through participation in the community. In short, the communal practices of asceticism allow persons to function in a reenvisioned world: "Through ritual, new social relations, different articulations of self and body, and through a variety of psychological transformations, the ascetic learns to live within another world."[9]

Contemporary persons often assume that the function of ascetical and monastic groups is retreat from the "real world" into the cloister, but historically many of the members of these groups had regular contact with and served the broader culture. Monasteries were used for educational and healing functions, and members of religious orders served as spiritual advisors to persons outside their communities. Monasteries also provided hospitality and sanctuary to travelers and refugees. Members of ascetical communities were often intimately linked with the broader social world around them, but they interpreted this work in the world through their formation into an imaginative world quite distinct from the broader culture. This formation was rigorously embodied in the shared practices of deconstruction and reconstruction of the self in the community.

You may be thinking, how exactly am I supposed to establish an anticonsumer monastery for young people? An ascetical community does not have to be a cloistered environment. I have shared stories of the youth group I worked with in Atlanta. Arguably, they engaged in ascetical practices that formed a separate culture in participants, an alterative imagination informed by faith in something outside of consumer culture. Blart, fried-chicken talk, the shoe ministry, non-targeting humor, and free recreation all are bodily practices that generate a different subjectivity. The fact that these practices were

9. Ibid., 550. Valantasis lists some of the elements of ascetic culture as "narrative, biography, demonic and angelic psychology, as well as systems of theological anthropology and soteriology" (ibid.). Clearly these are not everyday concepts present in broader cultural settings. This function of formation into an alternative imagination can occur in more common contemporary pedagogical communities. For example, Lydia's family clearly and self-consciously nurtures an alternative identity in its members.

shared in community reinforced their formative power. When new youth arrived who operated in ways that made fun of vulnerability or otherwise violated the alternative forms of interaction, the youth were known to say, "We don't do things that way here." A youth group could address issues of consumer practice even more directly in its worship life, but even the haphazard amalgamation of practices that we established formed an alternative subjectivity in the members of the group.

Closer to home, this is a place where taking the family seriously in youth ministry becomes important. The family is the primary culture-setting norm for most adolescents, despite the cultural myth that teens do not listen to their parents. Both Lydia's and Michael's families set up counter-consumer norms in their practices of household economics, media engagement, and other choices. The mantra in Lydia's home was that everyone should have "all that they need and some of what they want," and her parents worked to be sure that family members understood the difference between an actual "need" and a consumer-culture-generated "want." These families served as ascetical communities that engaged in practices that helped their members' formation into a faithful imagination quite distinct from consumer faith.

Support and accountability for ongoing transformation process: The example of Wesley's bands

As a person deeply influenced by monastic and ascetical communities, particularly the Society of Jesus,[10] John Wesley understood the pedagogical value of small groups removed from broader society for the purpose of formation into an alternative worldview. When a person had begun the process of transformation into a more engaged Christian life, Wesley encouraged the new believer to seek the "means of

---

10. Wesley historian Albert Outler notes: "The Methodist notions of corporate Christian discipline were derived, at least in part, from Wesley's interest in the Roman Catholic religious orders — the Society of Jesus in particular." Outler, Editor's introduction to "Church and Sacraments," in *John Wesley*, ed. Albert C. Outler (New York: Oxford University Press, 1964), 307.

grace" as a way of cooperating with the Holy Spirit's ongoing work toward their salvation.[11] For Wesley, this included participation not only in the traditional means of grace of the church (communion, prayer, regular worship, care of the sick, etc.), but also in a distinctively Wesleyan interpretation of the means of grace: participation in a small pedagogical group.

The classic Wesleyan structure for these means of grace is the small covenantal group that he called a class meeting. Historically, the class meeting had its roots in Wesley's experience with Moravian societies as well as his experience with holy societies or small student groups of prayer and service while at Oxford University.[12] Wesley defined the purpose of these small groups as follows:

> Such a society is no other than a company of men having the form and seeking the power of godliness, united in order to pray together, to receive the work of exhortation, and to watch over one another in love, that they may help each other to work out their salvation.[13]

While Wesley had experience as a self-selected participant in such a small group during his time at Oxford, he rather stumbled upon their pedagogical usefulness during the beginnings of the Methodist movement. Initially, persons involved in the movement were organized into twelve-person classes in order to facilitate the collection of money to pay for a building that the group had built as a meeting place. Eventually, the leaders making rounds to collect the offering and meet with their members began to discover problems both physical and spiritual in the lives of members. Wesley began meeting regularly with his class leaders, and charged them with the authority to provide spiritual guidance and correction to the members of their classes. Logistical concerns caused the classes to begin meeting together in one place, and the greater ability of a small group to provide support and a

11. For a discussion of the means of grace in Wesley, see note 12 on p. 166.
12. Richard Heitzenrater, *Wesley and the People Called Methodists* (Nashville: Abingdon, 1995), 104.
13. Wesley, "The Rules of the United Societies," in *John Wesley,* 178.

context to practice the way of love became evident. A pedagogical institution was born.[14]

As the societies and classes grew, an even more distinctively Wesleyan institution, the "band," emerged. The band consisted of five to ten people, often leaders of class meetings, who covenanted together for intense spiritual nurture and growth through confession and prayer. Wesley historian Richard Heitzenrater comments about the impetus for these groups: "Wesley was beginning to understand that holding and embodying the gift of righteousness (holiness) in the midst of a turbulent world was difficult for most people."[15] Thus, participants formed bands to provide mutual support and accountability for the process of growth in holiness of life in light of interaction with the difficulties of their everyday contexts. Unlike the classes, which had a clear leader responsible for the spiritual discipline of participants, these were collegial groups designed to encourage "growth in grace through Christian fellowship and religious conference."[16]

Participation in these structures was considered crucial for working out one's own salvation. In the activities of the small group, Wesley's nascent pedagogical strategies for the ongoing conversion of the believer are evident: (1) being held accountable to others who share a similar goal is essential for maintaining the process of ongoing conversion; (2) works of piety and mercy allow the believer to practice the new understanding of God's love in their life; (3) regular meetings and group rhythms allow members to establish an alternative identity in a new social setting. Wesley recognized that, while the affections are enlivened by the Holy Spirit, they are shaped by regular participation in the religious life of a community. The praxis of the life of

---

14. For a full description of this process, see Heitzenrater, *Wesley and the People Called Methodists*, 118–19.

15. Ibid., 104.

16. Ibid., 105. Wesley understood the process of "conferencing" to provide a connectional pattern of organization and accountability groups for the movement: "The primary purpose of these substructures of the Methodist societies was to support members' responsible participation in the transforming work of God's grace" (Maddox, *Responsible Grace*, 212).

holiness in a small group setting was crucial to individual growth in the life of faith.

For young people, the structure and rigidity of these bands would seem utterly foreign. However, networks of accountability among peers are more common than you might think. Witness Bryan, a seventeen-year-old talking about his best friend. When asked if he felt responsible to friends when he made life decisions, he responded:

> Only to people that are very, very close to me. Like my best friend, Tyrone. I've known him since I was in sixth grade, and he just graduated last year. And me and him take up responsibility for ourselves, both of us. He asked me what I'm doing; I asked him what he's doing. And we usually say, "That's not a good decision" or "Yeah, go ahead, go for it." That's what best friends are for. You care about what the friend does.... Friends can be a good responsibility or whatever it is.

Bryan describes a very common way in which adolescents seek accountability with each other.

Lydia also maintained an ongoing community of mutual soul-searching, confession, and accountability in relation to her commitments. While this community was rather informal in Lydia's story when compared to the more formalized network of accountability found in Wesley's bands, she had a network of family and close friends who were her conversation partners. For example, her definition of vocation as more than "getting paid for what you love to do" emerged from a conversation with a friend who was also struggling with vocational direction. They encouraged each other to structure their lives in a way that honored the values that they held dear. Through conversations with friends who shared her values and had left college when they found it to be out of line with their priorities of communal living and ecological sustainability, Lydia had begun to question her own decision to enter college. Some of her friends had dropped out, only to return later, and Lydia respected their decisions because she felt that they were the products of adequate self-reflection in light of named ideals. In her interview it became clear that Lydia valued candid conversation partners who helped her to gain an honest picture of her motivations and decisions in light of their commonly held commitments.

These adolescents are witnessing to the ways in which they seek each other out to hold themselves accountable to what they find important. I've also seen this kind of accountability in groups of young people supporting each other through intense training regimens for sports in the off-season months. These networks could be established around shared commitments to ecological practices, solidarity with the poor, or relational depth in order to maintain accountability for ongoing conversion from consumer culture.

Critical awareness and commitment to societal transformation: The example of Freire's culture circles

Brazilian educator Paulo Freire also established small groups called "culture circles" as part of his pedagogy for the development of literacy and liberation among the peasants with whom he worked. Freire understood the culture circle to be a place of dialogue in which participants learned to "name the world" together.[17] In the practice of naming the world together critically, they find themselves to be "re-creators" of the world through their reflection and action together.[18] Through the practice of regular dialogue in the circle the peasants began to understand themselves as a subject in the wider struggle of social transformation, and the practice of dialogue within the circles was understood as a sort of training ground for increased agency in the broader culture. The training ground was not the only extent of the work of the circle; praxis in the broader social context was required to fully transform consciousness: "The circle of culture must find ways, which each local reality will indicate, by which it must be transformed into a center for political action."[19] Thus, the unity of action and reflection is embodied in the institution of the culture circle.

---

17. Paulo Freire, *Pedagogy of the Oppressed* (New York: Continuum, 1997), 69.
18. Ibid., 51.
19. Freire, *The Politics of Education*, 157.

A culture circle was significant because Freire understood the act of gaining agency or "subject-hood" to be an inherently social act. The subject could only assess the world with the participation of another person.[20] Freire insists that conscientization requires not only the awareness that something exists but an understanding that "places it critically in the system of relationships within the totality in that it exists."[21] Because this knowledge only happens when one is inserted into the reality which one is trying to comprehend, the knowledge is not individual but social, and conscientization happens only within the context of real people in social structures. Freire goes further to state that this occurs solely in a context of love or "communion" with fellow revolutionaries, which he felt was fundamentally necessary for action for freedom.[22]

What would a culture circle to generate critical awareness and commitment to societal transformation look like among adolescents? Hayley, the young woman who struggled to counter her media-fed dissatisfaction with her body, gained her critical awareness of body-image distortion in a writing group sponsored by a feminist book-store. The young women in the group talked about issues that were important to them, and eventually generated an alternative imagination of women's roles in society to that proposed by consumer media. Other groups gather to discuss contemporary movies, popular books, or other works that highlight consumer commitments and use this as a beginning point to gain critical distance on consumer culture. Most of the examples of calls to awareness in chapter 4 (visiting Target, watching commercials, etc.) could serve as the beginning of a "culture circle" that would allow youth a place to begin to question consumer values and articulate alternative commitments.

---

20. Freire, *Education for Critical Consciousness*, 137.
21. Ibid., 148.
22. "Authentic communion implies communication between men, mediated by the world. Only praxis in the context of communion makes 'conscientization' a viable project. Conscientization is a joint project in that it takes place in a man among other men, men united by their action and by their reflection upon that action and upon the world" (Freire, *The Politics of Education*, 85).

Embodiment of a viable alternative:
The example of Ruether's women-church

Feminist theologian Rosemary Radford Ruether, in her work with women in the church to transform patriarchy, also recognizes the power of forming intentional small communities outside of official power structures. She suggests creating "women-church" as a temporary alternative space where women could be nurtured outside of the patriarchal church that hinders their full vocational development: "Women-Church means not only that women have rejected this system and are engaged in efforts to escape from it, but that they are doing so collectively."[23] Ruether assumes that the creation of an alternative public provides more power and significance to the move out of the church than a collection of individual exoduses.

Ruether asserts that the period of withdrawal into their own counterpublic allows women to create a critical culture, something they have lacked in comparison to other marginalized groups. A critical culture provides meaningful alternative visions of the identity and roles of participants that counter a dominant paradigm which offers oppressive visions. Ruether carefully indicates that this withdrawal must not be marked by ideological separation in which women are characterized as good and men as evil.[24] Rather, the feminist critical culture must be self-aware and attempt to be honest in its assessment of both patriarchy and the counterculture it sets out to establish.[25] This gathering of women who have experienced personal liberation serves as "a redemptive community rooted in a new being."[26] The community is meant to be a place of celebration, of communion, of

---

23. Rosemary Radford Ruether, *Women-Church: Theology and Practice of Feminist Liturgical Communities* (San Francisco: Harper and Row, 1985), 58.

24. Ibid., 59–60.

25. A need made all too plain by the critique of women of color who called the early second-wave feminists into account for their lack of attention to the complications of oppression multiplied by race and class as well as gender.

26. Ruether, *Women-Church*, 61. See discussion about the need for small groups to engage in group self-critique in chap. 9.

empowerment, of nurturing, and of being nurtured.[27] Here we see the function of withdrawal and regrouping, but Ruether recodes this function positively in terms of celebration and creation of critical culture. Ruether presents a third option to establishing a sectarian group completely outside of the church or continuing to participate in the church on its own terms: "It means establishing bases for a feminist critical culture and celebrational community that have some autonomy from the established institutions."[28]

Of the four examples of small groups that I have shared, Ruether speaks most directly to the way this small group can contribute to the broader transformation, both of the culture of the Roman Catholic Church and the broader culture of patriarchy. She imagines women-church as a necessary stage in a larger process in which men and women are both liberated from patriarchy and an alternative critical culture is formed.[29] Even though the feminist liturgical community may only gather for a few hours in a given week, the hope is that it can generate enough momentum as a critical culture to witness to an alternative possibility for shaping life. The community must make this culture clear enough that "some men feel compelled to try to understand it on its own terms and not simply to try to ridicule or repress it."[30] Ruether hopes to create a transformational conversation between the women in the liturgical community and women who have remained within the patriarchal institutions who can then adapt the creative alternatives developed by the intense work of the alternative communities.[31] Ruether recognizes that the exclusive and intensive imaginative work done in the alternative community

---

27. Ethicist Sharon Welch points to a similar role of community in one of her three elements of an ethic of risk (Welch, *Feminist Ethic of Risk*, 20). She notes that the ability to sustain responsible action in resistance to social injustice requires participation in a community that grounds the identity and vision of the actor in a shared imagination and hope.

28. Ruether, *Women-Church*, 62.

29. Ibid., 60.

30. Ibid., 61.

31. Ibid., 62.

is critical, but ongoing dialogue with persons within institutional churches creates the possibility of broader transformation.

Adolescents are not likely to have the resources to generate fully functioning alternative institutions like Ruether's women-church. However, they benefit tremendously from exposure to and connection with these kinds of institutions. Many organic farms, sustainable communities, intentional simple living communities, and communities that live in solidarity with the poor have programs that allow young people to participate in their ongoing work. Groups of young adults working through programs such as Americorps, Lutheran or Jesuit Volunteer Corps, or other programs can serve as a transitional version of the viable alternative. While adolescents may not be able to join fully in the daily life of these kinds of communities, they can be inspired and engaged by visiting the communities, talking to their long-term members, and sharing in their important work in appropriate ways. These opportunities of exposure allow young people to imagine other possibilities for how life together could be structured in communities that do not embrace consumer faith.

A delicate balance

In each of these four cases, the small community maintained the delicate balance between creating a set-apart intentional community for formation and renewal and critical engagement with the broader culture. The four functions I have explored through the four example communities can be interwoven in the life of any pedagogical community interested in cultivating a lively alternative imagination and engendering increased agency. However, forming a small group that functions as a smaller-scale subaltern counterpublic can go awry. The delicate balance of withdrawal from and engagement with the larger culture can be difficult to maintain. The group may become an enclave that loses touch with the broader cultures and thus loses the ability to speak to them in the transformational dialectic that Ruether imagines. The group may merely replicate the dynamics of the larger culture in a more intimate setting and undermine its ability to witness to a distinctive vision of how life together might be.[32] The group may become so enraptured by the experience of community and support that it fails to encourage self-critique and accountability. Any of these failures can damage the effectiveness of a pedagogical community hoping for individual and social transformation. The descriptions to this point have not clarified what makes these small groups pedagogically effective. Let us turn now to look at some of the necessary characteristics of such groups in order to sustain adequately both functions of alternative formation and support for vivid action in the world.

---

32. bell hooks speaks of the difficulty that many professors encounter when their classrooms replicate the politics of domination from the broader culture even as the professors attempt to create an alternative space where education is a practice of freedom. See bell hooks, *Teaching to Transgress* (New York: Routledge, 1994), 39. Freire also relates the ways in which the culture of silence becomes internalized in peasants so that they are unable to leave it behind when they enter the culture circles. However, while the goal is not a "pure" small group without any evidence of the outside culture (an impossible task), the group does need to articulate and embody the struggle for an alternative vision of how life might be.

Nine

Circles of grace

A circle of grace is a way station along the path of conversion for young people, a place to breathe, to be formed, to celebrate new visions, and to be connected with others who share them. I call these small communities "circles of grace" both because they are a gracious space of transformation for participants and because they embody the possibility of gracious alternatives to a broader culture. My imagination in describing these circles largely tends toward youth groups gathered in local churches because that is my experience base, but these circles can emerge in any setting where youth are allowed to establish communities with adult mentors. I have seen circles of grace established within "family friend" groups, whether formally or informally structured. I have also seen circles of grace spring up out of writing groups sponsored by feminist bookstores, among a dance troupe sponsored by the Boys and Girls Club of Atlanta, among book clubs established with parents and teenagers, and among yearbook staffs at a local high school. Circles of grace are spaces where adolescents can be fully themselves and seek together to grow into increasing understanding of their identities and the integrity of their commitments. They are places of growth and accountability, of challenge and support.

Circles of grace are part of the underground, the relational networks that nurture adolescents as they are converting from faith in consumer culture. In this chapter I move from outlining the functions of these small pedagogical communities to describing some of the characteristics necessary to accomplish their functions. While I have separated these into two sections, form and function, for the purposes of clarity, they are two sides of a whole. When religious educator

194

Maria Harris noted that "The church does not *have* an educational program; it *is* an educational program,"[1] she asserted the fundamental connection between the form of an educational community and its function. The manner in which a small group comes together forms its participants even before the "official" formative practices are engaged. Therefore, the characteristics, while descriptive, also point to the pedagogical life of the community. The following characteristics seem critical to the capacity of a small group to nurture ongoing conversion: an atmosphere of grace, confessional honesty, accountability in light of confession, a rhythmic pattern of common life, richness of imagery and worship, opportunities for nonconsumptive celebration, opportunities to live into new imaginations together, and encouragement for corporate self-critique. While not an exhaustive list, I hope these primary characteristics enliven your imagination for what such a group might look like in your own setting.

Atmosphere of grace

Grace is a complex theological category that merits a much fuller treatment than I am able to give it here, but I lean on John Wesley's assertion that grace conveys both the "pardon" and "power" of God. This understanding emphasizes two elements of grace. First, grace extends radical acceptance in the face of human frailty. The classic expression of grace as unmerited pardon in the Christian theological tradition is that Christ gave his life for us "while we were yet sinners." Second, grace becomes evident in the power granted to move on toward salvation. In this case, grace can take many forms: the gift of faith, a revelation of a new vision of the world and our place in it, loving mentors, the support of community, even increased self-awareness and a call to repent. Simply stated, grace is evident in whatever provides the possibility to move on toward renewed faith in alternative meaning systems to consumer culture.

---

1. Maria Harris, *Fashion Me a People* (Louisville: Westminster/John Knox, 1989), 47.

Tone of gracious acceptance

Shifting primary meaning systems that fund meaning making is a difficult and risky venture, particularly when you are leaving a meaning system that is supported by the broader culture for one that is countercultural. One of the characteristics of a community that makes this difficult work possible is that the community not only provides the support and modeling of others who share the new meaning-making structure, but also creates an atmosphere of graciousness that allows the person to explore alternative possibilities without the fear of condemnation. The extension of grace provides space to experiment and risk failure.

Turning to Wesley's bands as an example, Wesley emphasized that only the love of God allowed sanctification to occur. The bands were to embody this love in a vivid way for their members: "The point was to encourage faith working through love, that the love of God might be shed abroad in their hearts and lives. To this end, the bands met regularly (at least once a week) for intense spiritual intercourse."[2] How's that for a description for the work of a small group? Wesley's choice of words communicates an intimacy and a passion that seems well-suited to adolescents. While Wesley's sermons often embody a moral exhortation that seems more judgmental than gracious, his pedagogical design recognized that grace was a critical element for transformation. The band was to be a place of accountability, but within the atmosphere of gracious sharing and love. This atmosphere of radical acceptance was given ritual embodiment in the love feast, a Moravian practice that Wesley adopted as an important means of grace within the small groups.

Grace is not synonymous with permissiveness. Grace is not acceptance "no matter what you do." It is the careful balance of recognition that it matters deeply what we do and a sense that we will never be able to perfectly live into the vocations to which we are called. The balance of radical acceptance and high expectations is difficult to maintain, but critical for adolescents on the path of conversion.

---

2. Heitzenrater, *Wesley and the People Called Methodists*, 105.

Nontargeting humor

A major difference between Wesley's era and contemporary U.S. culture is that direct moral exhortation by an authority toward increased righteousness has even less power to effect transformation in contemporary contexts than it did in Wesley's time. Most of us have little belief in the basic depravity of humans, and condemnation of behavior comes across as judgmental and ineffectual, particularly to adolescents. Thus, the atmosphere of graciousness becomes even more important, and less direct manners of creating the self-awareness of repentance arise. Where condemnation and accusation can lead to defensiveness, humor can sometimes lead to illumination. When we can laugh at the ways that we get off track in our attempts for increased integrity in our new faith, we can be eased into greater self-awareness and possibility for transformation.

Humor provides a gracious buffer for that difficult look at ourselves, the moment in which you have to laugh or cry. When I have led workshops in which I ask participants to rewrite the Beatitudes as if they were to be included in a fictional "gospel of consumption," the reading of these new beatitudes often evokes great laughter. Here is an example of participants' creative efforts taking off on the Twenty-third Psalm:

> The wallet is my Lord; it buys everything I want.
> It makes me to lie down in the Ritz-Carlton.
> It leads me on Caribbean cruises; it restoreth my tan.
> It leads me to spend for the economy's sake.
> Yea, though I walk through a depressed job market,
> I fear no creditors.
> For the minimum payment is with me.
> My MasterCard and my Visa, they comfort me.
> My shopping bag overflows.[3]

---

3. This particular version was generated by members of the extended community of Iliff School of Theology at a "Lunch with a Professor" session on April 23, 2003.

The formalized and familiar language of sacred texts seems oddly connected with the crassest versions of consumer tenets. These statements often embody the caricature of consumer culture at its absurd extremes. At the same time, moments of self-recognition can occur where we see that we may be "a little like that." The gracious space of delight and laughter makes the self-recognition less painful.

Youth have to work particularly hard to cultivate an atmosphere of humor that is gracious, particularly because so much contemporary humor modeled for adolescents is humor at the expense of others. Adolescents value humor and fun, but often they find it hard to find fun with each other while avoiding cut-down forms of humor that target the frailties of others. This kind of humor is devastating to the atmosphere of grace, and makes the space unsafe to reveal struggles and frailties.

Toleration of ambiguity

Small groups also embody grace when they tolerate the ambiguity of the person in the process of transformation. People in the midst of ongoing conversion often display commitments to multiple faith systems in varying degrees; they are faithful to both consumer meaning systems and their new alternative imaginations at the same time. Communities that only tolerate undivided loyalty to a single meaning system and that reprimand the expression of doubt or mixed/divided loyalties do not invite persons in transition or provide support for the difficult work of ongoing conversion. Instead, they may invite increased self-deception both individually and corporately. The recognition of the conflicted nature of faithfulness is a critical component of providing an atmosphere of grace.

Youth are keenly aware of the social norms operating in situations, and they will respond accordingly. If they sense they must demonstrate their put-togetherness, their "fully committed Christian" or their "all about social justice" face to be a part of the group, they will not bring their struggles, questions, or doubts to the group. Adolescents are champions of telling powerful people (whether peers or adults) what they want to hear. Alternatively, they may avoid a group or actively disrupt it if they sense that they are not welcome to bring their full selves to the table. Either way, the small group fails to provide a space where young people can struggle with repentance and move on toward conversion.

Gracious mentors

Another embodiment of grace comes from mentors who hold positive visions of who we can be despite all current evidence to the contrary. When young people do bring to the table their struggles to be faithful, they need adults who recognize in those struggles the seeds of more mature, faithful living and who can encourage young people to keep walking the path. Mentors also encourage us on the path of conversion by their own honest sharing of their struggles to live into the vocations to which they have been called.

Mentoring that helps young people envision possibilities and feel agency in their capacity to bring those imaginations into reality is a rare and precious gift. Too often we find mentors who want to foist their unfinished dreams on us, or who want us to hike the trails they have already blazed. Sharon Daloz Parks has explored the critical roles of mentors and mentoring communities in the vocational journeys of young adults. She notes:

> The power of mentoring relationships is that they help anchor the vision of the potential self. They beckon the self into being and, in so doing, help to ground a place of commitment within relativism. As such, mentors exercise both a cognitive and affective appeal, offering both insight and emotional support.[4]

Finding mentors and mentoring communities provides a gracious space of exploration and movement toward increasing integrity of commitment.

This atmosphere of gracious beckoning is particularly critical for adolescents. Adolescents are in a developmental stage where they are keenly aware of the ways in which other people perceive and evaluate

---

4. Parks, *Big Questions, Worthy Dreams*, 81.

them.[5] When I interviewed young people who had years earlier been a part of an intentional community for theological reflection while in high school, a theme in the interviews was that one of the most transformational parts of the experience was that the community was a place where they could "drop all of the masks" and just be themselves.[6] In other words, they experienced the grace of a community that made them feel acceptable just as they were. This was important both because it provided the space for increased self-recognition and self-honesty that is crucial to transformation, but also because it was so unique in their experience as adolescents.

Young people, particularly those who are successful in the acceptable avenues of upper- and middle-class society (i.e., in school- and adult-sanctioned extracurricular activities), feel an enormous amount of pressure to measure up. They often structure their lives and extracurricular activities as if their college applications or resumes will always precede them into relationships. Coupled with the developmental stage that makes them feel that others are always watching them, this combination can be devastating.

Part of the grace extended to adolescents by good mentors is the acceptance of failure as a normal part of growth and learning. We live in a culture where failure is not an option. We watch our leaders, whether presidents or corporate executives, refuse to admit failure and spin mistakes rather than taking responsibility for poor choices. Religious educator Maria Harris noted in her *Portrait of Youth Ministry,* "No community can move to communion unless it

---

5. James Fowler helpfully connects the emergence of this "new burden of self-consciousness" in adolescence to the emergence of formal operational ability in Piaget's developmental schema and the "emergence of interpersonal perspective taking." Fowler notes: "The youth believes everyone is looking at him or her and may feel either a narcissistic inflation or a self-questioning deflation regarding 'the me I think you see' " (Fowler, *Stages of Faith,* 152–53).

6. These interviews were part of a research project evaluating the long-term impact of Emory University's Youth Theological Initiative on its participants. Both the summer academy and the follow-up research were funded by the Lilly Endowment, Inc.

is a place where failure is tolerated; communities are made up of sinful human beings."[7] An atmosphere of gracious acceptance becomes essential to invite young people into the work of ongoing conversion, where recognition of failure and struggle is central to the work of increasing faith.

Confessional honesty

An atmosphere of grace is necessary to generate the space for confessional honesty in a group. Confessional honesty is the practice of revealing failures to one another and to ourselves in order to find the grace to address them. Only in a group where people feel the safety of being affirmed and accepted even in their weakness will they begin the process of looking carefully at their own conflicts and difficulties in the life of faith. In a community where failure and frailty are unacceptable, recognition of one's own frailties and failures becomes dangerous. Deception about those frailties becomes the safer alternative.

Confessional honesty allows for the work of avoiding self-deception in the process of ongoing conversion. The initial formation and commitment into the consumer faith system will remain strong even after powerful experiences of justification. The practices of self-examination and confession allow group members to increase their awareness of the ways in which they continue to operate out of the initial belief system. As Salvadoran theologian Jon Sobrino advocates in *The Principle of Mercy*, it is crucial to name both what one believes in and what idols one is tempted to embrace in order to avoid self-deception. Sobrino uses the language of "idol" intentionally, noting that they are not "inventions of so-called primitive people" but rather real forces that are worshiped and that "demand victims in order to exist."[8] Sobrino names both capitalism and militarism as two of the

---

7. Maria Harris, *Portrait of Youth Ministry* (New York: Paulist Press, 1981), 119.

8. Jon Sobrino, *The Principle of Mercy* (Maryknoll, NY: Orbis, 1994), 9.

idols that he sees active in El Salvador. Confessional honesty is critical for Sobrino:

> In order to speak the whole truth, one must always say two things: in which God one believes and in which idol one does not believe. Without such a dialectic formulation, faith remains too abstract, is likely to be empty and, what is worse, can be very dangerous, because it may very well allow for the coexistence of belief and idolatry.[9]

Without such a dialectic of faith, Sobrino notes, one is likely to continue to serve the idol even as one believes oneself an unconflicted believer.

The dualism of belief and idolatry named by Sobrino may seem to contradict my earlier emphasis on the reality of multiple conflicting attachments in the person undergoing conversion. The naming of a belief system as idolatrous and judging it evil *can* be unhelpful when it leads to defensiveness and concealment about the remainder of that belief system. However, being clear about the commitments one embraces and those best left behind is important in the process of self-understanding and transformation. As Brian Mahan notes, the attention given to the conflicting belief system allows us to move toward greater coherence in our belief:

> Paradoxically, it is the simultaneous confession and careful study of our sometimes conflicting attachments to material, social, and moral scripts that hints at the possibility of joyful detachment and of a life given over more fully to vocation. If you wish to forget the self, study the self. If you wish to be compassionate, study how you are not compassionate.[10]

Sometimes companions who have a more external viewpoint on our struggles assist the process of honest confession that Sobrino and Mahan advocate. Wesley's weekly examination of heart within

---

9. Ibid.
10. Mahan, *Forgetting Ourselves on Purpose*, 113.

the bands was designed expressly for the purpose of examining to what extent participants were allowing sin to continue to reign in their lives. Wesley's bands exemplified this kind of honesty with one another, as is evident in the following rule of the bands: "To speak each of us in order, freely and plainly, the true state of our souls, with the faults we have committed in thought, word, or deed, and the temptations we have felt since our last meeting."[11] This confessional honesty was required even before someone was admitted to the band. A series of four questions asked of incoming members is particularly striking because of the questions' increasing threat of candor:

> Do you desire to be told of your faults? Do you desire to be told of all your faults, and that plain and home? Do you desire that every one of us should tell you, from time to time, whatsoever is in his heart concerning you? Consider! Do you desire we should tell you whatsoever we think, whatsoever we fear, whatsoever we hear concerning you?[12]

These questions make it clear that there will be no flinching in the face of difficult conversation about the shortcomings of members. This honesty was considered crucial for increasing self-knowledge to allow for productive work toward salvation.

In order to support confessional honesty, the bands were constructed in homogenous patterns with regards to gender, marital status, and age. Wesley scholar Richard Heitzenrater notes: "The purpose of this careful sorting was to allow for the highest possible degree of openness and candor within the bands."[13] This homogeneity removed the possibility that some members of the bands would have authority over other members that would keep the less powerful members from being honest about the state of their souls. With people who are in similar situations, one often assumes more readily that they will understand personal struggles and temptations enough

---

11. Wesley, "The Rules of the Bands," in *John Wesley*, 180.
12. Ibid.
13. Heitzenrater, *Wesley and the People Called Methodists*, 104.

to be compassionate and honest in their response. While homogeneity may not be desired in a contemporary incarnation of accountability groups, the insight that confessional honesty is difficult within situations where persons have different power and authority is an important one. This may be why teens like Lydia and Bryan named their friends as their system of accountability. They feel they can be more honest with their peers because they do not fear reprisal in admitting their weaknesses and missteps. Adults can model appropriate vulnerability through their own confessional honesty and invite the reflections of adolescents. "Appropriate" vulnerability is the key term here — sharing what is helpful for the growth of the adolescent rather than telling personal stories for your own self-aggrandizement or enjoyment. While adult mentors will benefit mutually from confessional honesty with young people, their primary community of support and accountability should be with other adults.

On an individual level, confessional honesty could take the form of an ongoing conversation in youth group among adolescents struggling to survive in middle and high school social environments that elevate consumption as a marker of status. Particularly around the beginning of the school year, winter recess, and other seasonal highpoints of consumption, a small community of confessional honesty could help adolescents recognize the ways in which they are faithful adherents to the consumer system. In such a group, they might begin to explore the particular ways in which their participation in consumer faith systems takes form (clothing purchases, video games, music collections, car envy, etc.) and to move toward practices that negate this faithful participation. These moments become opportunities to rehearse with each other what the shared alternative commitments might mean for their daily life practice and to share the struggles of living into them.

Accountability in light of confession

Because the work of confession in light of revelation is difficult, even so painful as to create avoidance, we need to have a community of accountability in which to engage the work. A community of account-ability provides mutual discipline in light of the faith toward which its members hope to move. The community includes persons with whom we are in close relationship who help us to stick with the work of self-knowledge even when it is difficult and we wish to avoid it. In addition, when we have had a moment of increased self-awareness, the community can hold us accountable to changes of behavior that sustain that new self-awareness.

Wesley modeled this accountability in his classes. The societies were divided into smaller classes of twelve men so they could more easily keep up with each other's progress on working out their own salvation. While the only condition to gain admission into a soci-ety was "a desire to flee from the wrath to come, to be saved from their sins,"[14] to continue in the classes members needed to evidence their desire for continued salvation. This evidence was measured by first doing no harm, and then by "doing good of every possible sort, and as far as is possible, to all men" both in body and in soul.[15] Finally, they were also exhorted to attend "upon all the ordinances of God,"[16] such as participation in public worship and sacrament, study of Scriptures, and spiritual practices. Members were unable to continue in the classes if they did not show this kind of evidence that they were struggling to work out their own salvation. Here, we become aware that the atmosphere of grace is not unqualified per-missiveness, but is balanced out by the expectation for responsible action in light of the grace extended.

To refer back to the fictional youth group discussing school cul-ture and consumer faith in the previous section, this group would become a community of accountability if members were not only exploring for increased self-awareness but challenging one another when new evidences of consumer faithfulness arose. Commitments about consumption might be made together, and members would

---

14. Wesley, "Rules of the United Societies," in *John Wesley*, 178.
15. Ibid., 179.
16. Ibid.

encourage adherence to those pacts when they saw each other outside of the group. In addition, such a group could embody other forms
of affirming an alternative value system, and encourage one another
in living into those alternative faith systems. Remember again Bryan
and Lydia, who found their peer networks of accountability critical
to their own growth and development in commitments.

It will become important to discuss with the youth the danger that accountability can pass into judgmentalism, and to help
youth explore graceful ways of addressing each other in the midst
of accountability. Probably Wesley's increasing threats of candor
would be useless with adolescents. Young people may be able to
name for themselves the questions of accountability that would be
useful within their group culture. Mentors might also demonstrate
gentleness and the extension of grace in the moment of calling into
account.

A rhythmic pattern of common life

In order to establish the environment of trust and shared accountability that allows for rigorous self-examination, extended time together
is required. This time becomes shaped into rhythms that establish
patterns of habit, disciplines of faith, new forms of relationship, and
distinctive forms of engagement with the broader world. The regular
manner and rhythm of gathering, meeting, and leave-taking also help
to generate group identity. To this end, Wesley exhorted his bands:
"To meet once a week, at the least."[17] Regular time together provides
space for the development of relationships and trust that allows for
mutual support. Because the process of ongoing conversion can take
quite a while, it is also important that groups meet regularly over an
extended period of time to support that long-term process. The regular rhythm of gathering gives the group increased depth of influence
in participants' lives.

---

17. Wesley, "The Rules of the Bands," in *John Wesley*, 180.

The regular rhythms and practices in small groups generate a new individual and communal identity within the particular symbolic system of the community. These characteristic patterns are part of what make us feel at home in a group, part of what expresses the identity of the group. We are a ritual people, and the regular movements of our lives in community honor that need for ritual and order. Wesley recognized the importance of patterned behavior, and instructed his bands accordingly with the following rule: "To begin (those of us who are present) exactly at the hour, with singing or prayer. To end every meeting with prayer suited to the state of each person present."[18] The stability of rhythms and patterns creates a sense of unity and coherence among a collection of individuals and fosters a sense of group identity.[19]

Ruether's conceptualization of women-church as a feminist liturgical community also points to the need for regular rhythms. The rhythms of celebration and remembrance that are a part of liturgical practice foster individual identity formation even as they assist in generating group identity. Ritual rhythms provide embodied experience of new faith and imagination, social relationships, and patterns of service. Practical theologian E. Byron Anderson points to this function of liturgical practice: "By this I intend the claim that liturgical practice is intrinsically formational and transformational. It is a means by which we come to know ourselves as people of faith and to know the God whom we worship."[20] These practices provide opportunities to reflect on daily life, to pray, to sing, and to dream in the new faith system that are critical to the renewing of the faithful imagination.

Beyond the boundaries of liturgical practice, opportunities for formalized, rhythmic interaction provide opportunities for groups to

---

18. Ibid.

19. Religious educator Charles Foster also points to this function of a community when he notes the way it can be disrupted in unexpected events: "They interrupt the rhythmic patterns, structures, and relationships that have given coherence and order to the way congregations function" (Charles R. Foster, *Educating Congregations* [Nashville: Abingdon Press, 1994], 46).

20. E. Byron Anderson, "Liturgical Catechesis: Congregational Practice as Formation," *Religious Education* 92, no. 3 (Summer 1997): 350–51.

connect with one another. Historian William McNeill investigates the role of ritualized coordinated movement in establishing group identity, particularly looking at the role of communal dance in establishing communal identity: "Euphoric response to keeping together in time is too deeply implanted in our genes to be exorcized for long. It remains the most powerful way to create and sustain a community that we have at our command."[21] McNeill notes that the group movement allows ideas and feelings to be gathered up and expressed in their gestural and muscular form.[22] In other words, the distinctive rhythms of human communities help give meaning and guidance to the individuals that participate in them by embodying the collective identity. It is this "keeping together in time," moving within the distinctive rhythms of a community, that help us to feel continually at home within the bounds of that community.[23] These rhythms smooth and regularize social interaction and allow for other, deeper connections to form in the community. The sense of identity generated by these rhythms is also essential to establish the trust necessary for the difficult work of conversion to an alternative meaning structure that the group is meant to engender.

Liturgical and ritual calendars of groups of young people may be quite different from those of adults. The academic calendar is likely to have a larger influence than in adult communities, with the beginning and ending of the school year, summer break, finals periods, and other time schedules playing an important part in the rhythms of young people. The ritual life of a youth group may also be marked by individual life milestones such as transitions from middle to high school, getting a driver's license or first job, graduation, joining of new members, and leaving home for a job or college. Rituals and rhythms to celebrate these significant events are important bonding moments for the identity of a group. Annual events in the life

---

21. William H. McNeill, *Keeping Together in Time* (Cambridge, MA: Harvard University Press, 1995), 150.
22. Ibid., 152.
23. Ibid.

of the group, such as retreats and service projects and festive communal meals, also establish a ritual and liturgical cycle unique to the group.

Richness of imagery and worship

One of the most important rhythms in small group life is the practice of worship and immersion in new images that embody the new objects of faith. I use the term "worship" to indicate that this is not the passive witnessing of images central to the new meaning system to which participants are hoping for conversion. Rather, the community vividly embodies the images that are central to the new life of imagination that the community hopes to engender, creating a passionate encounter and evoking an adoring attitude toward them.

Niebuhr notes that we worship those gods that give unity and meaning to our lives, those deities that combine with power an adorable goodness.[24] The practice of worship works to transform the self through encounter with new images:

> We attend the places of official worship to let the symbols of an ancient faith work on us, we know not how. Adoration, prayer, thanksgiving, intercession — these are our daily rites. From these experiences of ours we turn back to the images of mind and heart, to the abstract ideas of our philosophies, seeking to understand our natural religion.[25]

Niebuhr points to an understanding that has been confirmed by later liturgical theologians, namely, that practices of worship form deep dispositional awareness in the person.[26]

---

24. Niebuhr, *The Meaning of Revelation*, 137.
25. Ibid., 130.
26. See for instance James Fowler, who notes: "Any proper appreciation of the power of *leitourgia* begins with the recognition that prayer, praise, sacrament, and worship form deep emotions within us. With liturgy we deal with the *kinesthetics* of faith. Through the teaching power of sacrament and worship, faith gets into our bodies and bone marrow" (Fowler, *Weaving the New Creation*, 181).

Among the ways that this immersion in new images was achieved by Wesley were singing and prayer. Much of Wesley's theology was encapsulated in his brother Charles Wesley's hymns (which John Wesley often edited). These two forms allow for the immersion in images of the new faith of believers. His instructions for singing (printed in the front of the *United Methodist Hymnal* even today) indicate that one should "learn these tunes before you learn any others."[27] Wesley encouraged his classes in the practices of prayer, regular Bible reading, participation in the liturgy, and singing. Each of these activities allows for a reverent encounter with the images of a new symbol system. Although Wesley never spoke of the function of images per se, his emphasis on song and imagery in sermons demonstrates that he was aware of the formative effect of the poetic images of these forms of primary theology.

Congregational studies scholar Linda Clark also demonstrates the ways in which hymns allow persons to "body forth" the images and emotional connection with a tradition.[28] She notes: "A hymn is a highly complex set of images, both verbal and aural, set in motion through singing by a group of people who have intentionally gathered to worship God."[29] Hymns are a particularly apt form of carrying the indirect and emotionally laden aspects of a tradition because the poetic imagery and the rhythms and tone of the music connect to persons on a deeper level than words alone. She notes:

> When members of a congregation sing together, the words of the hymn come alive to them and mean more than just a statement of fact. In hymn-singing they are pouring out their own hearts. The hymn creates that faith by bringing it into

---

27. John Wesley, "Directions for Singing," in *The United Methodist Hymnal: Book of United Methodist Worship* (Nashville: United Methodist Publishing House, 1989), vii.

28. Linda J. Clark, "Hymn-Singing: The Congregation Making Faith," in *Carriers of Faith: Lessons from Congregational Studies,* ed. C. Dudley, J. Carroll, and J. Wind (Louisville: Westminster/John Knox, 1991), 57.

29. Ibid., 51.

being and therefore is functioning as a symbol of the singers' faith.[30]

The fact that hymn-singing is a communal event that embraces and pulls along the individual person into the connection with other persons increases its formative effect.[31]

This immersion in images is analogous to the immersion provided by advertising culture with its jingles and carefully wrought visual images. We not only worship images that are traditionally religious; we give reverent attention to many different kinds of authoritative images in other symbol systems. One way of assessing the extent to which we have given reverent attention to these images is by assessing to what extent they have become the touchstone by which we measure other experiences. The imagery of advertising culture elicits worship on a daily basis.

Alternative images must also be embodied for worshipful, passionate encounter. One of the places that many liberal Protestant traditions have faltered in their mentoring of young people is in their failure to offer youth rich images in worship to enliven their imagination. Sharon Parks notes,

> Even in a time between stories, if the great traditions offer their stories, symbols, and songs — less as dogma and more as gifts to the faithful imagination — then with critical awareness they can be received as finite vessels to be treasured, reshaped, or cast aside according to their relative usefulness.[32]

Parks describes an important distinction in the way that these images are offered — not as dogma but as gift. The stories and images of our tradition address deep human questions of meaning that people have been asking for thousands of years. To offer these to young people as they struggle to leave consumer faith is to offer them companionship on the human journey that is much broader and deeper than their

---

30. Ibid., 52–53.
31. Ibid., 54.
32. Parks, *Big Questions, Worthy Dreams*, 202–3.

contemporary sensibility. Devotional reading of sacred texts, choirs that sing together, and prayers that are prayed in vivid and poetic language are all invitations to worship within a different imaginative world than the one offered by consumer culture. In finding stories to tell and songs to sing, it is important to seek out songs and stories that embody the struggles and alternative visions that inform the commitments of the young people with whom you work.

Opportunities for nonconsumptive celebration

Related to the rhythms of communal life and participation in worshipful immersion are opportunities for genuine communal celebration. Philosopher Albert Borgmann calls celebration constitutive of "the concrete and hopeful center of communal life," and he has documented the ways in which the emergence of technology and the public/private split generated by the rise of capitalism have contributed to the impoverishment of public celebratory life.[33] A major shift in human culture occurs in industrialized societies; work and production become the acceptable activities for public culture, and leisure and celebration are relegated to the private realm. Borgmann points out that major public "celebrations" in American culture such as the Super Bowl and the celebration of the restoration of the Statue of Liberty are generally funded by the private sector, and they become a spectacle for private consumption of individuals either on television or by purchasing souvenirs. Rather than active, vigorous public life enacted in artful and stylized ways that generate collective identity and meaning, such "celebrations" become passive events with little communal depth: "Here again I have concentrated on the tendency of technology to dissolve the depth of a genuinely public and celebratory life into a sophisticated machinery that yields an easily and safely consumable commodity."[34] The only public celebrations that occur are spectacles for individual consumption rather than participatory

---

33. Albert Borgmann, *Power Failure: Christianity in the Culture of Technology* (Grand Rapids: Brazos Press, 2003), 37.
34. Ibid., 45.

performances of solemn or entertaining occasions. In such a context, opportunities for participative celebration as an end rather than as an instrumental means for consumption become centrally important to small groups. As Borgmann's analysis indicates, in a technologically driven culture, public communities of celebration are in themselves a countercultural experience.

Borgmann's analysis invites us to think about the relationship between entertainment and celebration as it is practiced by groups of young people. Youth groups often consume the manufactured fun of an amusement park or miniature golf. Of course, youth find space within these structures to express their own "artful and stylized" fun, which is what makes the experience interesting and significant for them. It's not just the physiological thrill of the roller coaster that is exciting; it is riding it with friends in the characteristic ways you engage it together that is fun. Youth desperately need to discover that they can celebrate without consuming, and a circle of grace is a fine place to try this out.

Once I attended a retreat for a church where an adult in the church invited everyone to bring whatever musical instrument they could play for Saturday night's recreation. Adults and youth brought everything from kazoos to a trombone to a full drum set. During the day, the adult wrote out music to the folk tune "Little Brown Jug" for all of the instruments present. Anyone who couldn't play an instrument was taught a simple polka dance, and everyone in the church, from two to eighty-seven, polkaed gleefully to the ragtag band. I remember putting down my tin whistle and looking in utter amazement at the collection of people and what they were doing. Of course, the youth wouldn't have been likely to show up if the person had said, "Come on out this Saturday. We're going to polka!" At the same time, the young people recognized intuitively the power of nonconsumptive celebration in community, and responded with great energy and vitality. Using the resources and talents available to them, they made a celebration out of it.

At both of the residential youth theological academies that I have worked with, Friday night coffeehouses have been a central opportunity for nonconsumptive celebrations. At these events, youth have the space to share their musical talents, poetry that they have been invited to write, funny and dramatic readings, and whatever else they'd like to do. This kind of opportunity to create a celebration is quite different from competing together in sports, because there are no winners and losers. Many young people in local churches have been given opportunities to create worship services for their faith communities. These events are practice in celebration that does not have consumption as its primary goal, but rather the connection of a community around significant meaningful expressions. Churches could be uniquely poised to help young people rediscover the possibilities of nonconsumptive celebration by reclaiming their ritual traditions in ways that do not emphasize consumption.[35]

Events of celebration provide an opportunity for the formation and transformation of communal memory and identity. Charles R. Foster names three critical movements that allow communal events to develop into their fullest expression of communal participation: adequate preparation, full engagement, and mutually critical reflection.[36] Only when participants have sufficient familiarity and competence with the stories and practices of an event in advance, the opportunity to enter bodily and imaginatively into the process of the event while it is occurring, and moments of shared processing and assessment of the meanings generated by the event after its occurrence do they begin to enter fully into the possibility of an event. For both Borgmann and Foster, celebrations can be festive or solemn in tone. What makes them celebrative is their participatory and event-full character. Celebrations engage us in the life of a community beyond our individual selves, and they provide opportunity for the enactment of alternative corporate identities.

---

35. Several Catholic high schools have begun to cancel proms in recent years because of the consumptive excess that had emerged around them: literally thousands of dollars spent on limousine rental, dresses, extravagant pre- and post-parties, etc. What was a coming-of-age ritual has been transformed into an opportunity for conspicuous consumption.

36. Foster, *Educating Congregations*, 47–48.

In consumer culture, we are robbed of something centrally religious in learning to ritually mark significant life events without consuming major goods. I once sat between three young adults in an airport, two of whom had been at a wedding over the previous weekend and were telling their friend about the event. The two said something like this: "You know in the South it's all about the Lord. They had a DJ instead of a band. The reception was in the church fellowship hall afterward, so there wasn't any alcohol. It was the worst wedding ever." The young people were assessing the value of the ritual per-formed within a Christian religious framework by consumer religious categories. Once limited to wedding celebrations, even bar and bat mitzvahs are increasingly being hijacked by consumer culture, spawn-ing the term "batzilla" to describe the honoree who hopes to have the perfect coming-of-age ceremony. Opportunities for nonconsumptive celebrations become more and more rare and precious as the value of the ceremony is increasingly calculated by the amount of money spent to host it.

Opportunities to live into new imaginations together

Not only does a small group create opportunities for members to be immersed in new images, but it also can provide a chance to work together outside the bounds of the small community in light of the values and images it embraces. This praxis is a criti-cal element in changing individual consciousness and commitment as well as an important part of bringing about the broader trans-formation that is central to the role of the small group. Political action can be the event that brings about the change in insight and imagination.

Wesley's sermon "On Working Out Our Own Salvation" indicates that he thought praxis was the necessary condition of waiting for and working out one's own salvation. In this sermon he asks, "But what are the steps which the Scripture directs us to take, in the working out of our own salvation?"[37] Taking his cue from the prophet Isaiah, Wesley directed his believers to first avoid all appearance of evil. Then he turned to the positive praxis:

> And "learn to do well"; be zealous of good works, of works of piety, as well as works of mercy....As ye have time, do good unto all men, to their souls and to their bodies. And herein "be ye steadfast, unmovable, always abounding in the work of the Lord." It then only remains that ye deny yourselves and take up your cross daily.[38]

These three steps — ceasing evil, doing all possible good, and self-denial of those things which did not draw one closer to God — were the practice of holiness that constituted an active waiting for salvation in the believer. One of the places where Wesley truly differed from his theological contemporaries was this emphasis on sanctification — the ongoing process and praxis of salvation through cooperative work with God toward present and eternal salvation. Wesley advocated works of piety and mercy both for their effect on their beneficiaries and for their therapeutic effect on the souls of believers. Wesley also refuted the idea that persons could not participate in the means of grace, those active practices of waiting for salvation, unless they trusted in them or believed them to be true.[39] Practicing them was what led to trust in them.

Sharon Welch notes that ongoing praxis in light of the images a community asserts as true is not only about generating and continuing a shift in faith, but it is also about having energy to continue the difficult work of a community that envisions the world in a non-dominant way. Without immersion in ongoing practice in light of that alternative imagination, critique of dominant culture can become discouraging and disempowering. Critique without practice decreases agency. Alternatively, praxis can nurture the fragile hope of another

---

37. Wesley, *Sermons*, 489.
38. Ibid., 490.
39. Ibid., 166.

possibility. Working with others for justice in a consistent alternation of action and critique helps us to maintain an alternative vision. Welch notes:

> There is a simple reason for the repeated emphasis on practice by liberation theologians. Without working with others on projects geared toward social change, it is impossible to maintain the vision and energy necessary to sustain long-term work. If one engages in critique in isolation from those who are the victims of social systems, critique can become despairing and cynical.... Middle-class numbness is a luxury of being able to avoid direct contact with victims.[40]

Welch's point in this passage is particularly important within the context of consumer capitalism. With its ubiquitous, beautiful images of style and ease, consumer culture masks its costs to persons who labor to produce goods cheaply and to the earth that provides the raw materials which keep consumption moving. It is a system in which it is easy to lose sight of the victims of consumption and to be caught up in the beauty it generates. Thus, work in partnership with those who are victimized by consumer culture can help maintain the vision of why an alternative is important.

Youth can be invited into work that shapes new imagination in a number of ways. Earlier, I shared the story of the group of adolescents who participated in gleaning spinach alongside migrant workers. After the spinach was harvested, the youth washed and cooked it so that it could be frozen and stored at a local food bank for distribution. Clearly they would never view frozen spinach in the grocery aisle in quite the same way again. This experience deeply affected the imaginations of the participating youth on issues including hunger relief, immigration and undocumented workers, economic justice, community interdependence, and their own capacity to make a difference. Praxis together that embodies alternative imagination is a major impetus to the nurture of youth agency in addressing such

---

40. Welch, *Feminist Ethic of Risk*, 168.

issues central to consumer culture. This experience could have been developed further in a congregational context to gather congregational support for legislation that pays living wage to field workers and that addresses their immigration status, a direction that some of the youth participants are currently pursuing.

Often the students I have interviewed with the most clear-spoken critique and evident life structure changes around consumer culture have had experiences in residential environmental education programs.[41] Why is this kind of education such a powerful experience in establishing resistance to consumer culture? The participation in a fairly lengthy immersion in an intentional pedagogical community offers a concrete alternative vision of "the way the world is" described through ecological interdependence and embodied in a social setting. The experience of living in community and having to share resources is often a unique experience for participants, as is working through the inevitable conflict that this close living creates. The fact that many of these programs involve working together on a farm or other labor that sustains participants' lives together introduces an ongoing physical praxis of environmental stewardship in light of the alternative vision of the world espoused by the program. The programs often involve ascetic withdrawal from practices of consumption and ritual sites of consumer cultures such as malls and television.[42] Participants are engaged in significant intellectual work about the costs of consumption on natural resources. In other words, these communities embody in intensive fashion many of the pedagogical characteristics I explored in the previous chapter.

---

41. For examples of these kinds of educational programs, visit the following organizations' Web sites: the Outdoor Academy (*www.enf.org/toa.htm*) and the Chewonki Foundation (*www.chewonki.org/pages/chewonki_MaineCoast/index*).

42. Of course, the educational experience itself can also buy into consumer models of education. The Outdoor Academy, for example, advertises on its Web site: "Immersing yourself in a unique learning adventure creates the opportunity to distinguish yourself for college." Here the educational experience itself is being touted as an opportunity to acquire an experience that is marketable within the educational market.

Encouragement for corporate self-critique

While I have described the importance of confessional honesty about the individual's condition in the process of ongoing conversion, it is also important to talk about the necessity for practices of group self-critique within those new images. Any of these aforementioned characteristics of small groups (save an atmosphere of gracious acceptance, perhaps) could describe the movement of Hitler Youth in Germany and its formation of members into an alternative worldview. This makes the final characteristic so vital to mention. In addition to the immersion in images of the new faith, small pedagogical communities need to engage in and to encourage practices of group critique from within those new images. The new imaginations must not only inform their actions as a community but also call them into account when the life of the community is not adequately embodying those imaginations.

Sharon Welch addresses this issue in thinking about how communities can energize the struggle for justice without building a movement based on critique of others, demonizing, or unambiguously "being right." She notes: "My aim in this book is to present a vocabulary of good, of hope, of power and chaos, contingency and change, that can sustain not just resistance but also the self-critical and creative formation of institutions and coalitions."[43] The question of how to avoid fanaticism and self-aggrandizement while still energizing and sustaining a movement toward change is critically important. Alternative communities and movements for social transformation cannot be based solely on critique of others; they also need images that are life-affirming and that can generate strong communal identity. They need images that attend to self-critique and fallibility. Since group self-critique can often dampen agency, the struggle is to find ways that the critique motivates the group to live into the integrity of their imaginations rather than leading them into despair. The dynamics here replicate Wesley's understanding of "right repentance" on a corporate level.

---

43. Welch, *Sweet Dreams in America*, xii.

H. Richard Niebuhr also addresses this issue of corporate self-critique when he writes about the need for moral theology and reflective criticism in the church. He points to the need for the church to define itself by examining "critically the mind of the church with particular concern for the practical principles present in it and expressed in its activities."[44] Niebuhr expresses the need to not only worship images but to seek out the ways in which the faith community expresses and lives them out. The images of faith must be able to critique the life of the community.[45] This calls for the self-examination of the community that looks a bit like a corporate work of ongoing conversion:

> By reflective criticism I mean that method of self-examination in which one who participates in the faith and work of the church, in its order and life, seeks to bring into his own and his companions' full awareness the principles of individual and communal believing and doing, to analyze the consistency and inconsistency, the origins and consequences of such principles.[46]

I would take this self-examination a step further, perhaps, to ensure that what any faith system hopes for its particular group is what it hopes for the whole of creation. Niebuhr points to this in his assertion that the adequacy of the imaginations of a community can be measured by their consequences to selves and communities in the same way that hypotheses and concepts are shown to be true or fallacious

---

44. H. Richard Niebuhr, "The Church Defines Itself in the World," in *Theology, History, and Culture,* ed. William Stacy Johnson, 63.

45. Michael Warren names this capacity the achievement of "Spirit resonance" in communities of Christian practice: "Those in a Spirit-resonant community are meant to develop a perceptive system attuned to the gospel the way a parent of an infant can be so psychically tuned to her person that he wakes at night to her slightest cry and immediately attends her needs. When the Spirit of Jesus resonates in our congregations, it becomes discernible in their gospel practice because resonance involves not just perception but action" (Warren, *At This Time, in This Place,* 124–25).

46. Niebuhr, *Meaning of Revelation,* 63.

by their results.[47] The consequences assessed must include those to selves and communities outside of the small group.

Youth often engage in practices of group critique with great proficiency. Adolescents tend to be attuned to hypocrisy, particularly in the community of faith. The challenge is for the broader faith community to be open to hearing these critiques from their young prophets and open to the possibility of making some changes. Also, adolescents tend to be better in recognition of hypocrisy in others than in their own groups. The movement toward group self-critique offers a challenge to mature into accepting the failures of their own communities — and to experience that as a self-implication as well.

Seeking "good-enough" circles

Having described the ideal characteristics of circles of grace that serve as a context to support adolescents in the midst of ongoing conversion, I recognize that the list may be a bit overwhelming for any one group to sustain at all times. Fortunately, adolescents are resilient, and perfection is not a prerequisite. Adolescents will make use of the resources offered them by any group or combination of groups in their lives. Attention to these characteristics will be helpful, but the gracious acceptance of failure, limitation, and mixed loyalties can apply to group identity as well as individual identity. As child psychologist D. W. Winnicott understood about parenting, contexts of nurture will never be perfect; they need only be "good enough." What adolescents need are "good enough" circles of grace to provide way stations on their journeys of conversion. In the next chapter, we turn to other cautions and reality checks for adults seeking to mentor adolescents as they seek conversion from consumer faith.

---

47. Ibid., 73.

Ten

Facing the fierce, wild beast
Cautions and reality checks

As All Saints Sunday was approaching this year, I taught several songs about saints to a gathering of children and their parents during the opening moments of Sunday school. One of the hymns we learned together was "I Sing a Song of the Saints of God," by Lesbia Scott. As we finished singing the song for the first time, I did a little recap of what the lyrics meant for the younger children present. In particular, I tried to explain the context of a particular line of the song: "And one was a soldier, and one was a priest, and one was slain by a fierce wild beast."[1] If you are unfamiliar with this hymn, the chorusing last line of each verse expresses the sentiment that there is no reason why the singer shouldn't be a saint as well. When I noted that being killed by a fierce wild beast might seem like a good reason to avoid becoming a saint, one of the parents burst out in relieved laughter. Clearly, destruction was not what she had in mind for her young daughter in this whole church venture. Willingness to offer up one's young to the lions seems a laughable rather than laudable example of faith to contemporary believers.

Fortunately, being a Christian no longer requires risking a literal trip to the Colosseum for contemporary young people. However, asking young people to embrace commitments that counter consumer culture does feel a little like inviting them to take on a fierce wild beast of another sort. The visions that inform an alternative belief system

---

1. Lesbia Scott, "I Sing a Song of the Saints of God." *The United Methodist Hymnal* (Nashville: United Methodist Publishing House, 1989), 712.

render young people useless within the values held commonly by our contemporary culture. To invite them into solidarity with the poor, into sustainability and interdependent community, or into valuing relationships over commodities is to ruin them for easy participation in the religious rituals of our culture. These rituals generate a powerful, shared consensus about the vocations to which humans are called which are embodied in our institutions, our collective unconscious, our valuing, and our status-granting norms. While perhaps not a threat to their bodily well-being, ongoing conversion does risk young people's respectability and success within the broader culture. This venture is not one we should invite young people into lightly. We must not ask them to enter the Colosseum alone. To issue calls to awakening, invite repentance, share revelations, and seek regeneration is to implicate ourselves as the traveling companions of our young people on the road to sainthood, with all of its attendant risks and difficulties.

Risking shipwreck:
Education as changing faith

Understanding education as an invitation to ongoing conversion from faith in consumer culture becomes an extremely risky venture with the recognition that faith in positive centers of value and power provides a coherence that is crucial for survival. The change in faith is twofold: movement toward increasing integrity in the life of faith as well as change from dependence on one object of faith to another. Often we do not respect the risks of this kind of transformation. The experience of a change in faith means a change in the deep, faithing parts of the self, which is a risking of the coherence necessary for functioning. As deChant paired it, in seeking to shift from dependence on consumer capitalism as the center of meaning making, we may discover how religious we really are and how difficult it is to change.

The depth of the experience of changing faith is described quite profoundly in the metaphors of human faith offered by Richard R.

Niebuhr: "shipwreck, gladness, and amazement."[2] Sharon Parks takes a moment to meditate further on these metaphors in her book about the young adult's search for meaning, purpose, and commitment. In the following passage, she describes the phenomenological experience of a change in faith as a shipwreck:

> Metaphorical shipwreck may occur with the loss of a relationship, violence to one's property, collapse of a career venture, physical illness or injury, defeat of a cause, a fateful choice that irrevocably reorders one's life, betrayal by a community or government, or the discovery that an intellectual construct is inadequate. Sometimes we simply encounter someone, or some new experience or idea, that calls into question things as we have perceived them, or as they were taught to us, or as we had read, heard, or assumed. This kind of experience can suddenly rip into the fabric of life, or it may slowly yet just as surely unravel the meanings that have served as the home of the soul.[3]

The metaphor of shipwreck provides a powerful description of the disorientation that can occur when our sense of self, world, and God — those connections that allow us to narrate our experiences with meaning and purpose — are challenged. As Parks notes, this change can be sudden, brought on by disaster or the unveiling of something that discredits deeply the earlier construction of faith. Alternatively, it can be a slow process that develops over time. Either way, the sense of shipwreck when we discover the inadequacy of our old ways of making meaning (or the old gods we depended upon) can feel threatening in a primary way. What once provided our sense of security and togetherness has been challenged and found unworthy, and this dissolution threatens the very foundations of the self.[4] We find out just how attached (emotionally, cognitively, and relationally) we are to our ways of understanding the world and how painful it is to lose that attachment.

2. Niebuhr, cited by Parks, *Big Questions, Worthy Dreams*, 28.
3. Ibid.
4. Ibid.

Not every new piece of information or every change in faith is an experience of shipwreck. As educators, it is important to recognize the gravity and profundity of the change in selfhood that a change in faith elicits, and correspondingly to recognize the depth of support required to navigate the potential experience of shipwreck in educational journeys that are designed to challenge basic faith assumptions. Niebuhr's other two parts of the metaphor of faith provide hope and a reason for risking shipwreck. If we survive the shipwreck and reach a new shore where we are able to perceive life with increasing adequacy, we experience gladness and amazement at the transformation. However, while a new reality may be discovered beyond the loss of earlier meanings, we rarely are able to replace completely the earlier understandings. Thus, experiences of profound transformation are often marked by grief and loss even as there is a deep gladness in the enlarged being and capacity to act.[5] Change in faith and selfhood can be costly, and must be respected as a difficult journey even as we celebrate the new shores of understanding that are perceived to more adequately capture the complex nature of reality.[6]

Can we change the broader culture?

As I have presented this work on resisting the religious formation of consumer capitalism in a variety of venues, many people have asked me if the underlying agenda of this project is actually to end consumer capitalism. On my more cynical days I think that nothing short of environmental holocaust or catastrophic economic collapse could end the American love affair with buying and owning as a way of life. This book is not about ending consumer capitalism any more than theologians writing on ongoing conversion believed that they

---

5. Ibid., 29.

6. The experience of time in the movement of persons from shipwreck to gladness and amazement can be quite elastic. For some, the grief and disorientation of shipwreck can endure for a long time. For others, the movement from gladness to amazement can be nearly instantaneous. However, persons rarely move through these stages quickly or without struggle.

could bring about the end of sin in human life. However, I do hope to provide resources for addressing the reality of consumerist forces over the course of a lifetime, much as understandings of ongoing conversion address the reality of sin over the course of a believer's lifetime. I also suggest creating small but significant communities of resistance that allow some persons to enjoy the freedom to make other vocational choices and that work to change the broader culture. I assume that the structures of meaning derived from the institution of consumer capitalism in the United States will not disappear and will continue to have power in the construction of human consciousness. This power can be imagined as roughly equivalent to the power of sin in theological writings on ongoing conversion. Such writings strive to describe how an encounter with God in ongoing conversion provides a person or community with the strength to struggle with the power of sin over the course of a lifetime. I find that these writings provide a helpful basis for considering the possibilities of ongoing conversion from consumer-dominated imaginations of the purpose and direction of human life.

In exploring ongoing conversion as a metaphor for assisting adolescent resistance to consumer formation, I have addressed the importance of encountering a new viable "faith" system to the process of education for resistance to consumer culture. While I have avoided saying that traditional Christian faith is the only option for what adolescents are converted to in the process of ongoing conversion from a deep faith in consumerism, new systems that provide ordering, meaning, and beauty must have some criteria by which they may be judged. For me, some of the significant criteria become clear in the failures of the consumer system. A primary one is that the meaning system must contribute to decreased suffering of those who are rendered less powerful by the consumer system. The ability of the desires cultivated by a meaning system to be sustained within the limits of the earth's resources is a second criterion. A third is the meaning system's contribution to human fulfillment and flourishing and its adequacy to assist meaning making in the face of difficult circumstances. These alternative faith systems are best encountered in a communal context to assist in individual formation and to increase the likelihood of broader social transformation.

Partnering grace:
Divine and human work in conversion

All of the conversation about how to provide communities of support for the ongoing conversion of young people from reliance on consumer faith may cause us to forget the work of God as partner in the process. Changes in imagination through ongoing conversion may feel as though they are initiated externally. However, persons often approach efforts for personal and social transformation as though only human effort and discipline can bring about change. Focusing on the metaphor of ongoing conversion pushes us to consider both God and humans as active partners in the experience of transformation. Sharon Parks, in talking about the experience of moving through shipwreck into gladness and amazement, notes:

> We rarely experience this as a matter simply of our own making. As the primal, elemental force of promise stirs again within us, we often experience it as a force acting upon us, beneath us, carrying us — sometimes in spite of our resistance — into new meaning, new consciousness, new faith.[7]

This vague sense of a force acting upon, beneath, and around us as we are transformed points to the active presence of God in the work of conversion. But how might we describe that active presence?

Gary Larson once drew a Far Side cartoon in which a scientist is working out a mathematical formula on a blackboard. He has written a number of numerical scribbles on the left side of the board; the middle says "then a miracle happens"; and the right has the conclusion to the formula. Another lab-coated scientist looking on says, "I think you need to be more specific at the middle step." Like the scientist writing on the board, finding the words to describe how God

---

7. Parks, *Big Questions, Worthy Dreams*, 29.

is present and active as a partner in the process of conversion is quite difficult. A miracle *does* happen, and people need to struggle to name how God partners with them, and how they include that partnership in pedagogical efforts to support ongoing conversion.

Having long since given up an image of a God who works in human history by moving people and events around like a divine chess player, articulating how God works in the process of conversion becomes more nuanced, and perhaps open to the critique of vagueness. What is the partnering responsibility of humanity with the Spirit?

Here I turn again to the work of John Wesley. To look at Wesley's understanding of the *via salutis,* the ongoing process of sanctification and conversion in the life of the believer, is to see a repetitive pattern of God's gracious gift and human response thereto. As Wesley directed believers, "Stir up the spark of grace which is now in you, and he will give you more grace."[8] A contemporary interpreter of Wesley, Randy Maddox, felt that this theme of the relationship between human and divine effort in the project of regeneration was crucial enough to be considered Wesley's orienting concern throughout his career. Maddox called this orienting concern "responsible grace," an almost oxymoronic phrase that captures both the sense of divine initiative in the process of transformation and the need for human response and partnership.[9] Wesley's understanding of the partnering efforts of humans and God in the ongoing sanctification of believers was expressed in the organic image of respiration. God breathes into the believer, and the believer breathes back out in response to God. This deeply intimate interconnection between human and divine work in the process of salvation consistently emphasizes the primacy of the work of God in enabling human response.

In his sermon which most directly addresses this topic, "On Working Out Our Own Salvation," Wesley describes the relationship

---

8. Wesley, *Sermons,* 491.
9. Maddox, *Responsible Grace,* 18.

between human and divine work in the process of salvation: "If it is God that worketh in us both to will and to do, what need is there of our working? . . . For first, God works; therefore you can work. Secondly, God works; therefore you must work."[10] Wesley believed that the nascent restoration of the image of God in all of humanity creates the possibility of responding to calls for repentance, involvement in spiritual discipline, and other efforts to enliven faith. From the first sign of preventing grace, which Wesley understood to allow for the nascent desire to please God, through the convincing grace that allows a larger measure of self-knowledge, to justification and the ongoing project of sanctification, Wesley understood God's gracious action as critical to the way of salvation.[11] At the same time, Wesley exhorted the believer to all works of piety and mercy that would hasten the process of salvation as well.

The work of ongoing conversion requires the partnership of humans in response to divine initiative. This element, while tricky to describe, provides a novel twist to the understanding of the learner seeking resistance to consumer-meaning structures. The capacity for resistance can be understood as evidence of divine grace intervening in one's life. For example, when I recognized that my imagination of "good neighborhood" had been transformed, I could understand this as a sign of grace working itself out in conversion. The true challenge in this insight is discerning how to integrate the role of grace and divine partnership in pedagogical efforts prior to transformation, in addition to recognition of its influence in hindsight. Whether understood as the energy and vitality encountered in the process of transformation or the graciousness of revealed images that reorient our faith system and provide other objects of devotion and commitment, attention to the way our work is inspired and partnered by the divine is critical.

---

10. Wesley, *Sermons*, 490.
11. Ibid., 488–89.

An ecology of support
for the long road of conversion

I have written much about the culture of consumer capitalism, how it functions as a faith system, and how we might begin to use a pedagogical understanding of ongoing conversion to engender resistance to consumer culture. My hope is that such a process would allow persons to find deep joy in alternative meaning systems and significant avenues of vocational expression. As I draw this book to a close, I confess my own complex relationship with the system of meanings that is consumer culture. I, too, participate ritually in the system. I cannot, with John Wesley, say, there but for the grace of God go I. When I think of Michael and remember his sermonette on the virtues of proper consumption, I see a clear reflection of my younger self. I may be slightly further along the road to conversion, but I still regularly find myself worshiping at the altars of consumption and immersing myself in its ritual texts. My desire to explore the possibilities of conversion from belief in consumer culture comes out of my own deep desire for salvation from it and for the possibilities of vocation funded by alternative imagination.

Because the development of vocational identity is a lifelong project, no ten-week or even yearlong educational program can adequately address the issue. This reality informed my decision to explore guidelines and dynamic elements of a pedagogy rather than constructing a five-step pedagogy or ten-week program. When I look back on my own conversion process from an adolescent whose sense of comfort depended on designer jeans to my current status of multifaithfulness, the path of conversion includes a variety of pedagogical efforts and mentoring communities that encouraged me on the path. Some short-term immersion events were critical to my gaining critical distance on consumer culture and imagining a different way that the world could be. A summer of work in rural Appalachia comes to mind, as does a month in Brazil doing community service and seeing the impact of the debt crisis on the lives of everyday Brazilians. There have been some long-term processes of coming to see my own ritual participation in consumer culture, as well as some critical junctures where I experienced calls to awakening about the failures of consumer culture to sustain meaning in my own life. Participation in a community of faith attempting to live in solidarity with homeless persons provided lived experience and practices of worship that contradicted consumer tenets. Members of that community also served as mentors who embodied alternative religious commitments in their economic life choices and provided a community of confessional honesty for me.

The aggregation of these experiences in my own life and the lives of the young people I have interviewed points to the need for an ecology of educational support beginning in adolescence (or better yet, earlier!) and continuing throughout the life span. The metaphor of ongoing conversion allows for a different conception of pedagogy to engender resistance to consumer culture that focuses on the transformation of complex loyalties over an extended period of time. This conversion is fueled by the experience of being grasped by an alternative imagination of the world, and lived into in community through slowly increasing agency to respond to the visions produced by that alternative image. Only over a lifetime can vocational integrity begin to emerge and perceptible movement toward social transformation be recognized. Stronger and weaker pedagogical approaches to support ongoing conversion exist, and I hope that I have begun to illuminate some of the characteristics of stronger approaches in this book.

As Wesley noted about the lifelong struggle to move toward full sanctification, this is gradual and incremental work. Progress toward fuller integration of a different belief system can often be recognized only in hindsight. But hope emerges from the incremental progression toward increased resistance and renewed vocation: "And as we are more and more dead to sin, we are more and more alive to God."[12]

---

12. Wesley, *Sermons*, 374.

Works cited

Anderson, E. Byron. "Liturgical Catechesis: Congregational Practice as Formation," *Religious Education* 92, no. 3 (Summer 1997): 350–51.

Athanasius, St. *On the Incarnation*. St. Vladimir's Orthodox Theological Seminary Printing. Cambridge: Cambridge University Press, 1993.

Augustine of Hippo. *Confessions*. New York: Penguin Books, 1961.

Baker, Dori Grinenko. *Doing Girlfriend Theology: God-Talk with Young Women*. Cleveland: Pilgrim Press, 2005.

Barth, Karl. "The Awakening to Conversion." In *Church Dogmatics* IV:2. Trans. G. W. Bromiley. Ed. G. W. Bromiley and T. F. Torrance. Edinburgh: T & T Clark, 1958.

Bass, Dorothy C., and Don C. Richter, eds. *Way to Live: Christian Practices for Teens*. Nashville: Upper Room Books, 2002.

Borgmann, Albert. *Power Failure: Christianity in the Culture of Technology*. Grand Rapids: Brazos Press, 2003.

Brickman, Philip. *Commitment, Conflict, and Caring*. Ed. Camille B. Wortman and Richard Sorrentino. Englewood Cliffs, NJ: Prentice-Hall, 1987.

Chin, Elizabeth. *Purchasing Power: Black Kids and American Consumer Culture*. Minneapolis: University of Minnesota Press, 2001.

Clapp, Rodney. "Why the Devil Takes Visa." *Christianity Today* (October 7, 1996).

Clark, Linda J. "Hymn-Singing: The Congregation Making Faith." In *Carriers of Faith: Lessons from Congregational Studies*, ed. C. Dudley, J. Carroll, and J. Wind. Louisville: Westminster/John Knox, 1991.

Conn, Walter, ed. *Conversion: Perspectives on Personal and Social Transformation*. New York: Alba House, 1978.

Csikszentmihalyi, Mihaly, and Reed Larson. *Being Adolescent*. New York: Basic Books, 1984.

Damasio, Antonio R. *Descartes' Error: Emotion, Reason, and the Human Brain*. New York: Grosset/Putnam, 1994.

Dean, Kenda Creasy. *Practicing Passion: Youth and the Quest for a Passionate Church*. Grand Rapids: Wm. B. Eerdmans, 2004.

deChant, Dell. *The Sacred Santa: Religious Dimensions of Consumer Culture*. Cleveland: Pilgrim Press, 2002.

Erikson, Erik. *Identity and the Life Cycle.* New York: Norton & Company, 1980 (reissued 1994).

———. *Identity: Youth and Crisis.* New York: Norton & Company, 1968 (reissued 1994).

Foster, Charles R. *Educating Congregations.* Nashville: Abingdon Press, 1994.

Fowler, James W. *Becoming Adult, Becoming Christian.* San Francisco: Jossey-Bass, 2000.

———. *Stages of Faith: The Psychology of Human Development and the Quest for Meaning.* San Francisco: HarperSanFrancisco, 1981.

———. *To See the Kingdom: The Theological Vision of H. Richard Niebuhr.* Lanham, MD, and New York: University Press of America, 1974.

———. *Weaving the New Creation.* San Francisco: HarperSanFrancisco, 1991.

Fraser, Nancy. *Justice Interruptus.* New York: Routledge, 1997.

Freire, Paulo. *Education for Critical Consciousness.* New York: Continuum, 1998.

———. *Pedagogy of the Oppressed.* New York: Continuum, 1997.

———. *Pedagogy of Hope.* New York: Continuum, 1992.

———. *The Politics of Education: Culture, Power, and Liberation.* South Hadley, MA: Bergin & Garvey, 1985.

Gardner, Howard. *Frames of Mind: The Theory of Multiple Intelligence.* New York: Basic Books, 1983.

Gergen, Kenneth J. *The Saturated Self: Dilemmas of Identity in Contemporary Life.* New York: Basic Books, 1991.

Giroux, Henry A. *Stealing Innocence.* New York: St. Martin's Press, 2000.

Greene, Maxine. *Dialectic of Freedom.* John Dewey Series. New York: Teachers College Press, 1988.

———. *Releasing the Imagination.* San Francisco: Jossey-Bass, 1995.

Groome, Thomas. *Sharing Faith.* San Francisco: HarperSanFrancisco, 1991.

Harris, Maria. *Fashion Me a People.* Louisville: Westminster/John Knox, 1989.

———. *Portrait of Youth Ministry.* New York: Paulist Press, 1981.

Heitzenrater, Richard. *Wesley and the People Called Methodists.* Nashville: Abingdon, 1995.

Hine, Thomas. *The Rise and Fall of the American Teenager.* New York: Avon Books, 1999.

hooks, bell. *Teaching to Transgress.* New York: Routledge, 1994.

Jaggar, Alison M. "Love and Knowledge: Emotion in Feminist Epistemology." In *Feminist Social Thought: A Reader,* ed. Diana Tietjens Meyers, 384–402. New York and London: Routledge, 1997.

James, William. *Essays in Psychology: The Works of William James Edition.* Ed. Frederick H. Burkhardt. Cambridge, MA: Harvard University Press, 1983.

Klein, Naomi. *No Logo.* New York: Picador, 1999.

Maddox, Randy. *Responsible Grace.* Nashville: Kingswood Books, 1994.

Mahan, Brian J. *Forgetting Ourselves on Purpose: Vocation and the Ethics of Ambition.* San Francisco: Jossey Bass, 2002.

Maritain, Jacques. *Education at the Crossroads.* New Haven, CT, and London: Yale University Press, 1941.

McCracken, Grant. *Culture and Consumption.* Bloomington: Indiana University Press, 1988.

McNeill, William H. *Keeping Together in Time.* Cambridge, MA: Harvard University Press, 1995.

Meeks, M. Douglas. *God the Economist: The Doctrine of God and Political Economy.* Minneapolis: Fortress Press, 1989.

The Merchants of Cool. PBS's *Frontline.* Originally aired February 27, 2001.

Miles, Margaret. *Practicing Christianity: Critical Perspectives for an Embodied Spirituality.* New York: Crossroad, 1988.

Moore, Mary Elizabeth. *Ministering with the Earth.* St. Louis: Chalice Press, 1998.

Nelson, C. Ellis, ed. *Congregations: Their Power to Form and Transform.* Atlanta: John Knox Press, 1988.

Niebuhr, H. Richard. *The Church against the World,* with Wilhelm Pauck and Francis P. Miller. Chicago and New York: Willett, Clark, & Co., 1935.

———. *The Meaning of Revelation.* New York: Macmillan, 1941.

———. *Radical Monotheism and Western Culture.* Library of Theological Ethics Edition. Louisville: Westminster/John Knox Press, 1943.

———. *Theology, History, and Culture: Major Unpublished Writings.* Ed. William Stacy Johnson. New Haven, CT: Yale University Press, 1996.

Palmer, Parker J. *The Company of Strangers: Christians and the Renewal of America's Public Life.* New York: Crossroad, 1996.

Parks, Sharon Daloz. *Big Questions, Worthy Dreams: Mentoring Young Adults in Their Search for Meaning, Purpose, and Faith.* San Francisco: Jossey-Bass, 2000.

Roberts, Donald F., and Ulla G. Foehr. *Kids & Media in America.* Cambridge: Cambridge University Press, 2004.

Rosenblatt, Roger, ed. *Consuming Desires.* Washington, DC: Island Press, 1999.

Ruether, Rosemary Radford. *Women-Church: Theology and Practice of Feminist Liturgical Communities.* San Francisco: Harper and Row, 1985.

Savage, Scott, ed. *The Plain Reader.* New York: Ballantine, 1998.

Scott, Lesbia. "I Sing a Song of the Saints of God." In *The United Methodist Hymnal*. Nashville: United Methodist Publishing House, 1989.

Shandler, Sara, ed. *Ophelia Speaks: Adolescent Girls Write about Their Search for Self*. New York: Harper Perennial, 1999.

Shank, Matthew D. *Sports Marketing: A Strategic Perspective*. Upper Saddle River, NJ: Prentice Hall, 1999.

Sobrino, Jon. *The Principle of Mercy*. Maryknoll, NY: Orbis, 1994.

Suchocki, Marjorie. *The Fall to Violence*. New York: Continuum, 1995.

Valantasis, Richard. "A Theory of the Social Function of Asceticism." In *Asceticism*, ed. Vincent L. Wimbush and Richard Valantasis, 544–52. New York: Oxford University Press, 1995.

Van Meter, Tim, and Katherine Turpin. "No Longer Guests: On the Dynamics of Agency and Formation in Ministry with Older Adolescents." *Journal of Youth and Theology* 1, no. 2 (2002): 7–22.

Warren, Michael. *At This Time, in This Place: The Spirit Embodied in the Local Assembly*. Harrisburg, PA: Trinity Press International, 2000.

————. *Seeing through the Media: A Religious View of Communications and Cultural Analysis*. Harrisburg, PA: Trinity Press International, 1999.

Way, Niobe. *Everyday Courage: The Lives and Stories of Urban Teenagers*. New York: New York University Press, 1998.

Weber, Max. *The Protestant Ethic and the Spirit of Capitalism*. Trans. Talcott Parsons. New York: Scribner, 1930.

Welch, Sharon. *A Feminist Ethic of Risk*. Rev. ed. Minneapolis: Fortress Press, 2000.

————. *Sweet Dreams in America: Making Ethics and Spirituality Work*. New York: Routledge, 1999.

Wesley, John. "Directions for Singing." In *The United Methodist Hymnal: Book of United Methodist Worship*. Nashville: United Methodist Publishing House, 1989.

————. *John Wesley's Sermons: An Anthology*. Ed. Albert C. Outler and Richard C. Heitzenrater. Nashville: Abingdon Press, 1991.

————. "The Rules of the United Societies." In *John Wesley*. Ed. Albert C. Outler. New York: Oxford University Press, 1964.

White, David F. *Practicing Discernment with Youth: A Transformative Youth Ministry Approach*. Cleveland: Pilgrim Press, 2005.

Wink, Walter. *Engaging the Powers*. Minneapolis: Fortress Press, 1992.

Young, Iris Marion. *Justice and the Politics of Difference*. Princeton, NJ: Princeton University Press, 1990.

Index

abstinence
  from consumer-oriented
    entertainment, 122–24
  from mass media, 120–22, 125–26,
    218
  from purchasing goods, 126–28
  from sexual activity, 119–20, 182
accountability, 159, 177, 181, 184–88,
  193–96, 204–6
adolescence
  and calls to awakening, 86, 96, 101
  and commitment, 19–20, 111–12,
    126–27, 156, 162–63, 175–76
  and community, 163, 170, 179–81,
    187–88, 204
  and consumer formation, 65, 105–6
  and developing economic commit-
    ments, 20, 97
  and embodied faith, 148–49, 160–62,
    208–9
  and entertainment, 123–24, 213–14
  identity development in, 17, 112,
    164–66, 175–76, 200
  and media consumption, 23, 46,
    121–22
  and marketing savvy, 36, 96
  muted agency in, 67, 94n
  passion in, 136
  primary institutions of, 13
  and repentance, 109–10, 152–53,
    221
  as targeted market, 15, 21, 46, 105
  theological understanding of, 18
  vocational development of, 13, 15,
    175–76

adults
  and consumer culture, 19, 20
  as mentors to young people, 94n11,
    139, 145, 151–52, 164–66, 194,
    199–201, 204, 223
advertising
  and adolescents, 22–23, 96
  as consumer institution, 32, 43
  critical reflection on, 66, 90–91, 95
  and formation, 2, 27, 32, 115, 168
agency
  and consumption, 5, 36–37, 46
  cultivation of, 5–6, 26, 67, 70, 88,
    143, 167
  definition of, 66
  as learned capacity, 55n2, 58n5,
    66–67
  and praxis, 87–88, 188–89, 216–17,
    219
  and vocation, 59, 231
  and young persons, 67, 112, 163, 199
Anderson, E. Byron, 207
asceticism, 65, 118–19, 125, 181–84
ascetic withdrawal, 118–26, 218
Athanasius, St., 69
Augustine, St., 50

Baker, Dori, 139n5
Barth, Karl, 5–6n2, 51–52
blart, 129–30, 183
Borgmann, Albert, 212–14
Brickman, Philip, 70, 154–56

camps, 107, 117–18, 139, 169
care for creation, 17, 99, 118, 145–47